BETTER
GREEN BUSINESS

Pearson employed a 100% green production method for the publication of this book.

This book was produced with paper made with 10% post-consumer recycled fiber. Using this type of paper saved the following:

3,142 lbs wood
A total of **10 trees** that supply enough **oxygen for 5 people** annually.

4,588 gal water
Enough water to take **267 eight-minute showers**.

3mln BTUs energy
Enough energy to power an average American household for **13 days**.

953 lbs emissions
Carbon sequestered by **11 tree seedlings** grown for 10 years.

279 lbs solid waste
Trash thrown away by **61 people in a single day**.

BETTER GREEN BUSINESS

HANDBOOK FOR ENVIRONMENTALLY RESPONSIBLE AND PROFITABLE BUSINESS PRACTICES

Eric G. Olson, PhD

FSC

Mixed Sources

Product group from well-managed
forests, controlled sources and
recycled wood or fiber

Cert no. SCS-COC-00648
www.fsc.org
© 1996 Forest Stewardship Council

Vice President, Publisher: Tim Moore
Associate Publisher and Director of Marketing: Amy Neidlinger
Wharton Editor: Steve Kobrin
Acquisitions Editor: Jennifer Simon
Editorial Assistant: Myesha Graham
Development Editor: Russ Hall
Operations Manager: Gina Kanouse
Senior Marketing Manager: Julie Phifer
Publicity Manager: Laura Czaja
Assistant Marketing Manager: Megan Colvin
Cover Designer: Chuti Prasertsith
Managing Editor: Kristy Hart
Project Editor: Betsy Harris
Copy Editor: Krista Hansing Editorial Services, Inc.
Proofreader: Apostrophe Editing Services
Senior Indexer: Cheryl Lenser
Indexer: Erika Millen
Senior Compositor: Gloria Schurick
Manufacturing Buyer: Dan Uhrig

Published by Pearson Education, Inc.
Publishing as Wharton School Publishing
Upper Saddle River, New Jersey 07458

Wharton School Publishing offers excellent discounts on this book when ordered in quantity for bulk purchases or special sales. For more information, please contact U.S. Corporate and Government Sales, 1-800-382-3419, corpsales@pearsontechgroup.com. For sales outside the U.S., please contact International Sales at international@pearson.com.

Printed in the United States of America

First Printing November 2009

ISBN-10: 0-13-701017-6
ISBN-13: 978-0-13-701017-2

Pearson Education LTD.
Pearson Education Australia PTY, Limited
Pearson Education Singapore, Pte. Ltd.
Pearson Education North Asia, Ltd.
Pearson Education Canada, Ltd.
Pearson Educación de Mexico, S.A. de C.V.
Pearson Education—Japan
Pearson Education Malaysia, Pte. Ltd.

Library of Congress Cataloging-in-Publication Data

Olson, Eric G., 1967-

  Better green business : handbook for environmentally responsible and profitable business practices / Eric G. Olson. — 1st ed.

    p. cm.

  ISBN 978-0-13-701017-2 (hardback : alk. paper) 1. Management—Environmental aspects. 2. Business enterprises—Environmental aspects. 3. Technological innovations—Environmental aspects. I. Title.

  HD30.255.O47 2009

  658.4'083—dc22

                         2009029875

Dedicated to Katelin and Cassandra

Contents

Contents   **ix**

Acknowledgments

I am thankful to Dr. Colin Harrison, David Lubowe, and Dr. R. Peter Williams of IBM for their thoughtful counsel throughout the conceptualization and writing of this book.

I am also thankful to the journals and contributing authors of the following articles for granting me permission to repurpose their content to use in this work:

- Dr. Eric G. Olson, "Business as Environmental Steward: The Growth of Greening," *Journal of Business Strategy* 30, no. 5 (2009): 4–13.

- Dr. Eric G. Olson, "Creating an Enterprise-Level 'Green' Strategy," *Journal of Business Strategy* 29, no. 2 (2008): 22–30.

- Dr. Eric G. Olson and Niall Brady, "Green Sigma and the Technology of Transformation for Environmental Stewardship," *IBM Journal of Research and Development* 53, no. 3 (2009).

- Dr. Ching-Hua Chen-Ritzo, Dr. Colin Harrison, Jurij R. Paraszczak, and Dr. Francis N. Parr, "Instrumenting the Planet," *IBM Journal of Research and Development* 53, no. 3 (2009).

Finally, I am thankful to all the professionals across many organizations whose work has influenced the writing of this book.

About the Author

Dr. Eric G. Olson has more than 20 years of experience in management consulting and industry, where he has worked with organizations of all sizes and across industries. His experience spans business, operations and technology strategy, e-commerce and e-business, innovation and product lifecycle management, process improvement and supply chain optimization, procurement and strategic sourcing, corporate mergers and joint ventures, and environmental stewardship.

He holds a Bachelor of Science degree and a PhD from Cornell University, an MBA from the Massachusetts Institute of Technology–Sloan, and a Master of Science degree from Rensselaer Polytechnic Institute. He is also a member of the American Society of Mechanical Engineers and a licensed Professional Engineer. You can reach the author at eric.olson08@gmail.com.

Preface

In today's information age, plenty of news reports and corporate pronouncements on environmental stewardship abound. But these show only a sample of the full breadth of activity underway. Business leaders and practitioners are exposed daily to a fray of news and magazine articles, television programming, "green" advertisements, organization announcements, and company press releases that describe plans, new products, and business benefits from initiatives that improve the environment.

Using this book, leaders and practitioners can begin to identify patterns in information. They can then learn what leading practices at other companies apply to their business, find areas where their enterprise should lead among its peers, and construct actionable plans to realize strategic objectives for environmental stewardship. You can appreciate that win-win-win scenarios still prevail in the green movement. For example, many businesses are benefiting from top-line revenue growth that has come from products, services, and business model innovations that are in line with environmental stewardship. Other businesses and consumers benefit from purchasing and using those products and services, from both increased efficiency and lower bottom-line costs. The global environment also benefits from lower greenhouse gas emissions and less resource consumption.

This book aims to give leaders and practitioners in any organization the practical insight necessary to help them move their enterprise toward a higher level of environmental stewardship, regardless of their current level of "green" maturity. It follows a holistic "strategy to implementation" approach, from strategy formulation to continuous improvement and beyond.

Chapter 1, "Driving Forces and Challenges That Organizations Face," examines why environmental stewardship is important for any business to pursue, and why that importance will likely grow stronger in the future. Chapters 2, "Formulate Green Strategy to Complement Traditional Strategy," and 3, "Green Strategy Supports Operational Improvements," suggest a framework for approaching and formulating a green strategy, and illustrate the benefits many companies have realized in each strategic area. Chapter 4, "Make Green Strategy Actionable with a Proven Approach," describes an approach for implementing a green strategy: developing a vision for the future, defining initiatives that fill gaps between the current state and the future vision, and constructing a roadmap for achieving the vision. The approach consistently maintains traceability throughout, from the investments made to fund specific initiatives, back to the driving strategic imperatives.

Chapters 5, "Transformation Methods and Green Sigma," and 6, "Applying Green Sigma to Optimize Carbon Emissions," introduce and explain business process transformation methodologies, with supporting technology and tools, that focus on increasing operational efficiency and reducing waste. IBM's Green Sigma is one methodology described in detail.

The concepts in Chapters 7, "Instrumenting the Planet for an Intelligent, Sustainable World," and 8, "Technology That Supports Instrumenting the Planet," are forging new paths on the frontier of environmental stewardship; they play a central role in achieving the full business benefits that are possible from our increasingly intelligent planet. We cover the drivers and rationale for instrumenting the planet, describe applications for the associated solutions, and explain key elements of the underlying technology. Chapter 9, "Business Considerations for Technology Solutions," describes the landscape of existing and developing technology solutions that apply to business operations and explains associated business considerations. Finally, Chapter 10, "Critical Trends Shaping the Future," concludes with a discussion of long-term trends that will play a role in shaping the future of business management.

This book will be useful for readers who want to understand what is happening around the world, as related to green business and environmental stewardship, as well as those who want to learn how to take action to achieve tangible benefits. We discuss strategic insights for top-line revenue growth, bottom-line cost savings, and operational transformation, all of which executives will value. We also address how to make green strategy actionable, and describe transformation methodologies that managers and project leaders can use to improve their organizational competencies, processes, technologies, and operations. All practitioners, at every level of any organization, will gain insight into how different actions can fit into a broader framework of holistic, global change. Readers in any size enterprise or industry will also benefit from our discussion of frameworks for such things as green product categorization, solutions and technology for environmental stewardship, and ways to build strength and differentiation from the lifecycle chain outside the four walls of an organization.

In some cases, we quantify and explain detailed environmental benefits, and discuss numerous other examples at a higher level in the context of specific frameworks. The objective of this book is not to evaluate and analyze public policies and legislation that impact global warming, nor is it to explore the detailed science of global climate and associated weather change. Beyond the intellectual exercise of understanding the complexities of global environmental change and the sophisticated science behind that understanding, is the capacity for organizations of all kinds to connect the driving forces of environmental stewardship with actual initiatives that improve the environment, strengthen business performance, and lower risk. Businesses are already applying these principles to grow revenue, operate more efficiently, reduce costs, and improve environmental sustainability—all at the same time.

PART I

Establish a Strategy and Transformation Plan

1

Driving Forces and Challenges
That Organizations Face

1.1. Environmental Stewardship Presents New Growth Opportunity

Since the turn of the millenium, environmental stewardship has gripped the collective intellect of humankind. Environmental issues have challenged our self-awareness and sparked a global initiative to respond to such critical issues as global climate change and natural resource conservation. As a result, attitudes toward the environment are changing to encourage innovation in conservation. The benefits that arise will surely outlive our current generation. Enterprises of all sorts and sizes are developing more environmental impact initiatives, a trend that continues to accelerate as more attitudes change. The U.S. government's executive and legislative branches, along with other governments worldwide, are also focusing on energy efficiency and alternative energy policy, along with their relationship to economic growth, employment, and national security.

Seldom has the need for large-scale transformation been so clear but the necessary course of action been so difficult to define. "Global warming," "global climate change," "greenhouse gasses," "resource scarcity," "environmental risk," and "carbon footprint" have quickly become common household terms and are mentioned daily in news and science reports. Business communities also are increasingly discussing these topics in company newsletters, in announcements to the investment community, and at shareholder meetings. Enterprises are certainly changing in ways that improve the environment, and environmental change continues to remain a top priority for many businesses, even as cyclical industry forces work to redefine other long-standing pillars of stability and growth. Environmental stewardship is one area of new business activity whose driving forces are so strong, responsibly compelling, and widely appreciated that the call to action can appeal to every industry, enterprise, and organizational level, from the most senior executives to the newest entry-level employees.

In the past, new legislation, community pressure, or customer safety concerns often prompted corporate environmental initiatives. Reactive calls to action for specific environmental concerns—such as acid rain, ozone layer depletion, excessive pollution, and smog, especially in and around urban areas—also drove these initiatives. In many countries, tremendous progress has been made through legislation to reduce automobile exhaust emissions, lower pollution levels in the air we breathe, and improve safety by eliminating the use of lead-based paint. All stakeholders, from government lawmakers to corporate executives and consumer advocates, helped enact these changes. However, scientific evidence tells us that global warming, and the associated climate change, is accelerating, fueling a growing consensus that more pervasive changes need to occur. Many people believe that government regulation should play a role in achieving effective change, but that it's only one of several forces that will drive the needed change into the future.

All governments, individuals, and businesses must play an important role in protecting the environment. By developing environmentally friendly strategies, adopting transformation methods that support environmental stewardship, and implementing solutions that reduce environmental impact, enterprises of all sizes and across all industries are already heading in this direction.

1.2. Leaders Are Already Taking Action

Many people believe that every business, government, enterprise, and even individual contributor can do something to reduce waste, improve the environment, and play an important role in achieving environmental sustainability. The slogan "Think globally, act locally" was coined during the 1960s, and has been used often to broadly promote recycling behavior and communicate the notion that anyone can make an impact and be part of a global environmental solution. Businesses are adopting that principle at the department/site, enterprise, and even country level through awareness programs, proactive guiding principles and policies, new legislation, and government incentives.

Not only is it becoming clear that virtually any stakeholder can do more, but it is also increasingly less acceptable for some stakeholders to do nothing. Today some of the largest companies in the world are developing new guiding principles and governance models that encourage proactive behavior and strengthen environmental stewardship. The reactive status quo, in which corporations and environmentalists would clash in a world of conflicting priorities, is becoming a thing of the past. Companies are designing new business models to accomplish a range of objectives, from recognizing and rewarding employees' knowledge and experience of sustainability practice, to enabling improvements in the extended value chain that include the activities of suppliers and business partners. Accolo, a provider of recruiting solutions for small to midsize companies, is one example of a company giving financial incentives to clients that are working to improve the environment through the EcoPartnership program. Accolo's program offers business partners a rebate on services equivalent to their investment in the environment, with an upper limit of 10 percent.[1] Business model innovations such as this are meeting little opposition from employees. One poll of attitudes in the American workplace found that more than three-quarters of U.S. workers said that it was important for them to have an employer that was going green in a significant way.[2]

Yet even to a sophisticated observer who sees a wealth of new information about the green movement on a daily basis, no clear picture emerges on the master plans at the enterprise level. In some cases, no master plan exists—only a group such as a program management organization (PMO) holistically prioritizing and managing a sophisticated portfolio of "green" initiatives. In other cases, companies are carefully formulating plans to help them realize more value.

More enterprises are consciously developing holistic green strategies that affect all organizational levels, from the enterprise down to departments, site locations, and even individuals. To support the implementation of such a strategy, businesses are also adapting and applying suitable transformation methodologies to achieve and sustain benefits to business operations and to the environment. Enterprises are also developing and implementing business solutions that creatively apply technology in new ways to achieve a more granular understanding of their operations and the impact they have on the planet. Using relatively new wireless technology, networked sensors, management dashboard reporting, and automated alarm management is one way for businesses to reduce waste and optimize their position as environmental stewards.

As more businesses invest in developing new products and improved infrastructure, it's not surprising that standards are also emerging to support cross-company, cross-industry, and cross-geography collaboration and require a high level of technical sophistication and management coordination. The notion of an instrumented world is emerging and even being tested in a number of industries. An instrumented world is, ideally, one in which the state of natural and human systems, and the interactions between them, is known through sensing, and in which computer software applications can lead in their management. The concept can be applied at all levels (global, regional, local, and site) and for multiple domains (company, government, and geography).

In the face of adverse global climate and weather changes, unpredictable energy prices of fossil fuels, increasingly scarce natural resources, impending government legislation, a growing trend for higher corporate social responsibility, and consumer sentiment that favors environmentally friendly products and services, it's not surprising that businesses, industries, and governments are responding in innovative ways that might have been unimaginable just a few years ago. But reducing waste, managing scarce natural resources, saving energy, and operating efficiently have always been good business tenets.

What is different in today's business environment that will enable a clear and sustained focus on improved environmental stewardship? In many respects, the driving forces behind the current wave of business transformation for improved environmental sustainability are more strongly aligned today—and can become even stronger in the future. Businesses are learning that being lean, efficient, and "green" all go together because they can simultaneously reduce costs, lead to revenue growth, and improve environmental stewardship.

The driving forces and science behind the "green" movement to improve environmental stewardship and the need to achieve environmental sustainability is widely documented. Some of these works focus on specific driving forces, such as Gore's *An Inconvenient Truth* [3], focusing primarily on greenhouse gas emissions and their unwanted effects on global warming and associated climate change. Another example is Campbell's *Oil Crisis,*[4] which discusses the force of natural resource scarcity (oil, in particular) and eventual depletion in authoritative detail. A third book, Lynas's *Six Degrees: Our Future on a Hotter Planet,*[5] paints a future picture of Earth after the consequences of unabated human pollution.

These and other works connect the driving forces with possible future scenarios, such as Kunstler's *The Long Emergency: Surviving the End of Oil, Climate Change, and Other Converging Catastrophes of the Twenty-First Century.*[6] Some works are highly specific, such as Brown's *Migration and Climate Change*, which predicts that climate change will displace 200 million people by 2050.[7]

Existing works vary widely in their approach to discussing a myriad of environmental issues, and many speculate on future impacts that will result if humankind's past behavior continues. Regardless of the approach, one common element that the vast majority of recent work shares is the viewpoint that current trends must be changed to avoid decidedly undesirable outcomes. The debate is already underway on whether the current green movement and its projected direction will eventually be sufficient, or whether more drastic and disruptive near-term measures are necessary.

Across industries and enterprises of all sizes, the capability to assess the driving forces that are pushing organizations to improve their environmental stewardship is also helping them to better identify and prioritize new opportunities. Businesses are identifying initiatives that are simultaneously improving both the environment and their own business performance. Esty and Winston's *Green to Gold: How Smart Companies Use Environmental Strategy to Innovate, Create Value, and Build Competitive Advantage*[8] is one work that explores such benefits in more detail. Megatrends and paradigm shifts such as those from the green movement, with so many win-win scenarios for such a wide range of companies, are unique in a world of ever-increasing challenges from hypercompetition. Companies offering products and services aligned with environmental stewardship are benefiting from top-line revenue growth, other companies and consumers that purchase and use those offerings are benefiting from bottom-line cost savings, and the environment itself is beginning to benefit from improved natural resource usage and lower greenhouse gas emissions.

1.3. Driving Forces Are Aligned Like Never Before

Among the difficult challenges business leaders and practitioners face today is understanding the driving forces that encourage environmental sustainability in the context of their own operations. Historically, many people have perceived that the driving forces behind profitable business decisions and efficient practices conflicted with environmentally conscientious behavior. Until only a few years ago, the most visible environmental stewards were often found chained to trees, lying in front of bulldozers protesting deforestation, or organizing and leading boycotts against the activities of "big business." Today these advocacy activities still play a role in promoting environmental stewardship, but it's also clear that all organizations can benefit from taking action to improve environmental sustainability. A positive spirit of collaboration and partnership is replacing the past perception of negativity and confrontation between environmental stewardship and profitable business activity.

Multiple forces pushing enterprises to become better environmental stewards have aligned in the right direction and changed earlier perspectives. The stage is also set for those forces to remain aligned far into the future. Figure 1.1 illustrates the topography of forces that drive enterprises to improve their environmental stewardship, presented in the context of the foundational drivers, their impacts that influence the global community, and risks that need to be mitigated. These forces don't exist in isolation; they're interdependent and often reinforcing. Although the specific relationships can be a matter of discussion, some forces clearly reinforce the strength of others. For example, if market risk from rapidly changing consumer preferences toward "green" products is high, the reputational risk for businesses that do not take steps to be more efficient and "green" will also be higher. As business leaders already know, when they can mitigate or manage risk in a topography such as this, opportunities exist to realize benefits and create value.

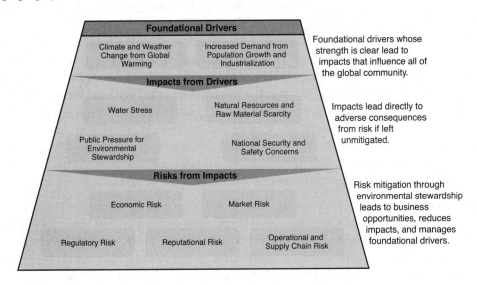

Figure 1.1 Topography of forces that encourage and drive action

Source: *Journal of Business Strategy*

1.3.1. Foundational Drivers

Foundational drivers are ones that the world must learn to manage, to avoid adverse impacts on the environment and Earth's natural resources. People pay attention to the global climate change, but population growth and industrialization are also important forces behind the need to improve environmental sustainability.

1.3.1.1. Climate and Weather Change from Global Warming

The often-studied, well-publicized, and sometimes-feared phenomena of global warming and associated climate and weather change from greenhouse gas emissions is one driving force that is encouraging businesses to become better environmental stewards. Although precise definitions vary, it's well known that global warming is the increase in global temperatures caused by greenhouse gas emissions into the atmosphere.[9] Greenhouse gas emissions include carbon dioxide and chlorofluorocarbons that contribute to an entity's (such as a person or business) "carbon footprint," which is often expressed in terms of a carbon dioxide equivalent.

Global warming and associated climate and weather change have received worldwide attention not only because of the accepted changes already caused to planet Earth, but also because of extreme predictions for the future that are being made based on increasingly sound scientific facts.

Some climate and weather changes that have already occurred are clearly documented, although complete agreement on specific details is still a matter of discussion and critics remain.[10] Scientific observations show that from 1900 to 2005, precipitation increased significantly in eastern parts of North and South America, northern Europe, and northern and central Asia, but declined in the Sahel of Africa, the Mediterranean, southern Africa, and parts of southern Asia.[11] During approximately the same time period, the sea level rose roughly 7 inches [12], and the snow cover in the Northern Hemisphere and floating ice in the Arctic Ocean have decreased.[13] Global surface temperature has also increased an estimated 1° Fahrenheit during the last century. Worldwide precipitation over land has increased by about 1 percent, and the frequency of extreme rainfall events has increased throughout much of the U.S.[14] Gore's book, *An Inconvenient Truth*, discusses increased hurricane activity as one specific weather pattern.

Scientific evidence supports a growing consensus that increasing concentrations of greenhouse gases will likely accelerate the rate of climate and weather change. Scientists predict that the average global surface temperature could rise by as much as 4.5° Fahrenheit during the next 50 years, and up to 10° Fahrenheit in the next century. Evaporation will increase as the climate warms, which will increase average global precipitation. Soil moisture will likely decline in many regions, and intense rainstorms could become more frequent. Sea level might eventually rise 2 feet along most of the U.S. coast.[15] One study from the U.S. National Oceanic and Atmospheric Administration (NOAA) concludes that the climate change taking place due to increases in carbon dioxide concentration is largely irreversible for 1,000 years after emissions stop.[16] Other work by McKinsey & Company concludes that potential exists for more than 200 greenhouse gas abatement opportunities to have a "good chance of holding global warming" below a critical threshold by 2030.[17] Because the entire planet suffers the effects of global warming and associated climate change, all stakeholders that contribute to greenhouse gas emissions can and should also contribute to a solution if the goal is to slow or reverse the effects.

For the anthropogenic greenhouse gas emissions (those that we can attribute to human activity and our combustion of fossil fuels), nearly every economic sector contributes significantly. Therefore, every sector can play a role in reducing emissions from human activity. Power stations make the highest contribution, at 21.3 percent; industrial processes follow, at 16.8 percent; then transportation fuels, at 14.0 percent; agricultural byproducts, at 12.5 percent; fossil fuel retrieval, processing, and distribution, at 11.3 percent; residential, commercial, and other sources, at 10.3 percent; and, finally, waste disposal and treatment, at 3.4 percent.[18]

Because business activity–generated carbon emissions account for such a significant portion of greenhouse gases (and, therefore, the effects of global warming from human activity), businesses and other enterprises are in a position to make a significant, positive impact as they improve their environmental stewardship. By understanding global warming and associated climate and weather change as driving forces for improvement, businesses can gain valuable insight into what actions to take.

First, by identifying and measuring key performance indicators that characterize the carbon footprint of an organization or significant operational area, an enterprise provides a solid foundation for managing and reducing greenhouse gas emissions. The often-heard phrase "If you can measure it, you can manage it" certainly applies here. Management can establish appropriate accountability if sufficient information granularity and reporting are achieved to show where greenhouse gases might be attributed to business activity in departments, plants, or products. By measuring emissions, reporting on them with business intelligence technology, and establishing workforce training and accountability for improvement, businesses can identify, achieve, and demonstrate significant reduction opportunities and significant cost savings.

However, don't underestimate the complexity associated with establishing an accurate carbon footprint for an organization. Setting appropriate boundary conditions for business operations and potentially business partner activity, defining and deploying a measurement system, establishing baseline data and monitoring performance, and adhering to standards that ensure that data is kept current and accurate can all pose challenges to any business. It's important to recognize that an enterprise can reduce its greenhouse gas emissions without knowing its carbon footprint. For example, United Technologies went from a $27 billion company in 1997 to a $48 billion company in 2006, but used

19 percent less energy by focusing its environmental programs on energy reduction instead of carbon emissions. Although the company had been measuring greenhouse gas emissions for some time, it wasn't until 2006 that it made the decision to shift from measuring and reporting energy use reduction to a greenhouse gas reduction–based model.[19]

Second, by understanding where the most significant sources of greenhouse gas emissions come from, businesses can evaluate all their options to prioritize and target the highest contributors to their carbon footprints for optimization and improvement. Whether the appropriate action is to replace inefficient machinery with devices that consume less energy or installing renewable energy–producing equipment, enterprises are now able to build business cases for different alternatives that support environment stewardship, reduce costs, and increase profitability. Some industries and business sectors can often predict where their major sources of emissions come from without detailed analyses because they already understand the data at a high level. For example, the branch offices and data centers contribute significantly in the banking industry, and refrigeration and transportation cause high emissions associated with supermarkets.

Third, by measuring and understanding how an enterprise's operations contribute to greenhouse gas emissions, business leaders can evaluate their extended value chain, or even wider "lifecycle chain," to make better decisions as environmental stewards and influence activity outside the walls of their own company. Some companies are already considering environmental stewardship performance in evaluating suppliers and business partners as part of a balanced-scorecard approach, and other companies are building stronger relationships with customers through recycling programs and incentives that build loyalty, encourage repeat business, and promote cross-selling and up-selling. Companies are also sharing the "carbon footprint burden" with specially designed programs. For example, some companies are purchasing "clean" electricity from the grid that is generated from renewable sources, such as wind farms and solar panels, and trading carbon credits in other programs. In 2008, Dell announced that it had become a "carbon-neutral" company, partly by increasing its purchase of green electricity.[20] Still, because no universally accepted standard exists for what a carbon footprint includes, every company calculates its numbers differently and the details behind claims of neutrality can be complex.[21]

Finally, a more sophisticated understanding of greenhouse gas emissions can open up opportunities for companies to develop new products, create relationships with new business partners, and even grow entirely new business segments that create higher value for new and existing customers, improve environmental impact on a very broad scale, and create a competitive advantage through sustained differentiation. Companies that are learning to master a more sophisticated view of greenhouse gas emissions, global warming, and associated climate and weather change already have the advantage of often being first movers—and, in some cases, the followers aren't far behind. These companies are deliberately formulating their green strategies to improve environmental stewardship through innovative business and operational improvement initiatives.

1.3.1.2. Increased Demand from Population Growth and Industrialization

Even after the threat of global warming and associated climate change is adequately addressed and sustainability of the planet's health has been demonstrated, the world's population will continue to grow (more than 30 percent from 2010 to 2050[22]) and draw from increasingly scarce natural resources, such as oil and other fossil fuels, water, minerals, agricultural land, and clean air. As different countries and geographic regions work to raise the living standards for their societies, industrialization will lead to additional demand. Developing regions of the world now have an enormous opportunity to industrialize, with the complementary objective of environmental sustainability and without some of the burdensome legacy infrastructure in other regions whose economies went through their industrial revolution more than a century ago.

Environmental risk, which is often described as the threat of adverse effects arising from human activity, includes a host of hazards that organizations have consistently worked to avoid in the past. Even though management of environmental risk has been a driving force behind environmental stewardship for many decades, new pressures from sources such as resource exploitation, unmitigated waste, residential and commercial real estate development, population growth, industrialization, and even climate change are gaining renewed attention. Avoiding such outcomes as oil and chemical spills, toxic waste contamination, health hazards, and unsafe environmental conditions continues to be a top priority for most businesses. Ineffective management and high consumption of scarce natural resources accelerate their ultimate depletion, or at least exacerbate their scarcity, which generates obvious business risk. Without the necessary supplies, businesses cannot manufacture their products. For example, pollutants that contaminate a river system that many businesses and communities depend upon pose clear risks that must be mitigated, especially if the water supply is already dwindling because of global climate change or population growth. In another example, if acid rain kills living organisms in a lake, and local businesses depend on activities such as fishing, environmental risk obviously jeopardizes that economy.

1.3.2. Impacts from Drivers Lead to Adverse Consequences Without Environmental Stewardship

Without widespread improvements in environmental stewardship, impacts from the foundational drivers will lead to adverse consequences around the world. Among these consequences are water stress, natural resource and raw material scarcity, public pressure, and national security and safety concerns.

1.3.2.1. Water Stress

Water is a natural resource that is sometimes overlooked as becoming increasingly scarce or placed under stress because its availability depends greatly on regional conditions. Some regions will continue to enjoy plentiful water even with global warming, but others will inevitably find their water in short supply as global climate change affects weather patterns and the distribution of fresh water.

According to the Intergovernmental Panel on Climate Change (IPCC), increasing temperatures and extreme weather patterns are already taking their toll on crop yields, which are declining in many parts of Asia. The panel reported in 2007 that future climate change attributable to global warming is expected to put 50 million extra people at risk of hunger by 2020—that rises to 132 million and 266 million by 2050 and 2080, respectively. This also suggests that rising air temperatures could decrease rain-fed rice yields by 5 percent to 12 percent in China, and net cereal production in South Asian countries could decline by 4 percent to 10 percent by the end of this century.[23] After those scenarios were evaluated, and with newer information available in 2009, C. Field of the Carnegie Institute for Science said that greenhouse gas emissions are "now outside the entire envelope of possibilities" considered in the 2007 report of the IPCC. Carbon emissions have been growing at 3.5 percent per year since 2000, which is up sharply from 0.9 percent per year during the 1990s.[24] Clearly, the imperatives to better manage natural resources, such as fresh water, and globally reduce greenhouse gas emissions are here to stay. Expanding industrialization and population growth also require increasing amounts of usable water and can lead to shortages even without drought or climate change.

1.3.2.2. Natural Resource and Raw Material Scarcity

The outlook appears equally risky for some raw materials when we consider long-term predictions. By some estimates, all the copper in existing ore, plus all the copper currently in use, is required to bring the world to the level of developed nations just for power transmission, construction, and other services and products that depend on the mineral. Platinum depletion is a potential risk in this century because few substitutes exist in such products as catalytic converters, and platinum is located only in specific sites around the world.[25] Even more troubling is that, at present rates of consumption, researchers predict that copper, lead, mercury, nickel, gallium, tin, zinc,[26] and phosphorous[27] will all be depleted within the next 50 years. Although most businesses and even government enterprises have difficulty formulating strategy around deadlines 50 years in the future, it's still important for today's businesses to recognize that the supply of some common raw materials is not infinite. And as global industrialization continues, price instability might represent a rising business risk. Even if predictions such as these are only partly true, businesses that take action to conserve today and explore different alternatives to stay "ahead of the curve" will be well positioned to reap enormous rewards as others strive to catch up in the future.

Oil and other fossil fuels are also natural resources whose capacity to meet growing demand might be limited, and their eventual scarcity routinely receives front-page attention. However, even scarcer than the fossil fuels, with many decades of supply still remaining, is our ability to burn them without causing adverse global climate and weather change.

1.3.2.3. Public Pressure for Environmental Stewardship

Climate change and adverse weather patterns, broader spread of infectious disease, increased glacial ice flow and melting, and redistribution of plant and animal life are only a few phenomena being linked to global warming, yet they serve to strengthen public pressure for improved environmental stewardship. The public is also sympathetic to endangered species that might perish because of global warming and associated climate change, especially "charismatic megafauna,"[28] which might be the case for polar bears as their ice-rich habitat melts without being replenished each year.[29]

"This time around, mainstream consumers are riding the green wave," and "Consumers are beginning to really vote with their feet and wallets in terms of green."[30] Public pressure as a driving force for the green movement is currently positive in most regions of the world and is pushing environmental improvement steadily forward. However, public pressure could shift from a positive driving force to a more negative, inflamed one. Public pressure in the form of unrest is certainly more likely when food production declines while population rises, basic natural resources become scarce, water supplies become more stressed, and other adverse changes occur in the environment, such as more frequent and more severe natural disasters.

1.3.2.4. National Security and Safety Concerns

Resource scarcity itself is enough cause for national and even international security concerns. In extreme scenarios, countries and regions that contain natural resources might raise protectionist economic barriers, forge new alliances with unexpected partners, and shift global economic strength. When this impact is combined with public unrest as resource supplies become scarce, national security concern is even more relevant. When global conditions become dire enough, riots, corruption, sanctions, and military action to protect sovereign borders all become potential adverse impacts.

Because impacts from climate and weather change cross country borders, additional concern arises, with the potential to unravel across boundaries that are literally on opposite sides of the world. In the past, blame for environmental impacts was often easily assigned and usually possible to mitigate through diplomacy and international law even before problems started. For example, the European Union has water protection directives that apply to all its member countries that share many common interests. However, diplomatic and legal solutions might be more difficult to achieve when the most severe adverse impacts from global warming are experienced by one country or region whose interests are poorly aligned with other regions that contribute the most to greenhouse gas emissions that might not share a common physical border. Notions of accountability and liability become unclear. This risk is a driving force behind environmental stewardship that is certainly important to mitigate before any of the direst predictions unfold and the current course of global cooperation changes.

The safety of all living organisms and their habitats is another obvious concern from increased severe weather patterns, floods, fires, and other events of nature. For example, increases in fires, floods, and hurricanes all pose a safety risk to people and property.

1.3.3. Risks That Require Mitigation to Manage Drivers and Capture Business Value

Appropriately mitigating risk can lead to significant business value. Environmental stewardship improvements can also result in differentiated products, more efficient operations, and a more sustainable world.

1.3.3.1. Economic Risk from Energy, Water, and Other Natural Resource Prices

The economics driving energy and raw material prices is one force that many businesses are working to understand better. Businesses are then leveraging that understanding to improve their environmental stewardship. How high energy and commodity prices can rise in a given economic cycle, or how long a retreat in prices can be sustained with the headwind of global industrialization is a matter of great debate, and economists and industry analysts continue to have differing points of view. Speculation on how long-term demand will be met is often made part of the same debate, which can include discussion of substitute raw materials, alternative energy sources, renewable energy sources, and conservation of traditional fossil fuels. Despite the ongoing debate, one fact has become clear in recent years: As long as energy and commodity prices for scarce raw materials remain unpredictable and long-term global demand sustains heightened levels, initiatives that reduce energy consumption and raw materials waste have stronger value propositions and, therefore, make more business sense to implement. One notable exception might be for water management: The price for water in many areas of the world is still much lower than its actual economic value.

Until recently, many businesses didn't consider energy, natural resource availability, and the cost of resources as impacting overall business risk enough to drive widespread conservation initiatives. In a 2008 interview, David J. O'Reilly, the chairman and CEO of Chevron, commented, "We have been too cavalier about our use of energy."[31] However, with wide fluctuations in petroleum prices and cheap energy being harder to rely upon, businesses across all industry segments are now taking a close look at their energy usage, learning where the significant energy use takes place in their business, and formulating a plan to reduce consumption or shift to a less risky source with a more stable long-term cost. For some enterprises, the first step has been simply to install straightforward technology devices, such as motion-sensitive light switches, and training employees on energy-saving practices they can use in their everyday work. Other companies have taken larger steps to instrument their inventory of energy-consuming equipment, implement new technology to monitor and optimize energy consumption, or appoint new roles in the organization with ownership and accountability for achieving business and environmental benefits. Still others have reconfigured their operations to use alternative and renewable energy sources, to reduce dependence on fossil fuels that have more volatile and unpredictable price fluctuations.

Efforts to reduce energy consumption and natural resource waste also reduce overall greenhouse gas emissions and improve environmental stewardship. However, conservation activity for raw materials is more sensitive to advancing or retreating prices because they don't mitigate greenhouse gas emissions. Economic risk associated with increasingly scarce raw materials has spurred conservation activities across all industries (although less vigorously when prices retreat), which include innovative efforts to reduce waste, recycle existing material, and search for lower-cost and more sustainable substitutes.

Economics—price volatility and the associated risks—are insufficient driving forces to sustain the current green movement. It's easy to justify business decisions that reduce energy consumption and natural resource waste when commodity prices are high and global economies are growing rapidly. However, the impact of reducing demand from conservation efforts, even in an active and vibrant economy, is an inevitable drop in price. This will remain true as long as businesses can reduce consumption of natural resources faster than the resources themselves are truly depleted from their source. Economic recession and slower growth also contribute to lower consumption as economic cycles occur. If improved environmental stewardship relied on price pressure alone as a driving force, the world would be destined to experience an endless ebb and flow of cyclical activity without new taxation or "cap-and-trade" mechanisms. As prices rise, initiatives for environmental stewardship would become popular; but when global demand and prices declined, the improvement activity would also decline.

As improved environmental stewardship reduces the global consumption of scarce natural resources, global demand is more easily met with existing supplies, and the risk premium built into commodity prices can potentially disappear quickly. For example, in 2004, when crude oil was trading at $40 a barrel, the "fair value" was estimated to be only $27 a barrel.[32] The risk premium has varied up to 30 percent and potentially higher over time[33] and will likely be highest during times of strong demand, constrained supply, and uncertain hazards, such as international conflict, adverse weather patterns, or disruptions in the supply chain.

1.3.3.2. Market Risk from Poor Response to Changing Consumer Preferences

Consumers' heightened awareness and changing preferences are also driving businesses to become better environmental stewards. Consumers are looking not only for new products and services that simultaneously address global warming and volatile energy prices, but also for environmentally conscious companies from which to make their purchases. Consumer demand for environmentally friendly products has spurred new product and service strategies, new business models, and entirely new businesses. For companies of all sizes, product portfolios and marketing focus is shifting from an environmentally cavalier atmosphere to an eco-friendly one. Although individuals and organizations that support actions such as living in trees to disrupt logging activities are still far from mainstream, it's becoming increasingly difficult for a business to be too eco-friendly, from a consumer's point of view. Because market risk and reputational risk are mutually reinforcing drivers of environmental stewardship, companies must mitigate both as they protect and grow their brands. For example, as consumers increasingly expect green products in the marketplace, businesses must mitigate market risk by offering those products, and mitigate reputation risk by positioning themselves as environmental stewards that are socially responsible.

The change in business strategy to capture the attention of customers can sometimes be simple, such as increasing recycled content and accentuating that fact in product labeling. Starbucks has been doing this with its beverage cups and heat protectors. Other subtle product changes can also be effective, such as redesigning a water bottle to reduce plastic content and explaining the reason for the new eco-friendly design to customers through low-cost label changes. For other companies that are making larger research and development investments to support more sophisticated eco-friendly products, risks and potential rewards are both higher. Eco-friendly automobiles have been in development for years and are just now growing in popularity. A few years ago, the trend was toward larger, fuel-insensitive sport-utility vehicles and light trucks.

New business success stories are occurring in areas that have previously struggled to be profitable. Companies that assess real estate properties for renewable energy opportunities and others that install new equipment are benefiting because of a new emphasis from consumers on reducing their own carbon footprint. Other businesses that extend the scope of recycling programs are also more successful now that consumers increasingly view recycling as an obligation instead of a nuisance.

To heighten consumer awareness, labeling standards are emerging, such as "carbon labeling," first introduced in the United Kingdom in 2007.[34] Carbon labeling articulates the total carbon emissions from bringing a product to the store shelf. In California, new cars being sold are required to include labeling with "global warming scores."[35] As more companies claim to have eco-friendly products, standards, oversight, and regulation are certain to follow to identify false claims and clarify the meaning and importance of others. One example comes from Green Seal, an organization that provides science-based standards that strengthen credibility and transparency in the marketplace.[36]

1.3.3.3. Regulatory Risk from Government Action and Legislation

The combination of regulatory risk from new legislation and global agreements is a driving force that is expected to accelerate the trend of environmental sustainability.

In 1997, the United Nations held a conference on climate change in Kyoto, Japan, that resulted in an international agreement to fight global warming and associated climate change. The Kyoto Protocol, which took effect in 2005, calls for industrialized nations to reduce greenhouse gas emissions. A broad host of countries participate in the Kyoto Protocol, but debate continues about its effectiveness. The prescribed emission reductions and timing are considered legally binding, but many of the protocol's obligations are limited to monitoring and reporting, without actual provisions for enforcement and penalties if reductions are not achieved.

At another meeting in Japan in 2008, the Group of Eight (G-8) leading industrial nations endorsed halving world emissions of greenhouse gases by 2050 but set no near-term targets. This accord could succeed the Kyoto Protocol when its first phase expires in 2012, but support beyond the G-8 countries is uncertain.[37]

Other, more binding proposals are also being developed and becoming law. The United Kingdom Climate Change Act, proposed in 2007 and made law in 2008, aims to move the United Kingdom to a low-carbon economy and society, with an 80 percent cut in emissions by 2050 from a 1990 baseline. Even though aviation and shipping are excluded, the impact to businesses will be substantial.[38] As with establishing compliance with Sarbanes-Oxley legislation in the U.S., technology is expected to play a significant role in monitoring and demonstrating compliance with climate-change regulations such as the U.K. Climate Change Act.

Regulatory proposals are being actively developed not only at the global and country levels, but also at the industry, state, and local levels.

The U.S. Army, which consumes roughly 22 percent of the facility energy that the entire federal government uses, has estimated that a 1 percent reduction in its energy use results in a savings of $10 million. It adopted the U.S. Army Energy Strategy for Installations in 2005, which identifies five tenets to the strategy: eliminate waste, increase efficiency, reduce dependence on fossil fuels, conserve water resources, and increase energy security. To ensure that objectives are met, the strategy even mandates "extensive use of electronic energy monitoring and control equipment to validate performance of energy systems and focus corrective action accordingly"[39].

Real estate markets recognize that state energy-efficiency standards are becoming stricter. The California Energy Commission says that, by 2020, all new homes will need to be zero-net-energy homes.[40] In 2007, it was predicted that future legislation would require commercial buildings to be zero-net-energy consumers by 2050.[41] For this to be even partly true, a paradigm shift is needed in the construction industry, with solar water heating, photovoltaic electricity generation (using solar panels), and water-conserving technologies all playing a role. Renewable, environmentally friendly building materials and energy-efficient fixtures and appliances are already playing a significant role in new construction. Although legislation in this industry is still developing, many incentives have already been enacted that encourage adoption through discounts and tax deductions. The foundation to enable this paradigm shift is already falling into place with standards and certifications that we can measure building practices against. For example, the Forest Stewardship Council (FSC) certifies some wood as sustainable when it meets established criteria.[42] The U.S. Green Building Council (USGBC) has created Leadership in Energy and Environmental Design (LEED), a third-party certification program for the design, construction, and operation of green buildings.[43] Standards and certifications are also emerging for appliances. The Environmental Protection Agency (EPA) and the Department of Energy approves Energy Star products. GreenPoint Rated products are also becoming more common.

Many governments regulate water as a valuable and scare resource, and the associated regulatory risks can be significant. For example, in 2002, India revoked the Coca-Cola Company's operating license to use ground water in Kerala, India, because of water management and supply concerns.[44] In another example, the town of Shapleigh, Maine, denied Nestlé permission to take water.[45]

Other industries are also facing a more restrictive legislative environment that is pressing—and, in some cases, mandating—businesses to become better environmental stewards. In 2003, the European Union enacted the Waste from Electrical and Electronic Equipment (WEEE) and the Restriction of Hazardous Substances (RoHS) directives, both pieces of legislation focused primarily on reducing damage to the environment from using certain hazardous substances in electrical and electronic equipment (EEE). More recently, Germany integrated the intent of both directives into its own laws with the Act Governing the Sale, Return, and Environmentally Sound Disposal of Electrical and Electronic Equipment, also known as the ElektroG. This law establishes new responsibilities for companies that sell their products in the German market. Among other responsibilities, firms must take back, recycle, and dispose of the products they sell. The information technology and electronics sectors are two industries that this legislation clearly affects. Others affected include sectors that produce household appliances, lighting equipment, electrical and electronic tools, toys, sports and leisure equipment, medical products, monitoring and control instruments, and automatic dispensers.[46] In the U.S., 18 states have developed recycling laws for disposing electronic waste, and more states are expected to follow.[47]

EEE products are a likely and sensible target for legislation such as the ElektroG. Many electronics products have relatively short life spans. And because of the constant stream of innovations that improve performance, planned obsolescence often encourages product replacement with new versions before the end of their functional lives. Without proactive recycling programs, excessive and hazardous input into landfills can result. Some electronics companies, such as Lenovo and Dell, have already voluntarily initiated their own take-back, recycling, and disposal programs. In 2006, Dell announced that it would take back any of its products from consumers for free, anywhere in the world.[48] Lenovo has also created a completely free take-back program for its products.[49] Sony offers free disposal and recycling to its customers for some products, and for other products it offers trade-in credit toward new electronics.[50] Hewlett-Packard, Apple, Asus, and Toshiba also have take-back programs.[51]

As some companies voluntarily adopt practices in one country that are being enforced through legislation in another, the broader trend toward increased corporate social responsibility plays an important role.

1.3.3.4. Reputational Risk from Failure to Strengthen Corporate Social Responsibility

The increased reputational risk as corporate social responsibility strengthens is another driving force that is making it easier for companies to improve their position as environmental stewards.

Corporate social responsibility (CSR) is no longer viewed as simply a regulatory or discretionary cost of doing business. Instead, it is increasingly viewed as an investment that brings financial returns. Environmental stewardship is a significant part of corporate social responsibility, which also includes societal and market responsibilities. In 2008, a survey of 250 business leaders on corporate social responsibility found that 68 percent of them are now using CSR as an opportunity and a platform for growth.[52] With the onset of the information age, society can more readily judge the highly visible actions of an enterprise, its leaders, and its employees. Not surprisingly, when this visibility uncovers actions that are perceived to originate from low ethical standards, regardless of their actual legality, companies can lose business value and customer loyalty, both of which are difficult to regain. Stakeholders in the investment community will perceive the enterprise with higher risk, customers will choose competing products when other factors in their decision are equal, and community support might disappear. For example, reputational risk from "failing to address social concerns associated with water use could prove damaging to a company's reputation or brand."[53]

Although many CSR actions focus on improving responsibility toward society and social values, a growing number of them target environmental stewardship. In one straightforward example, Catalyst Paper Corporation, a Canadian pulp and paper company, uses its own by-products (biomass) to power its operations. It also regains heat from effluence to warm process water, further reducing its carbon emissions.[54] Such efforts reduce waste and lower costs, while also demonstrating a visible, differentiated position on environmental stewardship.

Tesco is the fourth-largest retail chain in the world, with more than 2,800 stores in central Europe and Asia, and expanding into North America. The company operates in the grocery and other industry segments, and has a leadership position in corporate social responsibility from efforts to strengthen environmental stewardship. The company runs 75 percent of its delivery fleet on biodiesel fuel, had labeled 70,000 of its products with carbon counts for consumer awareness by 2008, and will meet the electricity and heating needs of a distribution center in Goole, U.K., with a straw-powered combined heat and power plant that will generate enough electricity to run eight Tesco stores. The electricity is almost carbon neutral because the amount of greenhouse gas emissions is about the same that the straw absorbs while growing, according to Tesco. To extend the benefits even further, the ashes from the process will be made available for other industries or local farmers to use, and all excess electricity will be sold back to the grid.[55] Tesco's efforts are not limited to the United Kingdom. Tesco U.S.A.'s CEO, Tim Mason, has said that the company will set "a global example by measuring and reducing our greenhouse gas emissions, helping to stimulate the development of low-carbon technology, and empowering consumers by providing then with choice, value, and information." With a $13 million solar roof installed on its five-building, 820,400-square-foot distribution center in California, Tesco will have one of the largest roof-mounted solar installations in the world.[56] Wal-Mart has also installed the largest sun-operated photovoltaic installation in Latin America, which will provide about 20 percent of the energy needs for one of its stores.[57]

In many cases, businesses that adopt ethical standards for environmental stewardship that go beyond current legislative requirements are also gaining competitive advantage, winning customer loyalty and market share, and lowering their business risk. Reducing environmental impact often leads directly to higher profitability through increased sales or decreased costs, but it can also lower the risk from adverse environmental impact events. When adverse environmental events occur, companies that are known for high levels of environmental responsibility might more easily maintain customer trust, loyalty, and support. However, because many leadership positions in CSR have little direct responsibility for core supply-chain or manufacturing decisions, successful CSR programs often require broad leadership commitment and a culture that supports that commitment.

1.3.3.5. Operational and Supply-Chain Risk from Inefficiencies and Environmental Change

Operational and supply-chain risk from inefficiencies, environmental hazards, and extreme adverse weather patterns is another driving force that is pushing businesses to invest in the necessary initiatives to become better environmental stewards. For example, as some enterprises improve their efficiency and lower their resulting cost structure, other businesses that don't are increasingly at risk of being unable to compete effectively because of higher operating costs. Polluted water supplies and increased hurricane activity are examples of other kinds of risk to business operations.

One emerging practice that some businesses are now adopting is to favor upstream suppliers and other business partners that run environmentally conscious businesses to deliver supplies. A complete transition to such practices requires fundamental changes to well-established procurement processes and supplier performance measurement systems, so it will take time to accomplish. However, the risk is growing for suppliers that don't improve their environmental stewardship in the future, and they will have more difficulty competing for business with low environmental-stewardship status.

Luckily, businesses can apply a growing number of mature, proven solutions and innovative, high-impact new ones to improve their operations and become better environmental stewards. However, businesses shouldn't overestimate the maturity of available solutions and must consider the pace at which improved solutions might become available when making long-term commitments. Most of the solutions that are available, some of which are "off the shelf" or turnkey, fall into one of four broad categories: targeted point solutions (solving one particular problem), diagnostic tools, transformation methodologies, and macro-level environmental models. Without this breadth of available solutions for companies to evaluate and utilize, the task of improving environmental stewardship would certainly be more difficult. Chapter 9, "Business Considerations for Technology Solutions," describes some of these solutions.

Opportunities have been available to improve environmental stewardship in most enterprises for many years, but only recently have all the driving forces aligned in the right direction to prompt the worldwide call to action that is being witnessed today. The widespread availability, use, and adoption of comprehensive diagnostic tools, solutions, and transformation methods that help companies identify and realize opportunities have only recently been popular in the mainstream global business community.

1.4. Develop Green Strategy with Rigor

The movement toward doing better green business is not solely the result of grassroots efforts that develop inside companies from individual initiatives and grow in an ad-hoc way into larger programs. According to one cross-industry study on how large, multinational corporations are addressing their carbon footprints, more than 77 percent of the companies surveyed had either already developed or were in the process of developing a carbon-offset strategy.[58] This isn't surprising, considering the level of strategy-formulation capability many enterprises already possess. During the past two decades, both large multinational companies and nimble, smaller organizations have made strategy formulation a core competence to compete in the marketplace. Using this competence, companies can refocus from traditional business strategy to green strategy for environmental stewardship.

Businesses are not alone as they develop enterprise-level green strategies for environmental stewardship and take steps toward achieving environmental sustainability. The academic community, business-strategy practitioners, and industry peers are creating and sharing their methods and points of view to help others develop their own visions for the future, and to construct practical roadmaps that achieve those visions. For example, the Pew Center on Global Climate Change provides a report that guides companies on how to integrate climate-related concerns into their corporate strategies.[59] In 2007, Deloitte's U.S. Manufacturing Industry Practice published a "practical guide to driving shareholder value through enterprise sustainability" that defines and describes strategic issues for businesses to consider.[60] The *Harvard Business Review* has also consolidated a collection of its articles into the *Harvard Business Review on Green Business Strategy*.[61] With businesses of all sizes and across all industry sectors embracing the green movement, it's clear that benefits are attainable. This is especially true when investment decisions are aligned with a well-developed green strategy that complements and strengthens traditional business strategy.

2

Formulate Green Strategy to Complement Traditional Strategy

2.1. The Role and Scope of Green Strategy Is Broad

A green strategy fundamentally helps an enterprise make decisions, transform its operations, and sustain improved performance so that it makes a positive impact on the environment. A green strategy also helps the organization define its role in environmental stewardship, communicate its role to the world, and determine how aggressively opportunities and investments to "go green" will be pursued. As noted in the previous chapter, operating a greener business brings with it opportunities to grow top-line revenue from developing and selling environmentally friendly products and services, and reduce bottom-line costs from better managing natural resources and energy usage.

A green strategy for an enterprise, whether public or private, government or commercial, complements or transforms the business, operations, and asset strategies that the enterprise already understands and articulates. As in any other aspect of strategy formulation, cost reduction and revenue growth are only two important dimensions to consider. Other areas include meeting existing regulatory compliance, anticipating new legislative measures, establishing a competitive position and brand image, and building appropriate perceptions in the global community. Green strategy also offers opportunities for enterprises to consider the consequences of their activities, products, and services beyond the four walls of their own business.

The principles that form the basis of a green strategy should lead an enterprise to make decisions based on solid business logic and good business sense, but also to improve environmental stewardship. The four principles in Figure 2.1 could be the tenets of any company's enterprise-level green strategy. We discuss each of these principles next.

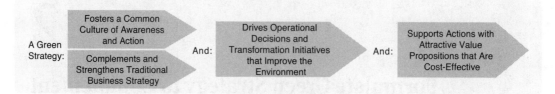

Figure 2.1 Potential tenets of enterprise-level green strategy

Source: *Journal of Business Strategy*

As with any new strategy formulation, green strategies need to consider and address interdependencies with other corporate programs and projects. In fact, an enterprise-level green strategy can be one key ingredient of a broader corporate social responsibility program, which companies are now formalizing more prevalently than in the past.

2.2. Foster a Common Culture of Awareness and Action

Creating a green culture often involves reinforcing behavior that people already want to adopt, but the appropriate tools and training are required for change. Without focused efforts, workforce attitudes might likely reflect those of society at large. That is, some people will be enthusiastic and proactive on their own, some will be neutral, and others will be skeptical. Transforming such a culture to a common one of awareness and action will certainly require a combination of investment, direction from leadership, and resetting of some priorities. Conversely, of course, when companies can successfully change attitudes in the workplace, they contribute to changing societal attitudes.

Businesses that cultivate a green culture today often stand out as being unique; other times, the differences in a green culture are imperceptibly small yet effective. In the former case, an environmentally sound culture is often part of the core business strategy to encourage "green" considerations in every decision that is made. In the latter, reinforcing simple courtesies that each employee can give to the environment might also have a significant impact on a company's bottom-line expenses—and even top-line revenue performance.

At some companies, the very idea of discarding an empty beverage container anywhere other than a designated recycle bin makes employees uncomfortable. At other companies, failing to turn off the lights in a conference room as the last person exits is a minor taboo. Still other companies measure and report the quantity of recycled office-use paper as a percentage of new paper purchased through its procurement organization, and set performance targets to increase the amount of recycling as part of continuous improvement efforts. Recycled paper that outside vendors purchase is sometimes considered a revenue stream.

In one straightforward example, a Fortune 500 global corporation in the industrial sector identified a critical need for global warming and climate change training so that employees could easily make connections between their daily activities and the improvement they could make to global environmental trends. In another example, IBM organized a community-building event in California so that employees could volunteer to pick up trash at a neglected beach.

Leading practices that cultivate a common culture of environmental awareness and support a green strategy are already emerging and developing in many companies. Effectively managing change to achieve a common culture of awareness and action that supports a green strategy should anticipate and provide for such organizational needs as leadership, tools, training, performance measurement, roles and responsibilities, and communications. Figure 2.2 shows a few key leading practices, which we briefly describe next.

Figure 2.2 Leading practices that cultivate a common culture

2.2.1. Lead by Example

The importance of leading by example applies to any business circumstance, but leadership visibility is especially important when cultural change is a key objective. Simple gestures from managers, directors, and executives can go a long way toward changing enterprise culture. Turning off lights when exiting conference rooms, walking a few extra steps to discard recyclables in the appropriate bin, and issuing straightforward requests to add recycling bins in convenient locations are all examples that pave the way for an entire workforce to adopt the same behavior. Communications to employees can emphasize that people at all levels of the organization should lead by example.

Senior-level support and sponsorship of environmental improvement initiatives with other business partners or in the global community, such as an investment in reforestation, can be another powerful driver of cultural change. This visible investment also enables a workforce to better understand how corporate priorities are changing. As companies organize volunteer efforts that build teams and improve local communities, communicating how these efforts align with broader environmental stewardship goals can drive cultural change.

2.2.2. Install Appropriate Tools

In creating a common culture of awareness and action, companies should give the workforce appropriate tools to support change. Clearly labeled recycling and waste receptacles can be placed where they are most likely to be used. Other tools, such as videoconferencing, can provide an alternative to face-to-face meetings that require travel. Tools that allow employees to telecommute from a home or remote office location also help reduce energy consumption by eliminating automobile mileage from commuting. Targeted, point solutions can solve one particular problem yet assist in virtually any industry. For instance, most companies that manage a fleet of vehicles for product deliveries could benefit from route-optimization software that minimizes the miles driven across multiple deliveries and across many delivery vehicles.

Reporting tools (ideally, with real-time reports) that inform every employee about how the company is doing with respect to its environmental goals can also foster a common culture of awareness and action. Such tools can report on energy or waste reduction to build a quality-centered culture. As in building a quality culture, the tools and measurements are similar, the business processes are largely the same, the role of leadership is still crucial, and new accountability is still assigned.

2.2.3. Provide Training

Companies should provide training for employees to foster a common culture that is sensitive to business impacts on the environment. Straightforward awareness training can be both simple and effective so that when recycling and other efficiency tools are put in place, employees are aware of their availability and understand the appropriate use. Awareness training can also help a workforce understand how some seemingly simple tools that are intended to improve environmental stewardship actually fit into a broader context of enterprisewide change. For example, in its Internal Revenue Manual, the U.S. Department of Treasury's Internal Revenue Service (IRS) describes its approach to employee training as addressing "the role of individual employees in relation to the IRS environmental policy, goals, and objectives" and emphasizes "the benefit of improved environmental, energy, and transportation management to the mission of the IRS."[1]

Training that connects the science of global warming, the associated climate and weather change, and depletion of scarce natural resources with actions that employees can take to make a difference represents a level of sophistication above awareness training. Many companies are now in a position to effectively provide this type of training to their employees. Environmentally conscientious companies can adapt employee new-hire training and refresher training to strengthen conservation behavior, such as turning off lights and recycling paper. The method by which training is delivered can also offer a case example or a learning exercise. For example, using online, web-based, or webinar-style training tools eliminates travel and the need for classroom facilities. If training is onsite, instructor-led training can be combined with other essential business activities that require co-location, such as job skills training, to avoid additional travel. In a third scenario, offering training on-site in the workplace minimizes environmental impact.

2.2.4. Measure and Report Performance

Measuring and reporting performance against key performance indicators for environmental impact can help establish an environmentally friendly enterprisewide culture. These measures can be cascaded through an organization and tracked at different levels—such as the employee, process, plant, or product levels—to enable accountability and empower people with authority to take action and make improvements.

Simple measures, such as number of bottles and cans recycled from different facilities, weight of paper recycled, and number of people who volunteer for environment improvement projects, can facilitate cultural transformation. These performance indicators can apply to all employees in an organization, whereas others might be customized for a specific division, site, or department. Fuel consumption, weight of scrap material, and volume of byproducts from chemicals consumed might apply specifically to manufacturing facilities. Office facilities might measure electricity usage and percentage of electricity supplied by renewable methods, or the level of telecommuting, web-conferencing, and videoconferencing in lieu of air or automobile travel. Public or investor relations departments might qualitatively measure favorable and unfavorable news reports and articles that have been written, or possibly capture announcements from local city officials that recognize the community contributions from employees.

After identifying the key performance indicators, implementing a measurement system, and establishing baseline performance, an organization is well positioned to begin setting improvement targets and communicating how each employee can help meet those targets. Even though everyone can contribute to improvements, explicit ownership and accountability should be assigned so that as plans are implemented and performance targets are achieved, "benefit owners" and their teams can be recognized. Likewise, when improvement targets fall short, benefit owners can lead efforts to identify the root cause and implement corrective action. Beyond individual accountability, departments, sites, and business units can all have environmental stewardship goals aligned with enterprise objectives.

2.2.5. Make It Everyone's Responsibility

In establishing a common culture of awareness and action, companies must encourage everyone to help improve a company's environmental stewardship position. Senior executives should take ownership of and accept responsibility for establishing priorities and guiding principles, to support an enterprisewide culture of awareness and action. Managers should be empowered to apply the guiding principles and make operational decisions that align with a green strategy. Employees should be encouraged to complete projects and continually improve operations with a greater degree of environmental benefit, and identify "grass roots" opportunities for new, innovative improvements.

Enterprises that already have a portfolio of human resource, innovation, and knowledge-management tools can apply them to support a green strategy and ensure that every employee has responsibilities and defined roles to help move a company toward environmental sustainability. For example, Centers of Excellence (COE) can include elements of environmental stewardship in their charters. Many existing performance-management approaches also allow employees to document their goals, discuss them with their managers, and then review progress toward achieving those goals at regular intervals. Typical goals include contributions to cost reduction, revenue generation, thought leadership, and product innovation. By adding dimensions of responsibility for improving environmental stewardship, reducing a company's carbon footprint, or organizing other employees to generate new ideas, every employee can have an important, recognized role as part of a common culture of awareness and action.

2.2.6. Communicate with the Workforce and Others

Communicating with the workforce and others is also critical in achieving effective cultural change and enabling a holistic green strategy. Forward-looking communications inform a workforce of future plans, allow employees to understand the big picture, and explain how the company sets high-level priorities and makes significant investment decisions. Such communications can also help individuals learn how to get involved in areas of high personal interest, areas where their professional development goals align with company goals, or areas in which they have specific subject matter expertise. Rearward-looking communications can celebrate success stories early and often, recognize leadership actions, capture lessons learned, build a knowledge base, and summarize progress against key performance indicators. Real-time communications can provide a support network, answer questions, and provide facts. General communications can highlight relevant trends and emerging technologies, competitor actions and competitive positioning, and collaborative relationships that will affect the company and its operations. A range of stakeholders can benefit from clear communications, including suppliers, customers, business partners, investors, and community members.

2.2.7. Manage Cultural Change and Risk

Finally, the practice of managing change and risk must be deliberate, planned, and flexible over a specific time horizon. Some corporations have taken a straightforward project or program management office (PMO) approach that centrally manages different aspects of cultural change. This approach significantly reduces the likelihood of duplicate efforts, poorly coordinated timing across events, and inconsistent communications. Other companies in which divisions operate with a high level of autonomy develop guiding principles that support a uniform yet decentralized approach to identifying and launching projects that improve environmental stewardship and strengthen awareness and action. One research study that included input from supply chain and retail executives concluded that best-in-class companies work to centralize responsibility for corporatewide sustainability initiatives, allowing them to take a coordinated, end-to-end, holistic approach to socialize enterprise goals.[2] This approach increases and widens visibility, and more firmly establishes stakeholder buy-in. BHP Billiton, whose products include metals and energy such as coal and oil, serves as one illustration. When BHP Billiton launched its 2007 revised climate change policy, the policy applied at the enterprise level. The policy covered areas such as research and development of clean coal technologies; behavioral change; and a strategy for working collaboratively with customers, communities, and employees to reduce emissions.[3, 4]

Centralized, decentralized, and even hybrid (combination) models for managing change are all legitimate for companies to consider adopting, and each of them can appropriately manage the risks associated with cultural transformation. Most enterprises operate using at least some principles of scarce funding resources, in which decisions to invest in projects that align with a green strategy could divert funds and sponsorship away from other, more traditional projects. As these decisions are made, it is critical to ensure that the company does not suboptimize core business needs or encounter unwanted risks. For example, a company would want to scrutinize a decision that could divert funds away from scheduled (or even overdue) manufacturing facility and equipment maintenance in favor of installing photovoltaic technology to reduce future electricity costs.

2.3. Complement and Strengthen Traditional Business Strategy

Setting a clear vision and strategy enables people to make better decisions, align actions with a company's priorities, and ultimately provide goods and services to the global marketplace in a more environmentally friendly way. Unlike a company's other areas of strategy formulation, green strategy can affect decisions across the entire enterprise, including business strategy, operating strategy, organizational strategy, technology strategy (information and applications), and supporting infrastructure. Figure 2.3 shows the different areas of strategy formulation (the strategy pyramid) and the tactical areas they govern.

Figure 2.3 Strategy pyramid and operations influenced by a green strategy

Source: *Journal of Business Strategy*

2.3.1. Brands and Market Positions

The green movement has uncovered new avenues for companies to reposition themselves in the global marketplace and even establish new market positions that might have been unthinkable just a decade ago. To an environmentally minded business strategist, the current times are as challenging and exciting as megatrends from the past were to other business leaders. In the early 2000s the dotcom era saw the rise of the Internet and, along with it, new business models, products, and services. Some of the accompanying business ventures have stood the test of time and have matured and become part of our everyday life. Amazon.com's online book and merchandise store, eBay's online auction service, and Bank of America's online bill-payment service represent a sample of such ventures.

The green movement is now transforming the landscape of business in another new way. New business models can help companies focus on improving environmental stewardship and establish profitable new market positions. Intel, traditionally a manufacturer of semi-conductor computer chips and chip sets, entered the business of manufacturing photo-voltaic solar cells for makers of solar modules. In 2008, Intel spun off its SpectraWatt business to focus on this area and capture new growth opportunities in the solar arena.[5] Applied Materials, a company that traditionally has developed and manufactured the semiconductor manufacturing equipment used by companies such as Intel, is developing a position in the business of solar-generated electricity. Initiatives to build a new business model in this area at Applied Materials range from making acquisitions to pursuing technology innovation. Applied Materials' acquisition of Baccini, a leading supplier of automated metallization and test systems for manufacturing photovoltaic cells,[6] accelerated and strengthened its solar-oriented business model, as did its development of technology such as the Applied SunFab thin film line, for manufacturing thin-film silicon solar modules.[7] As early as 2006, Applied Materials had in place a strategy to reduce the cost per watt of solar power.[8] Other traditional companies in the semiconductor manufacturing industry are also gaining strength in the photovoltaic (solar energy) market. IBM's researchers have developed a new technology based on thin, flexible films that is being pursued as a competing product to films based on silicon wafer technology.[9] Even the funding and business leadership structures that companies are using to establish new market positions and support environmental stewardship are reaching an impressive level of sophistication. Intel has leveraged its New Business Initiatives group and Intel Capital, the company's global investment organization; IBM has launched Project Big Green and a Big Green Innovations leadership team to manage a variety of large-scale programs and collaborations, including its Green Data Center offerings.

The high-tech sector is only one area in which traditional, sometimes mature business models are innovating to establish new market positions. For example, General Electric's Ecomagination business initiative aims to meet customer demand for more energy-efficient products while also driving growth for the company. Reflecting a commitment to finding innovative solutions to environmental challenges, this business initiative helps bring such technology as wind turbines and solar energy to customers.[10]

As early as 2006, Sir Richard Branson, chairman of Virgin Group, sought to advance Virgin's environmental stewardship initiatives. That year, he announced Virgin Fuels and a new business model to fund environmentally friendly projects and business ventures to combat global warming and promote alternative energy. The products and services that the Virgin Group offers span such areas as mobile telephony, transportation, travel, financial services, leisure, music, publishing, and retailing. Although most of its business operations are in well-established markets, Virgin Group invests some profits from those businesses to fund initiatives for environmental stewardship.[11] By 2009, the Virgin Green Fund had become the primary clean energy and energy-efficiency vehicle for Virgin, making investments in areas such as turning biomass into butanol (a fuel more similar to gasoline than ethanol)[12], building a factory to manufacture flexible thin-film CIS (copper indium diselenide and related alloys) solar technology,[13] recycling petroleum and metal[14], using efficient lighting[15], and investing in automobile driver safety and efficiency technology.[16] But companies do not need to invest billions—or even hundreds of millions—on "make-or-break" business decisions to establish a market position in environmental stewardship and benefit from favorable brand recognition.

Many companies today are gaining at least some level of recognition in the marketplace for incremental improvement efforts for environmental stewardship, thus building their brands at the same time. Meaningful progress toward becoming a greener business can establish a clear position of higher social responsibility for virtually any organization; this is becoming increasingly important to consumers and other business partners. This is true even when the products and services that a business offers are not necessarily themselves better for the environment. Indeed, a company can legitimately make large strides toward becoming carbon neutral in today's business environment by simply purchasing electricity that has been generated from renewable sources instead of from burning fossil fuel.

Efforts to increase awareness and improve customer perceptions of corporate brands are made visible through traditional means such as press releases and all forms of advertising, and by making significant "green" investments and entering new partnerships with objectives to improve the environment. Office Depot, for example, opened a "green" store in Texas in 2007 that incorporates an energy-efficient green building design and new approaches to green visual merchandising.[17] This is only one move that Office Depot has made to build a greener brand and meet the needs of a customer base that is increasingly asking for environmentally friendly products. In one survey of 2,500 business professionals, more than half indicated that they are interested in making their office greener.[18] The United States Postal Service (USPS) is another enterprise that has tied its brand to environmental stewardship: The USPS has announced that it will cut energy use by one-third by 2015. The range of tools the USPS plans to use range from simple steps such as turning off lights, to significant equipment changes that involve renewable energy systems and alternative fuel vehicles.[19] PepsiCo has analogous goals, to reduce electricity and water consumption by 20 percent and fuel consumption 25 percent by 2015.[20] Its competitor, Coca-Cola plans to improve water efficiency 20 percent by 2012, among other goals [21], with an aspirational goal of being "water neutral."[22] PricewaterhouseCoopers, LLC (PwC), a leading business audit services firm, plans to cut its greenhouse gas emissions 20 percent by 2012 from better managing travel, office space, and commuting. PwC recognizes that the benefits of these actions go beyond improving environmental impact; they also affect the firm's reputation and can strategically differentiate a company in the marketplace in areas such as recruiting and workforce engagement [23]. By 2012, JPMorgan Chase is another company that wants to achieve "green" brand recognition by working to reduce carbon emissions 20 percent through facility efficiency improvements, conservation, and the purchase of renewable energy.[24] An online entertainment guide in the U.K., Localnightsout.com, has taken carbon-neutral positioning a step further and established itself as a "carbon growth negative" company, partly by pledging to plant a tree for every new paid display on its web site. It even issues each customer a certificate confirming the planting.[25]

Google, Cisco, Kodak, Wal-Mart, Duke Energy, and Yum! Brands represent only a handful of other companies whose brands are benefiting from a relatively early adoption of green practices and objectives.[26] History reminds businesses that even differentiation based on megatrends has a finite lifespan. It has been years since automatic transmissions were widely advertised as a differentiator in automobiles, and even longer since color differentiated televisions from their black-and-white predecessors.

Government organizations, analyst opinions, new industry awards, and watchdog organizations are leading other efforts to improve perceptions and position corporate brands for a greener world. The U.S. Environmental Protection Agency (EPA), for example, maintains a "Green Power List" of organizations that purchase electricity generated from clean, renewable resources, such as solar, wind, geothermal, biogas, biomass, and low-impact hydro sources.[27] The EPA also presents a prestigious Climate Protection Award.[28] Innovest has developed its proprietary EcoValue'21, an assessment tool that correlates eco-efficiency with financial performance and value-creation potential.[29] Similarly, the Ceres investor coalition ranks leading companies for their climate change strategies.[30] Innovest and Corporate Knights maintain an annually updated list of the "global 100 most sustainable corporations."[31] Energy Star, the World Environmental Center (WEC), the Council on Economic Priorities (CEP), and the International Energy Agency (IEA) are just a few organizations that bestow awards on companies for their leadership roles as environmental stewards. Also, analysis from research organizations such as Gartner, Inc., and Forrester Research, Inc., increasingly recognizes companies that demonstrate strength in green business practices. Being at the top of environmental stewardship ranking lists, receiving awards, and gaining favorable analyst coverage has become a competitive tool for companies to advertise and strengthen their brand. At the other end of the spectrum, rankings such as the "Climate Watch List" of laggards compared to industry peers [32] may have different implications for brand recognition.

Not all industries are displaying their green activities with the same degree of enthusiasm, though. Most companies are quick to declare carbon neutrality or establish environmentally friendly practices before definitions and standards for compliance are fully mature, but others are more careful. The wine industry, for example, recognizes that being green, biodynamic, sustainable, and organic all have important and potentially different implications for their various customer segments. Cohesive and meaningful answers are needed for marketplace questions regarding green involvement in this industry.[33] For example, one winery that uses fewer harmful pesticides in its vineyards might want to project a certain image of "being green" to its target customers. Another winery that uses environmentally conscious packaging with its products might use a different image of "being green." Without a way to remove the ambiguity in the meaning of "being green" for two such companies, confusion in the marketplace could result around product attributes that customers deem important.

Regardless of the specific approach, pursuing valuable and environmentally beneficial initiatives is undoubtedly helping companies reposition their brands in the global marketplace and achieve a sustainable competitive advantage. All businesses have many options to create stronger brand recognition and improve their market position; they simply need to consider which options and actions to take when identifying, prioritizing, implementing, and communicating progress toward environmental sustainability.

Environmental stewardship is one area of brand development in which companies can benefit from communicating both internal and external progress: They can emphasize more efficient operations and environmentally friendly practices internally, and they can point to external progress by offering "greener" products and services to customers—who, in turn, provide benefits to the environment when using those products.

2.3.2. Products and Services

Green strategies have enormous potential to influence the products and services a business offers to its customers, and thus can contribute to significant revenue growth. Within the context of brand and market-positioning goals, companies can open new channels for generating ideas by prioritizing product-development projects and service offerings based on their contribution to environmental improvement. Although green concepts are still emerging and competing companies are learning how to incorporate them into their offerings, this area is effectively allowing enterprises to establish product differentiation that is sustainable for at least some period of time. Evidence also suggests that green products are differentiated enough to be somewhat resistant to economic recession.[34] In fact, by 2008, an estimated 56 percent of manufacturers had already deployed some form of design for a greener products strategy. Another 26 percent of manufacturers planned to adopt a similar strategy by 2010.[35]

Every business has its own perspective on the customers and customer segments it serves, as well as a viewpoint on how to effectively sell to each of those segments. When rethinking a company's product and service portfolio to improve environmental stewardship, companies must understand the value created from the customer's perspective. Certainly, companies can view green products and services in more than one way based on customer value, but useful categorizations might focus on performance, ingredients, substitutes, and innovative new values. Each of these categories are discussed next.

2.3.2.1. Efficiency-Based Green Products

Efficiency-based green products and services make customers more efficient users, with no changes in use: Consumers simply use the products or services as they always have, except that now they benefit the environment while doing so. These products also often benefit the customer directly, by lowering usage-based waste, reducing energy consumption and related costs, and improving environmental impact. Technology improvements are often the reason these products and services are more efficient. In this category, environmentally friendly products compete directly with traditional offerings. These products are often easy to differentiate in the marketplace because they typically benefit end customers directly by improving their financial bottom line.

Some consumer-oriented products that fit into this category include energy-efficient household appliances such as refrigerators and ovens, efficient lighting technology, motion-activated light switches, and fuel-efficient automobiles that burn traditional fossil fuels. Energy-efficient heating, ventilation, and air-conditioning equipment also fits into this category. Alternative, energy-efficient building materials also have been growing more popular for several years. In fact, a number of products in this category are already mature enough that legislation likely will become more pervasive and will accelerate market adoption. For example, recent actions by some governments to phase out incandescent lighting will likely accelerate the adoption of more efficient lighting technology.

Other consumer-oriented products are evolving in the efficiency category, and more are yet to be invented. Sony's green television is an example of a product that consumers use every day: Adding an easily described feature that more efficiently delivers lighting to conserve energy can help Sony differentiate its product with existing customers and reach a potentially new customer segment.[36] Sanyo has also announced plans to launch a green TV[37] that can conceivably compete in the same space.

Business-oriented products and services are also developing in this category. In 2007, IBM announced that it would partner with APC to create an energy-efficient Green Data Center for Bryant University. About the same time, IBM announced that it is using state-of-the-art technology to build a Green Data Center as part of Project Big Green to help the company and its clients reduce energy costs.[38] Market adoption has continued: IBM announced in 2009 that it would deploy energy-efficient, green Scalable Modular

Data Centers in a $3.1 million agreement with Religare Enterprises Limited (REL), one of the leading integrated financial services groups of India [39].

Companies must communicate performance improvement information to customers and articulate an explicit connection with environmental stewardship. Communicating the cumulative environmental benefits over the product's lifetime and comparing the overall environmental impact with that of traditional alternatives can be effective.

2.3.2.2 Ingredient-Based Green Products

Ingredient-based green products and services are often nearly identical to their traditional counterparts in form, fit, and function. However, they make customers part of a larger community of conservationists simply by using those products instead of the traditional alternatives. Products in this category are typically produced using more efficient and environmentally friendly manufacturing processes and equipment, or using raw materials that have a lower environmental impact (such as recycled metal, paper, and plastic). McDonough Braungart Design Chemistry's (MBDC) Cradle to Cradle Certification now includes product ingredients.[40] This might help consumers better judge ingredient-based products using criteria such as use of environmentally safe and healthy materials, materials reutilization, use of renewable energy and energy efficiency, and efficient use of water.

Some ingredient-based green products have been available and widely used for many years. One example is recycled paper in its many different forms. Unleaded gasoline is another early example of an ingredient-based, environmentally friendly product; it replaced leaded gasoline several decades ago.

More recent examples of ingredient-based products are emerging in virtually every industry. Consumers can now purchase bottled drinking water from brands such as Arrowhead [41] and Poland Spring [42] in eco-designed bottles that have a smaller environmental impact. Although these bottles are still made of plastic, which is a subject of ongoing debate over bottled versus tap water,[43] they use less material to manufacture, are lighter to transport, and are easier to crush for recycling. Organic jeans made by Greensource are now part of private-label clothing lines that Wal-Mart and Kmart stores offer.[44] Businesses can now purchase electricity that has been produced from renewable energy sources, wood can be purchased from forests that were replanted after logging, and reclaimed water can be used in some areas for irrigation. In fact, any product that is produced from recycled materials or manufactured by more efficient, environmentally friendly means falls into this category.

Businesses are also developing innovative ingredient-based services that differ little from traditional offerings but still improve the environment. Many hotels replace towels and bedding only when the customer wishes (the customer usually places them on the floor or leaves an indicator card on the bed) instead of automatically doing this every day. In this case, the customer experience is virtually unchanged, but the impact on the environment from water usage, detergent chemicals, and washer and dryer energy consumption is significantly lower. Starwood, Hilton, and Marriott hotels are just a few that offer this service.

AISO.net, a company that has partnered with IBM, claims to be the first company with 100 percent solar-powered web hosting. Moreover, the company has reduced its power and cooling costs associated with the company's IT operations by 60 percent through a massive consolidation effort.[45] This company provides another ingredient-based product whose environmental stewardship role is valuable to customers only if it is effectively communicated.

Companies must communicate the essential "ingredients" that go into the product before it reaches the customer and why they are important to the environment. Whether the ingredients are recycled content, less wasteful manufacturing processes, or more efficient transportation and delivery modes, customers need to have access to the information so they can make an informed purchasing decision to improve their role as environmental stewards.

2.3.2.3. Substitute-Based Green Products

Substitute-based green products and services, as the name implies, offer a viable substitute to traditional offerings, with a key difference: They have an improved impact on the environment. Alternative-energy automobiles that use fuel from renewable resources, and artificial lawn turf that does not require irrigation are two examples of green substitutes to traditional offerings.

Other substitute-based products include many mature but still-improving solutions that consumers are more rapidly adopting. These include on-site photovoltaic or wind-driven generators as a substitute for utility-supplied electrical power, solar or geothermal water and air heaters as an alternative to gas-powered systems, and modes of transportation that consume less fuel and result in a smaller carbon footprint. For example, public transportation and carpooling are well-established substitutes for individual automobile transportation.

On an enterprise, macro scale, nuclear power facilities, hydropower, or "wind farms" can represent substitute electricity-generating solutions for utility companies that might otherwise construct more traditional coal-burning power plants. To the end user of electricity, however, the product is an ingredient-based one.

2.3.2.4. Innovation-Based Green Products

Innovation-based green products, services, and solutions can be developed by bundling traditional offerings with additional, environmentally valuable features. These enable customers to proactively improve their environmental stewardship positions in ways that they could not have in the past. Other innovation-based offerings can represent entirely new solutions in the marketplace.

Companies should carefully consider where the sources of green ideas will likely come from and how they should develop those ideas. Sometimes identifying and evaluating green ideas can leverage traditional stage-gate processes from existing research-and-development (R&D) practices. For example, "IBM's Big Green Innovations was built extensively on innovation with the corporation's existing core competencies."[46]

GE Money, a unit of GE Corporation, introduced its Earth Rewards credit card in 2007. GE advertises that it will invest 1 percent of a cardholder's purchases in emission-reduction projects. Promotional material claims that $9,000 a year in purchases offsets all the emissions the cardholder is expected to produce in a year from travel and home energy use.[47] The Nature Conservancy Visa credit card offers an analogous product: Among other benefits, trees are planted based on enrollment and use.[48] These are clearly differentiated from other points-based consumer loyalty programs.

"Green rooftops" are another innovation-based solution that helps building-management companies, owners, and occupants to improve their impact on the environment while benefiting from an improved rooftop space. By 2006, Chicago had installed more than 200 green roofs, covering 2.5 million square feet of space with garden plants and other foliage that both absorbs carbon from the atmosphere and provides vegetables and new recreation space.[49] The 2008 Green Roofs for Healthy Cities Awards went to designs in a diverse group of cities, including Chicago, Vancouver, and Austin.[50] The Schwab Rehabilitation Hospital in Chicago uses its green roof as a place for patients to practice life skills or participate in horticulture-oriented physical therapy without having to leave the security of the hospital.[51]

Green financial products are another example of an innovation-based offering that allows investors to channel money into companies that are recognized for their environmental stewardship. For example, Green Century Capital Management administers Green Century Funds, a family of environmentally friendly mutual funds that include the Green Century Balanced Fund and the Green Century Equity Fund.[52]

Innovation-based information services are also developing and being offered to consumers. In 2008, Hewlett-Packard started its Eco Solutions program with an ambitious goal of allowing companies to reduce their environmental impact by 30 percent. The program includes a carbon footprint calculator and a printing assessment that measures a company's impact and costs from its printing activity.[53] Xerox also offers a carbon calculator as a service to customers, to track the environmental impact of office equipment usage.[54]

Capital.com, a hub for small businesses, highlights that companies can benefit from energy audit services that help business leaders learn how to better conserve energy by taking advantage of solar power, water conservation, and other energy-saving methods. Taking appropriate post-audit action not only increases energy efficiency, but reduces operating costs and gives the company some positive "We've gone green" publicity.[55]

Other innovation-based products and services have been developed to help businesses focus on capturing and managing information, to make better decisions to improve environmental impacts. IBM offers its Green Sigma solution, which combines sensor-based measurements with statistical analysis and dashboard-reporting technology to show business leaders their carbon footprint and other areas of waste. Microsoft's Environmental Sustainability Dashboard also makes businesses more aware of their impact on the environment.[56] In 2008, the Accenture Green Technology Suite was introduced to help organizations use information technology to assess their green agenda, including a green maturity model to assess environmental efficiency.[57]

Every industry has examples of new products and services that germinate from green strategies, and the number of them grows every day. Clearly, top-line revenue growth can benefit from an enterprise-level green strategy. Companies still have enormous opportunities to differentiate themselves from competitors through products and services based on efficiency, ingredients, substitutes, and innovation. First movers are already strategically positioning themselves in the marketplace and establishing market share early.

2.3.3. Channels and Partners

Common objectives, synergistic technologies, and complementary core competencies are all themes that bring businesses together in collaborative partnerships. Internet technology is one area in which the global business community has seen a large number of new partnerships and business models develop rapidly and mature almost as fast. Companies with enterprise-level green strategies are already starting to form and nurture partnerships that develop from a shared, common interest in improving the environment.

Some partnerships are forming for enterprises to more effectively take action in the community and improve infrastructure for public use. In one partnership formed in 2007, the San Jose Unified School District, Chevron, and Bank of America collaborated to establish the largest K–12 solar power and energy-efficiency program in the U.S. This collaboration is expected to yield benefits of $25 million over the life of the solar power system and is heralded as a model for other public sector renewable-energy programs.[58] Without a partnership such as this, the project simply might not have been possible.

The Green Highways Partnership (GHP) is another example in which concepts such as integrated planning, regulatory flexibility, and market-based rewards allow for environmental streamlining and stewardship in all aspects of the highway lifecycle. Global corporations such as Chevron have supported this partnership, and it also includes members of government agencies, such as the U.S. Environmental Protection Agency (EPA), the U.S. Federal Highway Administration, and the Maryland State Highway Administration.[59]

Other partnerships have formed with the objective to improve business performance for environmental stewardship. Ricoh, a $17 billion Japan-based company that offers digital office solutions, has organized a comprehensive network of green partnerships to promote effective environmental conservation. These green partnerships include customers, logistics companies, recycling companies, nonprofit and nongovernmental organizations, suppliers, and administrative organizations.[60]

The EPA Green Power Partnership is a voluntary program that supports the procurement of green power by offering advice, support, tools, and other resources. Participating in this partnership can help companies lower the costs of buying green power, reduce their carbon footprints, and communicate their leadership in environmental stewardship. This partnership explains to participants that buying green power is one of the easiest ways for a company to improve its environmental performance.[61] The Global Water Challenge (GWC) is one example that focuses on water and sanitation, not carbon. This coalition of companies has a common goal of universal access to safe water and sanitation.[62]

Other partnerships have formed to help companies develop new products that might not have been possible with the businesses working separately. For example, International Paper and Green Mountain Coffee Roasters won a Sustainability Award in 2007 from the Specialty Coffee Association of America (SCAA), the world's largest coffee trade association. The award came in the category of "Sustainable Business Partnerships Resulting in a Sustainable Product" for the partnership that resulted in the ecotainer cup, the first hot paper beverage cup made from fully renewable resources.[63]

As businesses invest in partnerships and alliances to improve environmental stewardship, they must consider their alignment with strategic business objectives. Partnerships can complement core competencies to better meet market needs, jump-start involvement in local and global communities, and support philanthropic efforts that boost brand recognition and public perception.

Suppliers, channel partners, and logistics partners are also important business relationships to consider in the context of green strategy. Many companies already recognize that improving the environment involves not only their own environmental stewardship position, but also the position of their upstream suppliers and downstream channel and logistics partners. For example, Dell has told its major suppliers that it plans to take their emission levels into account when deciding whether to continue doing business with them. This message came at a time when many of them had not yet even calculated their emission levels, according to Dave Parker, Dell's director of environment, health, and safety.[64] A 2008 cross-industry survey of more than 200 procurement professionals showed that many businesses support practices like this, although opportunities to improve in this area still exist. The survey found that one-third of the respondents are already following green practices according to established company policies, and nearly a quarter said their companies have written their green purchasing policies.[65] A different survey in 2009 strengthened the finding that a gap remains to be closed: It concludes that only one in ten companies actively manage their supply chain carbon footprint, and that more than one-third do not know the level of emissions in their supply chain network.[66]

Wal-Mart provides an example of a company that is successfully working with its suppliers and other stakeholders to improve environment stewardship throughout its value chain. One of its many "sustainable value networks" aims to reduce the amount of packaging for products on the shelf. In one successful case, General Mills straightened the noodles offered in its Hamburger Helper product. Straight noodles lie flatter than curled ones and require less space, so this made the packaging box smaller. As a result, the company saved 900,000 pounds of paper fiber every year, reduced General Mills' greenhouse gas emissions by 11 percent, and took 500 trucks off the road. Moreover, the effort increased the number of Hamburger Helper boxes on Wal-Mart shelves by 20 percent.[67] This is only one of many successes that the sustainable value networks have achieved. Another company, Tesco, introduced earlier in Chapter 1, "Driving Forces and Challenges That Organizations Face," works with its customers by allowing them to return excess packaging to stores for recycling.[68] This practice essentially allows customers to share the burden and cost in a "reverse logistics" channel for recyclable packaging.

In addition to suppliers, logistics and channel partners are important to consider. Even though transportation often accounts for only a small part of a product's carbon footprint, its contribution varies by product category and should not be overlooked as a potential area of opportunity. Some companies own and operate their own retail stores and logistics operations; others partner with distributors, retailers, and third-party logistics providers for the services. Companies that partner for these services to bring their products to the marketplace have essentially externalized the environmental impact of the associated activities so that the impact occurs outside the four walls of the enterprise. Many times the business drivers to outsource are well aligned with environmental stewardship and take advantage of economies-of-scale and efficient retail schemes. However, paradoxes do arise. For example, service agreements with logistics companies might prescribe reliability and on-time freight-delivery metrics that drive the provider to use air and truck transportation modes instead of more efficient means such as ships and rail. Reducing the need for company-owned warehousing can also paradoxically result in inventory shifting to public roads or into containers that contribute to highway congestion and inefficient space utilization. Some estimates show that congestion costs account for 8.5 percent of the gross domestic product (GDP). Clearly, the negative effect on waste can be large when logistics are not managed with environmental stewardship in mind.[69]

Channels through which companies offer products to customers are evolving under green strategies. For example, today consumers often have a range of shipping options for products they order through catalogs or web sites. Overnight air versus ground shipping is a common combination. A new option, "green delivery," is easy to imagine as an enhanced shipping option: The shipping company could consider not just timing, but also the greenhouse gas emissions from each transportation mode to minimize environmental impact. And with enterprises such as the USPS setting goals to cut energy use by one-third by 2015, offering choices like this might make more sense as the future unfolds over the next several years.

When developing a green channel strategy, businesses can follow channel strategy best practices from areas outside environmental stewardship. For marketing and sales, channels with low carbon footprints, such as Internet portals, virtual shopping carts, online order status tracking, electronic billing, and online customer (self) service are all low-cost, low-energy-consumption ways to reach, service, and sell to customers. For distribution channels and transportation modes, some air freight can be shifted to trucks or ships; and some truck cargo can be shifted to railways through transportation optimization. Outsourcing to logistics companies can take better advantage of economies-of-scale, with container shipments more likely to be full and making the most efficient use of each transportation mode. Further steps might include giving priority to fleets that consume alternative fuel. Some products, such as software and entertainment media, can shift from physical to online distribution channels that have a lower environmental impact.

2.3.4. Locations and Geographies

A green strategy should at least consider the environmental implications of entering, growing, or sustaining business in different global regions. The advanced legislative environment in Europe brings with it a set of unique opportunities and risks because adoption of environmentally friendly products might be more rapid there than in other places in the world. Similarly, rapid growth in countries such as China brings a different set of opportunities and risks. Companies also must balance opportunity with risk in decision making. For example, if carbon taxation and other costs associated with poor environmental stewardship are at risk of going too high for a certain region that does not prioritize reduced emissions, that region could lose some of its global competitive advantages from, for example, having low-cost labor. Outsourcing trends to such a region could slow or even reverse if the cost of poor environmental stewardship becomes too high and outweighs the benefits of labor arbitrage.

3

Green Strategy Supports Operational Improvements

3.1. Drive Operational Decisions and Initiatives That Improve the Environment

In addition to complementing and strengthening the effectiveness of a traditional business strategy, green strategy drives decisions and transformation initiatives at the operating, organizational, information, and applications levels of the strategy pyramid. (Refer back to Figure 2.3 to see this pyramid.) Transformation initiatives that are aligned with a green strategy can also improve the supporting infrastructure (bottom) layer of the strategy pyramid, which includes hardware and equipment. This section addresses each of these lower levels of the strategy pyramid.

3.1.1. Processes, Supply Chains, and Facilities

Green strategies have frequently targeted facilities. Office buildings, manufacturing operations, retail sites, and other key facilities are areas where businesses can easily measure energy consumed and identify improvement opportunities. Environmental impact–improvement efforts and initiatives in this area range from targeting human behavior and small retrofits, to focusing on large-scale construction and renovation.

For example, one Fortune 50 company in the industrial sector has retrofitted the light switches in its U.S. office buildings with motion-sensitive switches. If a conference room or common area of a building is not being used, the lights turn off automatically to save energy and reduce costs. This kind of retrofit is now common. Although this seems like a relatively low-impact activity, it's easy to envision the potentially significant impact of having every light switch in developed countries operate by motion sensitivity.

In another example, the Ben & Jerry's ice cream company started testing more environmentally clean freezers in 2008.[1] In a much larger move in 2008, the University of California, San Diego, launched construction on a sustainable-energy program as part of a goal to be the "greenest university" in the U.S. Photovoltaic solar arrays will be installed on the university's rooftops, and the project also includes biogas fuel cells and wind-generated energy.[2]

Numerous technologies are available, and companies need to evaluate what green technology makes the most sense, depending on the local climate and facility function. The availability and effectiveness of items such as solar cells and wind farms to generate electricity, or solar water and air heaters will vary based on geographic location and business purpose.

But not all organizations have proactively improved their facilities. In one example, a recruiting officer from one Fortune 500 global company recently interviewed university seniors to fill open positions. In the interviews, nearly half of the candidates asked what the company was doing in terms of green building and facility initiatives. Without an enterprise-level green strategy, the answer to their question was unimpressive to the interviewees. In this scenario, the most freshly educated minds were asking something that one of the most forward-looking companies could not answer. Shortly afterward, the department responsible for business real estate put the wheels in motion to develop a green strategy whose scope included all facilities.

Green strategies have also targeted process improvement opportunities. Six Sigma, a business management strategy and related set of quality-management methods, and Lean practices for organizing and managing business processes, have already made significant progress in reducing waste, especially from manufacturing and back-office processes. Chapter 5, "Transformation Methods and Green Sigma," further explains Six Sigma and Lean practices. Muda, a Japanese term for anything wasteful that does not add value, from Lean practices, provides a basis for identifying waste that can be reduced or eliminated. However, when a green strategy is considered along with cost reduction and optimization in process-transformation initiatives, outcomes can be different and additional opportunities can be captured. How many times has a gap assessment between a current process and a desired process included analysis of pain points and deficiencies such as "very little recycling of paper and plastic" or "too much paper and raw materials used"? Gap assessments are frequently used in business-process reengineering and other transformation initiatives, but "green" gaps are often neglected.

Process improvement opportunities to increase efficiency, reduce waste, and reduce a company's carbon footprint represent only a small part of the value companies can capture as environmental stewards in this area. Companies can transform and leverage processes throughout the traditional supply chain, value chain, and entire lifecycle chain to achieve not just cost-reduction goals, but also revenue growth, customer loyalty, and brand recognition.

Figure 3.1 shows how the lifecycle chain is constructed from the traditional supply chain inside the "four walls" of a company. It also includes processes from the traditional value chain that include supplier and customer activity, and expands beyond traditional boundaries to include farther-reaching processes for both upstream and downstream operations. The lifecycle-chain view of an organization, and visibility to the full scope of processes a company depends upon, provides new insight into proactive measures that business can take to positively impact the environment.

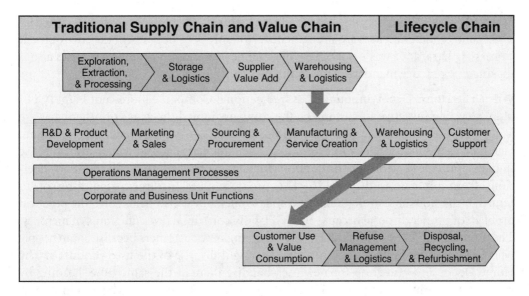

Figure 3.1 Lifecycle chain

As with many elements of green strategy, a number of companies have already applied lifecycle-chain principles to innovate and establish some leading practices. For example, Hewlett-Packard has sold its inkjet printer cartridges with an envelope that customers can use to recycle their old cartridges at no cost and with relatively little effort. This seemingly simple tool enables an original manufacturer to reliably retrieve its used products, dispersed over millions of sites, back to a central location for refurbishment or disposal. The obvious cost and environmental impact advantages of efficient refurbishment instead of original manufacturing are only a few of the benefits from this kind of program. Participating in the recycling program strengthens customer loyalty and brand association with environmental stewardship. Motorola is another company that offers a similar option to its customers: Customers can use prepaid envelopes that are bundled with many new cellular phones to send old phones back to the company for recycling.[3] Motorola, Nokia, and Sony Ericsson are just a few companies making it easy to recycle products from their industry by enabling consumers to print prepaid envelope labels directly from the Internet.[4, 5] Equipment manufacturers that are taking responsibility for the refurbishment and recycling of their products, and also involve end customers in the process, might be viewed as just a sophisticated version of reusable soda and milk bottles that were common decades ago. Today the practice still strengthens brand recognition and customer loyalty.

Some companies in the consumer electronics industry are taking this concept a step further by offering to take back any of the products they have sold in the past (discussed earlier in Chapter 1, "Driving Forces and Challenges That Organizations Face,"

Section 1.3.3.3). Manufacturers bear the cost of refurbishment or disposal, but customer loyalty and brand awareness are strengthened. Not only does this benefit the environment by keeping hazardous waste out of landfills, but new legislation in some countries also is making this practice mandatory for companies to sell their products there.

When The Home Depot announced its free national Compact Fluorescent Light (CFL) bulb–recycling initiative to customers, the company joined the ranks of others that are innovating their offerings and services in ways that consider the broader lifecycle chain. Heralded as the first service of its kind that a U.S. retailer made so widely available, the initiative provides customers with options for making environmentally conscious decisions, from purchase to disposal.[6] This program gives customers a good reason to return to the store and strengthens customer loyalty, but it also helps solve the practical problem of proper disposal because each CFL bulb contains a few milligrams of mercury. The program might even be a catalyst for acquiring new customers because some people who purchase CFL bulbs from other retailers might dispose of the used product at The Home Depot and also shop for new merchandise there at the same time. Leading by example, the company announced at the same time that it would switch from incandescent to fluorescent lighting in its retail store showrooms, to reduce energy consumption and improve the company's impact on the environment. For an idea of the waste reduced, one study from Greenpeace estimates that households in the U.K. could save 15 percent on electric bills simply by switching to CFL technology.[7] Best Buy followed a similar strategy when it launched its free e-waste recycling program.[8]

Large and medium-size companies are also leveraging knowledge of the lifecycle chain by instituting programs to collect and properly dispose of batteries and electronic equipment from employee use. By recognizing that disposal of these products should be treated differently than disposal of other biodegradable refuse, and instituting appropriate recycling programs, companies are proactively reducing their negative environmental impact. To extend the benefit, some companies encourage employees to leverage such hazardous waste–disposal programs by bringing their personal-use batteries and small electronics into the office for disposal instead of discarding them with household trash.

Innovative approaches to improving environmental stewardship from lifecycle-chain insights are large in number, but they are still only beginning to reflect their full potential. Radio frequency identification (RFID) technology is already being use to manage returnable containers and optimize logistics in the automotive industry.[9] RFID technology has also been tested where it could streamline checkout procedures in grocery stores and retail locations, and Global Positioning System (GPS) technology is being applied to track and optimize logistics functions around the world. Conceivably, companies could apply similar technology further down the lifecycle chain, to help automatically identify and separate recyclable material from refuse headed for dumping or landfill sites.

Not all the lifecycle-chain innovations come from improvements to downstream activities. In the pulp and paper industry, traceability of wood products and recycled raw materials back to the forest or other source is already important for paper manufacturers to make sure they are following established environmental stewardship practices and can confidently communicate compliance to customers. For example, International Paper is able to demonstrate its commitment to sustainable forest management through third-party certification to a number of independent standards, including the Sustainable Forestry Initiative (SFI), the Switzerland-based Programme for the Endorsement of Forest Certification (PEFC), the Forest Stewardship Council (FSC), and the Brazilian Forest Certification Standards (Cerflor).[10] For building materials such as lumber, organizations such as the FSC and the U.S. Green Building Council have developed certification standards. Companies can stamp their wood products with a mill's FSC chain-of-custody certification number, which enables it to be traced back to the originating forest. Such traceability gives lumber mills a means of communicating to their customers that the wood they purchase was harvested in a sustainable manner.

More companies are also finding ways to improve their environmental stewardship by "fracturing and splicing" lifecycle chains together from different industries. For example, when the U.K. online entertainment guide Localnightsout.com pledged to plant a tree for every new paid display on the web site[11], the company essentially fractured its lifecycle chain at its sales and marketing link, and spliced it with a "manufacturing" step in forestry.

Corporations that have taken a lifecycle-chain perspective to identify strategic, environmental improvement opportunities are already benefiting from an early-mover advantage, establishing favorable market positions with their increasingly green customers.

3.1.2. Organizational Roles, Skills, and Core Competencies

When a company creates and pursues a green strategy, its plan will undoubtedly affect its organizational strategy and core competencies. Some studies estimate that up to 500,000 new jobs across all income levels in ecologically responsible trades will be created in just a few years.[12] When the U.S. House of Representatives passed the Green Jobs Act in 2007, it paved the way for government funding of "green-collar" job training by authorizing up to $125 million per year to create an energy efficiency and renewable energy worker training program as an amendment to the existing Workforce Investment Act (WIA). The Green Jobs Act targets skills in a range of industries that include energy efficient building, construction, and retrofits; renewable electric power; energy-efficient vehicles; biofuels; and manufacturing that produces sustainable products and uses sustainable processes and materials.[13] The act has achieved some success, although the $22.5 million approved in the 2009 budget for the green-collar jobs training initiative "is well short of the $125 million that was authorized" originally.[14] If U.S. President Barack Obama's campaign policy objectives from 2008 are fully realized, $150 billion will be invested over ten years to create a much larger population of five million green-collar jobs.[15]

Entirely new core competencies are foreseeable to effectively execute a green strategy. Product engineers will need to have the competency to design products that use less energy and fewer raw materials to produce, and consume less energy and fewer resources when in use. Energy auditors will be in higher demand as the need for facility energy audits increases and building energy-efficiency analysis needs increase. Environmental management skills will need to be developed to monitor performance, and protect and conserve natural resources. Today's landscapers and maintenance workers will benefit from acquiring arborist competencies that give them an understanding of conservation and renewable resource use.[16]

Other existing roles will need to adapt to accommodate a greener job market. For example, finance and accounting professionals could learn how to manage and take advantage of carbon emission offsets. Drivers of all sorts, from pizza delivery workers and commuters to cross-country truck drivers, will benefit their employing organizations by learning energy-efficient driving practices. Countries such as Sweden already incorporate learning these eco- and energy-efficient competencies into the knowledge requirements to receive a driver's license. A new European Union directive on mandatory periodic training of bus, coach, and truck drivers includes sessions on fuel-efficient driving and safety.[17] Office workers at many companies that have not already started telecommuting programs will need to learn remote-work practices and the associated technology to reduce the environmental impact from commuting. Others in business operations will learn how to reduce carbon emissions and lower natural resource consumption, such as water and energy, at least partly by using traditional measures, such as cost, quality, cycle time, and inventory levels.

Few organizational roles are unaffected when a company adopts a green strategy. Facilities managers become more accountable for energy conservation, custodial staff has a higher responsibility to handle recyclable material, managers become responsible for reporting performance against environmental key performance indicators and are accountable for results, and executives become accountable for environmental stewardship, sustainability progress, and regulatory compliance.

In addition to skills and competencies, other organizational development tools should be aligned with the objectives of a green strategy. Performance management reviews are more likely to reward green contributions in the balanced scorecard that employees are assessed against, typically on an annual, semiannual, or project-by-project basis. High-potential employees and recruiters will likely recognize a need for environmental awareness in candidates. Training will likely include green elements and the impact employees can have on improving the environment. Communication and awareness campaigns will likely emphasize green objectives, highlight key successes, and recognize significant green contributors.

Many scenarios are being tested and turned into leading practices, with more options yet to explore. We can imagine a day in the near future when it's feasible for companies with effective recycling programs to match the redemption value of recycled beverage containers to fund, for example, an employee-chosen donation program. Or perhaps the day will come when human resource professionals require training on the legal implications of hiring practices that discriminate against employees with long commuting distances that result in a larger carbon footprint for the organization.

Ultimately, new roles will evolve, with critical responsibilities for delivering results on a green strategy. The Chief Sustainability Officer (CSO) role is just one such example.

3.1.3. Data Visibility, Reports, Systems, Platforms, Hardware, and Equipment

Information visibility and the enabling technology should be aligned with a green strategy so that investments in information technology (IT) are not wasted and expected benefits can be achieved. Although IT accounts for only 2 percent of global carbon emissions, it can contribute significantly to controlling and reducing as much as 98 percent of the carbon dioxide–equivalent emissions caused by other activities across all industries.[18] We can leverage technology to significantly manage and reduce environmental impacts of all sorts. More companies are applying RFID and GPS technology, along with vehicle and container routing-optimization software, to optimize supply-chain activities. Companies are also using optimization technology to support carbon trading and enable such capabilities as model-based optimization of supply chains and logistics activities.

Technology solutions that simply increase the efficiency and effectiveness of business activity while reducing waste can have a significant beneficial impact on the environment. Mature solutions already exist to enable web conferencing, videoconferencing, online chatting, virtual collaboration, e-mail, and voice over IP. Many companies are deploying these solutions to reduce the need for air travel and employee commuting into a physical office space. Wireless and portable technologies, such as cell phones, personal data assistants (PDA), highway-navigation computers, laptop computers, and Internet access, have made it much easier to do business practically anywhere. But fewer enterprises have taught employees the proper use of these technologies to reduce environmental impact. Using e-mail instead of traditional mail, traditional mail instead of overnight delivery, virtual conferencing instead of air travel, and electronic files instead of paper printouts are all technology-enabled practices that are apparently obvious, but barriers often exist to their full adoption. Sometimes the barriers are eliminated by training employees on how to use the technology, and other times cultural and policy barriers are strong enough to prevent their effective use. For example, by traditional policy standards, videoconferencing infrastructure and its use might appear costly. However, savings from less air travel could more than offset those costs. Through information technology, companies can monitor enabling tools, set improvement targets, and report progress. For example, an increase in telecommuting can correspond to a measurable decrease in physical commuting, and an increase in videoconference usage can correspond to a measurable reduction in air travel.

A different kind of opportunity exists for reducing paper consumption at some companies that are learning to operate in a more virtual, paperless office environment. For many companies, the information age has only led to faster printing technology that spurs increased paper consumption, instead of motivating a more paperless work environment. By monitoring the printer infrastructure, understanding improvement areas, and setting waste-reduction targets as part of a holistic green strategy, reducing waste can often be a simple matter of education and cultural change.

Companies can also apply technology to manage and report information so that business leaders can make better decisions that improve environmental stewardship. Solutions are now available that enable wired or wireless sensors to feed data from processes and other business operations into a data warehouse, and software can analyze and report on trends, apply limits, and even initiate and manage alarms so that process owners can take immediate action when real-time corrections are beneficial. Chapter 5 discusses this approach and its corresponding benefits.

The electronic and computer infrastructure itself also deserves consideration in green-strategy formulation. Green data centers are growing their market share and beginning to replace older, less energy-efficient server systems. Companies are also beginning to consider environmental impact along with other factors, such as labor pools with appropriate skills and labor rates, when choosing locations for new data centers. Because data centers generate heat and require sophisticated temperature controls, one consideration could be to choose a location that has a lower average outside temperature, to lower cooling costs through heat exchange. Other considerations could include alternative uses for the heat generated by a data center. A straightforward application of heat-exchanger technology could use the heat energy from a data center to heat air, water, or other liquids, to reduce the overall environmental impact from other facility operations.

Because the majority of computer electronics have ever-shortening lifecycles and include some toxic materials, procurement from responsible suppliers and disposal through appropriate channels easily fits within the scope of a green strategy. One study from Forrester Research, Inc., found that 85 percent of IT procurement and operations professionals in U.S. companies said environmental concerns were important in planning their IT operations. And 72 percent were aware of efforts by their vendors to promote "green IT" in the design, operations, and disposal of IT products. The needed awareness to act on a green strategy is largely in place. However, 78 percent of the study respondents said that they haven't included green IT in their evaluation and selection criteria for IT systems and devices.[19] Having a green strategy in place could easily fill this gap between awareness and action. Being green could be as simple as emphasizing energy efficiency in computing, but it could also put preference on selecting products from vendors that have environmentally friendly sourcing, manufacturing, delivery, and disposal operations.

As in other areas of business strategy, the most sophisticated technology solution is not always the answer to enabling a green strategy. The trend of using plasma or LCD display screens in place of printed or mechanical displays represents a move toward larger carbon footprints. These television-style displays are now used for everything from advertising in shopping malls and travel information at transportation hubs, to announcements and other messages posted at building entryways. Motion-sensitive switches could be one way of lowering the impact of this trend without reversing it.

Electronics manufacturers will inevitably face the challenge of balancing the production cost and retail price of their products with energy efficiency and functionality. In one example, the trend to move from analog to digital solutions makes it easier to integrate different products such as printers, copiers, and fax machines, but still might represent a move toward higher energy consumption. But the trade-offs are not simple to evaluate. If businesses purchase one integrated digital product instead of three traditional ones, the lifecycle-chain impact to the environment could be lower. Electronics suppliers that provide relevant, quantified information so that their business customers can weigh the trade-offs and make decisions to support green strategies would be providing a useful service in support of environmental stewardship.

Technology infrastructure is much broader than electronics and computer hardware. Businesses that own car fleets can explore including hybrid vehicles in their mix. For example, Enterprise Rent-a-Car and Wal-Mart have both increased the number of hybrid or alternative vehicles in their fleets.[20] In other examples, some of the world's most advanced warehouse facilities have already eliminated forklifts and heavy machinery with engines that consume natural gas in favor of electric-powered equipment.

Facilities across all industries are using renewable electricity from solar-, wind-, and water-generation technologies to reduce greenhouse gas emissions and carbon footprints. Many industries are also using technology to manufacture biofuels such as ethanol and biodiesel from corn grain or vegetable oil to replace fossil fuel consumption. Some industries are applying technology to operate and maintain water treatment plants and manage water supplies, as water management becomes more critical. Industry-specific technology solutions are also being developed, tested, and deployed as companies implement green strategy. For example, clean coal technology includes a portfolio of tools to reduce the environmental impact of burning coal as a source of energy.

These are only a few of the many examples that illustrate how an enterprise-level green strategy has the potential to impact nearly every area of a company's operations and can significantly impact both top-line revenue growth and bottom-line cost savings.

3.2. Support Actions with Attractive Value Propositions

Assigning value to environmental benefits that are typically qualitative is important when understanding a program's total green value proposition. Green value propositions include benefits to the company's working environment by improving buildings and facilities, benefits to the community, and impacts that improve the global environment. A green strategy should generally lead to cost-effective transformation initiatives that meet or exceed regulatory requirements.

Net present value (NPV), return on investment (ROI), and internal rate of return (IRR) are all frequently calculated measures of value used to prioritize business transformation initiatives and other projects. Cost reduction, revenue growth, level of fit with corporate strategy, strength of support for regulatory compliance, and risk reduction are all carefully evaluated. However, environmental benefit, carbon footprint reduction, water management improvement, and other factors that improve environmental stewardship aren't yet routinely included in prioritizing new initiatives and programs. This new dimension of value is not always difficult to evaluate. For example, as the economic value of carbon emissions becomes clearer through such programs as carbon trading, it's also easier to quantify that aspect of environmental stewardship in a value proposition.

When compared to traditional approaches, evaluating the green elements of an initiative involves a number of differences. Enterprises must understand these differences as they prioritize opportunities and make investment decisions as part of a green strategy.

First, the timeline for achieving a break-even ROI will likely be longer where startup costs are high but benefits are steady. Businesses can easily compute financial benefits from many initiatives that positively impact the environment by comparing current methods with their lower-cost green counterparts. Solar-, wind-, and hydro-generated electricity offer relatively high initial startup costs when implemented on-site—but after installation, they typically offer a positive financial return during their useful lifespan when compared to the usual utility bills. For businesses that look for their investments to break even after two to five years or sooner, the decision to make an investment in sustainable energy with a break-even point that is further out in the future can be difficult. Long-range business cases such as this require assumptions for items such as energy price over a long period of time. If actual prices are higher than originally assumed, the realized benefits will be better than expected. But if energy prices are lower, the realized benefits will be worse than expected. Accounting for traded carbon credits can further increase financial benefits when excess credits that result from emissions-reduction initiatives are sold at a prevailing market price.

Now that many enterprises have the choice to purchase electricity from utility companies that is generated from renewable and sustainable sources, they can make quantitative comparisons between installing on-site energy generation and relying on utilities to provide it for them. Skeptics that question the practice of purchasing green power from utilities argue that, by doing this, companies are avoiding their potential to move toward being carbon neutral within the four walls of the enterprise. Yet if every business was willing to bear the higher cost of electricity from renewable sources from utility companies, economies of scale would inevitably lead to lower prices that could be virtually unaffected by fluctuations in fossil fuel prices.

Second, product differentiation can be easier to achieve, and possibly easier to sustain, while the green movement continues to strengthen and its mass appeal widens. Differentiation in the marketplace frequently leads directly to market share and revenue growth, higher margins for a longer period of time, and stronger customer loyalty for cross-selling and up-selling opportunities. With the appropriate assumptions, businesses can quantify these benefits as an input into the value proposition and business case. For example, Lighting Unlimited, a company based in Florida that sells lighting fixtures and ceiling fans, learned that investing in carrying and promoting Energy Star–qualified products was an easy way to gain local market share. In just one year, sales of these differentiated products grew from 0 percent to 5 percent of total sales. According the company's president, Bert Heuser, "Advertising the Energy Star products we sell was a simple investment with a huge payback."[21]

Third, new initiatives and programs with soft benefits might receive more consideration under a green strategy, such as employee morale, lower attrition, favorable press releases, community goodwill, and more sustainable costs in a trend of rising or fluctuating fuel prices. Analysts predict that the green movement and changing consumer preferences will ultimately require businesses to routinely consider environmental stewardship in their investment decisions. In one 2008 survey of CEOs in northeastern Wisconsin, nearly 70 percent of the executives said that customer demand for an improved environmental impact was an important motivator for them to do so in their business.[22] Another survey of retailers identified competitive advantage as the top driver of sustainability programs in that industry.[23] Everything from product-development projects and process-improvement initiatives, to customer service and community involvement will be affected.

Fourth, legislative action and government incentives might contribute more to the value proposition of initiatives and programs that align with a green strategy, whether in place or anticipated, local or national, domestic or global. Legislation is already being drafted and passed that increases requirements for businesses to improve their environmental stewardship, and those that are staying ahead of the regulations are able to proactively transform their products and operations instead of reactively responding to government-imposed constraints.

Fifth, new risks and risk-mitigation approaches will emerge as new technology, new organizational skills, and change-management needs are considered. For example, low aspirations for environmental stewardship and correspondingly small investments would certainly be low-risk from a transformation perspective for many companies—where maintaining the status quo might be all that is required. However, the downside risk of noncompliance with new legislation—losing preferred supplier status with environmentally advanced business partners, losing market share to more advanced competitors, or experiencing increased employee attrition—could drive companies to set aspirations higher and increase the value of initiatives that meet those aspirations. Chapter 1 showed that businesses can view the driving forces behind environmental stewardship from the perspective of risk in different areas. With this perspective, it's clear that businesses can achieve tremendous value from having a green strategy and mitigating risk with the appropriate initiatives.

Business leaders and decision makers increasingly miss out on significant benefits because they do not consider green opportunities in a strategic context. S. L. Hart appropriately describes "greening" as being about more than cost reduction and explains that it can actually be a major source of revenue growth.[24] Stonyfield Farm, the third-largest yogurt producer in the U.S., has had an enterprise-level green strategy since it was founded in 1983. Its CEO, Gary Hirshberg, emphasizes that businesses need to be convinced of the "economic benefits of going green" and that "Stonyfield proves that you can make money working for the planet instead of against it."[25]

3.3. Steps to Develop a Green Strategy

As most business leaders already know, simply because a strategy has not been written or formally articulated doesn't mean that one isn't being followed, and vice versa. However, when a strategy and its objectives are well described and communicated to an organization, it's easier for employees to align their activities in collaborative environments, allocate their time appropriately with competing priorities, and make decisions that drive progress toward common goals. In addition, when successes are achieved and an explicit strategy is in place, it's easier to capture and widely disseminate lessons learned, sustain improvements and maintain best practices, and leverage the experience so that similar benefits can be captured across the entire enterprise.

The first step for an enterprise to develop a green strategy is to assess the current green state of operations and initiatives that have been completed or are underway. A maturity assessment of each area of the strategy pyramid against a maturity model, along with assessing the adoption level of leading practices, can clearly show the areas of a business that are advanced and others that might not even have a basic level of green awareness.

Figure 3.2 illustrates a range of maturity for one green strategy maturity model. As companies move from a low, "aware" level of maturity to higher levels, the role of leadership changes, the role of policies and governance becomes more sophisticated, and actions become an increasingly integral part of a changed corporate culture that continuously scans for new opportunities to improve environmental stewardship.

	Aware	Developing	Practicing	Optimizing and Leading
Role of Leadership	• Create guiding principles and governance to operationalize a green strategy	• Sponsor pilots for significant, visible investments with a key green component	• Sponsor a broad range of initiatives that integrate green principles with traditional business value	• Support and institutionalize continuous improvement
Role of Policies	• Identify simple, enterprise level initiatives that demonstrate early commitment to a green strategy and reinforce the cultural change that is needed	• Communicate success stories, encourage all employees to begin thinking about opportunities in their local area of responsibility	• Manage a pipeline of green initiatives, monitor the external landscape for new green developments and industry trends	• Identify interdependencies across ongoing initiatives and manage skill sets through strategic staffing
Illustrative Actions	• Pursue recycling initiatives, add the "green" contribution dimension to prioritizing business initiatives, and add the "green" selection criteria to procurement's selection criteria	• Establish and report on green performance measures, such as revenue from recycled paper, bottles and cans, or lower energy consumption	• Build and maintain a green knowledge base • Share lessons learned across the enterprise and develop a Center of Excellence	• Identify where results from successful initiatives can be duplicated and leverage them in other areas of the business

Figure 3.2 Green strategy maturity model: maturity range

Source: *Journal of Business Strategy*

Even companies that rank low in a green-maturity assessment can start in sensible places to build a green strategy. When a maturity assessment is performed to characterize the current state, it's always sensible to consider future aspirations and how the assessment compares to other companies. Are the aspirations to have base-level capabilities, be competitive with peers, or achieve differentiation? For most businesses, the answer to these questions depends on the area of the strategy pyramid under consideration, and the possible trade-off between downside risk and upside benefit from transforming to achieve different levels of maturity.

Figure 3.3 illustrates one analysis framework that enables a company to assess its current state of green strategy against its own aspirations, and against industry leaders or averages for every level of the strategy pyramid from Figure 2.3. Detailed descriptions of aware, developing, practicing, optimizing, and leading companies; the positioning of other companies within and across industries; and a company's current level of maturity can all guide an organization in establishing its future aspirations. Wherever a company's aspirations are meaningfully different from its current maturity level, the company can formulate a green strategy to close the gap between the current and desired state. Chapter 4, "Make Green Strategy Actionable with a Proven Approach," describes one method for defining such gaps, based on strategic imperatives, and formulating actionable initiatives and roadmaps to fill them.

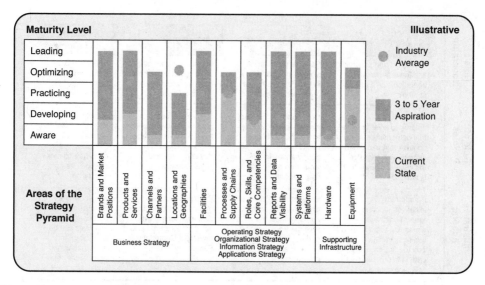

Figure 3.3 Green strategy maturing model: analysis framework

Source: *Journal of Business Strategy*

Many businesses have already made significant progress with initiatives that fit within the scope of a green strategy. However, few companies have taken the broadest view of the green possibilities that are available today, and the enormous potential those possibilities have when considered in the context of the whole enterprise. It's not difficult to find a corporation today in which employees are eager to discuss large, focused efforts of their company aimed at improving the environment, but they still have difficulty locating a properly labeled recycle bin for beverage containers when needed. Although most enterprises have undertaken some form of green initiative, few of them have yet to establish an enterprise-level green strategy.

Organizations can take advantage of well-developed assessment models. Maturity models and diagnostic tools can both play important roles in strategy formulation. Chapter 9, "Business Considerations for Technology Solutions," Section 9.4, describes these diagnostic tools.

Elements to consider when developing a green strategy include the driving and restraining forces in the enterprise, which make strategic transformation easier or more difficult to achieve. For example, an organizational culture in which business transformation and innovation are common and project management skills are strong represents one driving force that facilitates the implementation of a green strategy. Another driving force might be an advanced technology infrastructure and scalable information architecture that already enables effective business-process monitoring and reporting, to easily accommodate new environmental reporting measures. Existing competence and subject-matter expertise in essential areas of environmental stewardship, process optimization skills, and product development competencies can also be important driving forces for easier strategy implementation. Resource-allocation practices at some companies can represent a restraining force, requiring changes before initiatives for environmental stewardship get priority funding and the most skilled personnel. Employee performance management and company recognition and reward practices can also be restraining forces to strategy implementation without appropriate changes; realigning performance metrics might be necessary before initiatives for environmental stewardship attract the attention and interest of top talent.

After identifying the forces driving and restraining strategy implementation and the associated change, companies can use one frequently used tool to analyze them: the Force-Field Analysis.[26] A Force-Field Analysis enables companies to weight each force and visually shows both the driving forces pushing in one direction and the restraining forces pushing in the opposite direction. By reducing or eliminating the restraining forces and strengthening the driving forces, a company can dramatically reduce the effort required to implement a green strategy.

The benefits from having a formal, well-articulated green strategy vary by industry and even by individual business, but early adopters can still harness the enormous potential to opportunistically position themselves with a sustainable green strategic advantage. The results of a maturity analysis and subsequent green strategy formulation can then be the basis for developing a set of initiatives and an associated implementation roadmap to close gaps and reach aspirations. Companies should apply the same level of rigor to implement their green strategy as they do for any other element of traditional business strategy. Chapter 4 describes one methodology for accomplishing this task.

4

Make Green Strategy Actionable with a Proven Approach

4.1. Use Leading Practices for Making Strategic Visions Actionable

Businesses can effectively apply well-established methodologies for making business-driven operational improvements to areas of environmental stewardship. Such methodologies for implementing strategy or reaching strategic objectives in an organization often provide a clear way to trace the initiatives and programs back to the original vision and high-level objectives. Companies simply need to trace the initiatives in which investments are made back to the driving strategic imperatives. This traceability is important to maintain because it offers several significant benefits at relatively little cost.

First, creating initiatives and programs from a driving strategic vision with explicit traceability between the two ensures that the business transformation activities actually align with and support the strategic vision. Businesses often find that functional areas, such as IT departments, product development groups, sales and marketing groups, or customer service teams, launch their own improvement initiatives that align poorly with the business strategy. This can result in technology initiatives that don't meet business needs, products that don't meet consumer needs, marketing programs that don't support global brands, or difficulty portraying a "single face" to customers. Traceability weeds out pet projects and low-value investments that don't enable the business strategy.

Second, traceability between a high-level strategic vision and the initiatives that implement the vision enables businesses to incorporate changes and revise action plans when the vision or business priorities change. This is especially important in the area of environmental stewardship, in which high-level objectives can change due to technology breakthroughs, new legislation, or changes in the price trends of fuel and scarce raw materials. Businesses might launch some transformation initiatives proactively, based on future-state scenarios whose likelihood is uncertain. As trends change and predicted scenarios become more or less likely to occur, traceability back to the driving business strategy and strategic imperatives is crucial.

For example, new legislation might require an enterprise to change a greenhouse gas emissions–reduction target from 20 percent to 30 percent. Traceability enables an organization to quickly identify which existing initiatives and programs support such an aggressive goal.

Third, as the business environment changes, a company can use traceability to reprioritize its portfolio of projects, to keep investments aligned with the strategic direction. For example, if funding availability for an initiative changes, the organization could rapidly prioritize by tracing the initiative back to its strategic drivers and identifying its benefits and costs.

Fourth, from a change-management perspective, the importance of transformation initiatives and larger programs is frequently easier to communicate when their contribution to a strategic vision is clear.

Figure 4.1 depicts one methodology that businesses can use to develop and follow an action plan that implements a green strategy. Although Figure 4.1 implies that this methodology is sequential, it should actually be treated as iterative: Knowledge and insight gained from any step could influence content developed in one or more previous steps.

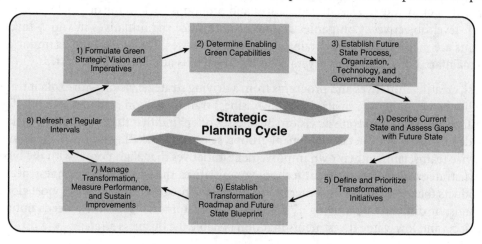

Figure 4.1   Green strategy implementation methodology

We next describe this methodology and then focus on a case study of a company whose current state includes few leading practices for environmental stewardship.

4.2. Formulate Green Strategic Vision and Imperatives

In Step 1 of the methodology, an enterprise formulates a strategic vision that describes its high-level objectives.

The green strategic vision is often guided by assessments against maturity models, reviews of benchmarks and leading practices from other companies and other industries, industry and global trends, analyses of market and customer segmentation, evaluations of new technology, and assessments of organizational core competencies. A company often communicates a strategic vision to its employees to facilitate organizational alignment and focus business activity toward key objectives in a uniform way.

However, because strategic visions are often articulated at too high of a level to be actionable, businesses must construct strategic imperatives so that the leadership of each business function can formulate plans to take specific action. Strategic imperatives align closely with the higher-level vision, but they also have a higher degree of clarity, to help drive the development of new business capabilities.

Consider an example of a company whose current state includes few leading practices for environmental stewardship. Although this is a hypothetical case, to illustrate the methodology and its application, its challenges and opportunities available are similar to those faced by thousands of companies around the world. As with many companies, this one has established offices and manufacturing facilities in the Americas and Europe, and plans to construct similar facilities in high-growth markets in Asia. This company has also recently completed a maturity assessment, benchmarking analysis, and customer segmentation assessment to compare itself to its key competitors and better understand its customers. The findings indicate that although no clear industry leader currently exists for environmental stewardship, competitors are actively working to establish an early-mover position by investing in product development and implementing sustainable-energy practices at some facilities. Customers across all segments now prefer products that are environmentally friendly, which represents a significant change in their behavior. Finally, through executive-visioning sessions, senior leadership has decided to add environmental stewardship to the company's strategic agenda and make certain investments to establish a leadership position in its industry.

Companies that fit the profile of our sample company could formulate a sensible strategic vision and associated strategic imperatives such as the ones shown in Table 4.1.

Table 4.1 Example of Green Strategic Vision and Associated Strategic Imperatives

Green Strategic Vision
Achieve industry leadership in environmental stewardship and be recognized by customers, business partners, and the global community for having sustainable business practices
Green Strategic Imperatives
1. Become an industry leader in environmental stewardship and sustainable business practices by providing products that exceed the expectations of environmentally conscious customers, transforming business processes and operations, and partnering with other businesses and organizations in the global community
2. Reduce carbon emissions 50 percent by 2025, using the current year as a baseline

The strategic vision addresses the most important issues to this company from an environmental-stewardship perspective. These include responding to changing customer preferences and establishing a competitive position in the industry. The lower-level, more actionable strategic imperatives address how the organization will achieve that vision, through changes to product offerings, facilities, and partnerships.

4.3. Determine Enabling Green Business Capabilities

In Step 2 of the methodology, companies determine enabling green business capabilities that focus on areas of the business that require new development to achieve the vision.

Companies can develop green business capabilities with relatively broad participation from senior leaders and managers because their knowledge of existing capabilities, and their understanding of the feasibility for developing new ones, is often helpful. This step is important because, without the capability-level detail, organizations won't have enough information for all the different business functions to define and launch the appropriate transformation initiatives. Traceability is maintained at this step because the capabilities remain tied to the strategic vision through their associated imperatives. After these green business capabilities are determined, it's much easier for leaders and managers to envision the level of transformation that will be required in their area of the business.

Now consider the case study and its two green strategic imperatives identified in Table 4.1. Table 4.2 summarizes a sensible set of enabling green business capabilities that are required to meet the strategic imperatives, and also shows how traceability is maintained as lower levels of detail are established.

The company can directly trace back the two sets of green business capabilities (items 1–8) to their associated green strategic imperatives. If either the vision or the imperatives change because of a shift in business priorities, the company will immediately know the implications to the enabling capabilities. The level of detail is still not exhaustive enough to require deep subject-matter expertise, nor is it sufficient to begin quantifying detailed benefits, costs, and environmental impact improvements. Also note that part of the first strategic imperative, particularly business capability 4, is strongly aligned with revenue-growth priorities.

However, the capabilities are described in sufficient detail that an organization can coarsely filter some of them out, if appropriate, to eliminate unnecessary work when constructing the action plan in subsequent steps. Although an organization would usually filter across all the green business capabilities—and potentially even across every capability that supports an action plan for all business visions (green and other), when green strategy and business strategy planning are integrated—we illustrate the approach for only the last two capabilities from Table 4.2. Table 4.3 summarizes the filtering results for these two capabilities.

Table 4.2 Example of Enabling Green Business Capabilities and Traceability

Green Strategic Vision	
Achieve industry leadership in environmental stewardship, and be recognized by customers, business partners, and the global community for our sustainable business practices	
Green Strategic Imperatives	**Enabling Green Business Capabilities**
Become an industry leader in environmental stewardship and sustainable business practices by providing products that exceed the expectations of environmentally conscious customers, transforming business processes and operations, and partnering with other businesses and organizations in the global community	1. Identify and capture energy efficiency and retrofit opportunities for offices and manufacturing facilities in mature markets of North America and Europe
	2. Utilize green building designs for planned offices and manufacturing facilities in high-growth markets in Asia
	3. Identify and remove excess waste from business processes
	4. Improve existing products to increase their efficiency without sacrificing quality, and innovate to create new products that meet the needs of an environmentally conscious customer base
	5. Develop governance and policies that improve environmental stewardship activities with business partners and global community organizations
Reduce carbon emissions 50 percent by 2025	6. Identify and pursue further opportunities that offset carbon emissions to meet the 2025 reduction target
	7. Reduce carbon emissions from employees' daily activities that support the organization
	8. Develop a new structure to outsource manufacturing and externalize the associated carbon emissions

Table 4.3 Framework to Filter and Eliminate Low-Value Green Capabilities

Green Capability	Green Capabilities Filtering Criteria					Overall Rating
	Strategic Fit	Revenue Benefit	Cost Savings	Environ-mental Impact Improvement	Operations Risk Reduction & Compliance Contribution	
7. Reduce carbon emissions from employees' daily activities that support the organization	High	Low	High	High	High	**High (keep)**
8. Develop a new operations structure to outsource manufacturing and externalize the associated carbon	Low	Low	Low	Low	Low	**Low (filter out)**

For these two capabilities, the company clearly should further explore the first one, capability 7, but it can filter out the second one, capability 8, and lose little value toward environmental stewardship. Although the filtering criteria can be customized for an individual business, the following analysis of capability 7 from Table 4.3 helps to more clearly define the criteria used here:

- A high strategic fit indicates that the capability aligns well with the driving strategic imperative and vision, which is easily established because traceability is preserved.

- A low revenue benefit indicates that the company should not anticipate a significant positive effect on revenue or revenue growth simply by having employees telecommute more often.

- A high cost savings indicates that a connection between increased telecommuting and reduced office facility costs is possible. For example, if 20 percent of the workforce is telecommuting at any particular time, the company could reduce office space or operate existing office space more economically with fewer people.

- A high environmental impact improvement indicates that the carbon emissions reductions from having an effective telecommuting program in place are significant.

- A high operations risk reduction and compliance contribution indicates that having this capability actually reduces the normal risk from daily operations, and also reduces the potential risk associated with future regulatory compliance for carbon emissions.

For green business capability 8 in Table 4.3, simply externalizing carbon emissions without the ability to demonstrate lower net emissions in the lifecycle chain could result in customer backlash if the transformation is positioned as one that improves environmental stewardship. However, if the company had a more traditional business imperative to transform fixed costs into variable costs, it might not filter out capability 8 at this step because of priorities other than environmental stewardship.

In practice, the decision to filter out capabilities at this step is not always clear, especially for capabilities that might have an overall rating of medium. Companies should avoid filtering out borderline capabilities at this early step because another filter, based on more detailed analysis, will be applied when potential initiatives are prioritized in Step 5. It's also important to consider prerequisite and interdependent capabilities when applying this framework. For example, a capability that has an overall rating of low might actually be a prerequisite for another capability, in which case it shouldn't be eliminated here. In a later step, one combined initiative might target those two capabilities together.

4.4. Establish Future-State Organization, Process, and Technology Needs

In Step 3 of the methodology, the organization establishes specific needs that will meet the objectives of the strategic vision.

The business establishes future-state needs to collectively cover what is required to fulfill the strategic imperatives. The organization, process, and technology needs to show business leaders, managers, and practitioners what will change and what will be new to the business at a deeper level of detail. Throughout every step of the methodology, traceability is maintained. In this step, each need ties back to its associated green business capability.

An organization could establish similar needs to support different capabilities. For example, the need for employees to conduct energy audits might support two different capabilities, such as one for capturing facility-retrofit opportunities (capability 1 in Table 4.2) and another for removing excess waste from business processes (capability 3 in Table 4.2). In later steps, an organization can combine these similar needs in such a way that they are met by the same initiative or as part of the same program of initiatives.

In this step, a business can map the future-state needs to any business model or business architecture, to analyze the areas that require change, how much transformation to expect, and what kind of transformation to anticipate in each business area—organization, process, or technology change.

Table 4.4   Example of Future-State Needs and Traceability

Green Capability	Future-State Needs	Type of Need
7. Reduce carbon emissions from employees' daily activities that support the organization	*Behavioral Training Needs*	
	1. New behavior-based training in which employees learn leading practices for environmental stewardship, such as operating in a paperless environment, substituting air travel and collocation with more remote collaboration, driving more efficiently, and exhibiting proactive conservation behavior, such as turning off energy-consuming devices when not in use	Organization
	Effective Recycling Program Needs	
	2. New recycle bins placed in convenient locations that enable employees to recycle metal, plastic, paper, and electronics waste	Technology
	3. Revised facilities procedure that collects and properly routes recyclable materials and disposes of hazardous waste	Process
	4. New awareness training that instructs on recycling activity and connects recycling objectives with improved environmental stewardship and lower carbon emissions	Organization
	5. New measurement and reporting system to capture recycling-performance information	Technology
	6. New accountability for establishing baseline performance, setting improvement targets, communicating progress toward goals, and taking action to meet recycling goals	Organization

Green Capability	Future-State Needs	Type of Need
	7. Updated incentives that are aligned with recycling objectives	Organization
	Telecommuting Program Needs	
	8. New access to telecommuting tools that give employees remote access to the company network and intranet, email and documents, the Internet, phone service, web conferencing, remote collaboration, and Internet-based video cameras for face-to-face discussion	Technology
	9. New governance and policies that establish when telecommuting is appropriate and how employee tracking is different when telecommuting	Process
	10. New training on how to use telecommuting tools, and the relationship between telecommuting and reduced carbon emissions	Organization
	11. Revised measurement and reporting system to monitor employee efficiency while telecommuting	Technology
	12. Revised descriptions of roles and responsibilities for managers and their employees impacted by telecommuting	Organization
	13. Updated incentives that are aligned with telecommuting objectives	Organization

Now consider the example in which one green business capability, capability 7, is passed through the filtering criteria in the previous step for further analysis. This example doesn't analyze the other green capabilities (1–6) because it's intended to only illustrate the methodology, not to provide a full implementation plan. Table 4.4 shows example future-state needs associated with green business capability 7.

Note that a deeper level of detail is provided in describing what must change. This gives functional leaders in a business a clear picture of what will be different in the end state, and they can even infer who should be involved to achieve the transformation.

Although a one-to-one relationship exists in this example between each need and its type, needs don't have to fall into just one category type. In practice, needs commonly require more than just one type of transformation; some require all of them—organization, process, and technology. Assigning a type of need here gives an indication of whether the transformation will be balanced or heavily biased toward technology, process, or organizational change.

At this point, the methodology has answered why transformation is needed from the driving strategic vision and associated imperatives, and what must change from the capabilities and associated needs. The next step identifies how the business must change to implement green strategy.

4.5. Describe Current State and Assess Gaps with Future State

In Step 4 of the methodology, the organization assesses the gaps associated with each need. Larger gaps require a higher degree of transformation to fill.

With an understanding of why change is needed and what must change, the organization performs a gap assessment to understand how the transformation can occur, how much change is actually needed, and what kind of transformation should take place. This is the final step before defining transformation initiatives to fill gaps that meet the objectives of a strategic vision. Again, traceability is preserved to clearly document how filling the gaps will contribute to meeting the original strategic vision.

For most gap assessments, the gaps themselves are sometimes not written explicitly if the current state and future state are sufficiently described. A gap is simply the difference between the current and future states. Similar to Step 3, an organization can assign gaps a type, depending on whether an organization, process, or technology transformation resolves them. However, unlike in the previous step, gaps usually fall into one type. By defining gaps in this way, an organization can easily combine them into natural groups. Natural groups can be a collection of gaps from any number of future-state needs that arise from any of the green business capabilities. The groups enable an organization to form initiatives that minimize duplication of effort and enable one initiative to potentially meet the needs of several strategic imperatives and many enabling capabilities.

An organization can assess all the gaps, along with their associated needs, to determine their importance in building the required capabilities. An organization can also assess whether they are required in the near term or whether they can be developed over a longer time period for more flexibility during implementation.

Leaders can assess organization gaps for their complexity, level of cultural change required, number of people in the organization affected, and fit with existing knowledge and skills.

An organization can assess process gaps for their complexity, level of process change required, and amount of new training needed.

Leaders can also assess technology gaps for the complexity of features and functionality, interoperability requirements, scalability requirements, and reliability expectations.

At this step in the methodology, the gap assessment details will add clarity to the initiatives defined in the next step, which fill the gaps. The last activity in this step is to identify an initiative title that will fill the gap. Initiatives titles in this step are closely aligned with the natural groups discussed earlier.

Turning again to the example, and focusing only on the telecommuting program needs (8–13) to illustrate the approach, Table 4.5 describes a set of corresponding gaps, along with traceability back to the future-state needs.

Gap assessments require detailed knowledge of the current state of the business, along with reasonably accurate knowledge of what the future state of the business will look like after the needs have been met. However, complete knowledge of the future state isn't always necessary at this step because an organization could defer additional depth of subject-matter expertise or time required to achieve a deeper level of detail until the initiative itself is funded, staffed, and launched.

In this example, the same initiative will fill multiple gaps. In an actual application of this methodology, a lesser number of initiatives might fill hundreds of gaps. Furthermore, in an actual application, an organization might want to assess the gap sizes in more detail. Experienced project managers can often judge the size of a gap and the level of effort anticipated to fill a gap, in terms of both investment and resources required based on previous knowledge of similar projects. One advantage from quantifying the size of each gap in terms of costs and resources in this step is that it simplifies the work of the next step to determine the cost of an initiative that fills multiple gaps.

Table 4.5 Example of Gap Assessment and Traceability

| Future-State Needs | Gap Assessment | | | | |
	Current State	Future State	Gap Type	Gap Size	Initiative
8. New access to telecommuting tools that give employees remote access to the company network and intranet, email and documents, the Internet, phone service, web conferencing, remote collaboration, and Internet-based video cameras for face-to-face discussion	Most employees have high-speed Internet access from potential home offices but have no way to access the company network or other tools remotely. However, the tools are accessible from the company network between facilities.	All office-working employees are able to work from home offices, to securely access the company network and documents seamlessly, and to access the complete portfolio of telecommuting tools already in use from office locations.	Technology	Medium	Telecommuting technology
9. New governance and policies that establish when telecommuting is appropriate and how employee tracking is different when telecommuting	Rough governance and policies are available to cover a limited number of employees that work from home offices part-time.	Existing governance and policies expanded and clarified to be applicable to all office working employees.	Organization	Small	Telecommuting governance, roles, and incentives
10. New training on how to use telecommuting tools, and the relationship between telecommuting and reduced carbon emissions	Training is available and deployed for using most tools from company facilities where the network is easily accessed, but with no connection to carbon emissions.	One- to three-day, onsite training deployed, with online refresher training available that teaches technology use and connection to carbon emissions.	Organization	Medium	Telecommuting training

Future-State Needs	Gap Assessment				Initiative
	Current State	Future State	Gap Type	Gap Size	
11. Revised measurement and reporting system to monitor employee efficiency while telecommuting	A manual measurement system is in place and used with a limited number of employees.	Automated measurement, monitoring, and reporting of employee efficiency while telecommuting.	Technology	High	Telecommuting technology
12. Revised descriptions of roles and responsibilities for managers and their employees impacted by telecommuting	Roles and responsibilities currently discourage telecommuting.	Roles and responsibilities encourage telecommuting on a part-time basis (from two to four days a week).	Organization	Low	Telecommuting governance, roles, and incentives
13. Updated incentives that are aligned with telecommuting objectives	No incentives are in place to encourage tele-commuting.	Telecommuting incentives are added to annual performance reviews, and a communication plan is designed to share leading practices.	Organization	Medium	Telecommuting governance, roles, and incentives

4.6. Define and Prioritize Transformation Initiatives

In Step 5 of the methodology, the organization defines the initiatives that fill the gaps assessed in the previous step.

The gaps were associated with natural groups that a single initiative could fill. In this step, the organization clearly articulates and documents the initiatives, estimates implementation costs, and benefits, and then prioritizes them.

Documenting each initiative entails identifying an owner, describing the initiative, and articulating the current and future state using details from the gap assessment. The solution that meets the objectives of an initiative and fills the associated gaps can be organizational, technological, process-oriented, or a combination of the three.

Initiative definitions also include information on alternate approaches for filling the gaps between the current and future states. Timing considerations that describe whether the opportunity should be considered a short-term quick hit or longer-term improvement are also captured, along with other timing considerations, such as estimated implementation duration.

Finally, initiative definitions include qualitative and quantitative costs and benefits, along with the criteria that will be used to prioritize all the initiatives.

Table 4.6 is a sample initiative-definition template for the telecommuting initiative from the case study.

Table 4.6   Example Initiative-Definition Template Completed for One Initiative

Initiative Title	Enable telecommuting technology		Initiative Owner	Owner's name
Description	Enable access to a portfolio of technology tools by employees from remote locations and home offices for effective telecommuting			
Current State Description		*Future State Description*		
Most employees have high-speed Internet access from potential home offices but no way to access the company network or other tools remotely. However, the tools are accessible from the company network between facilities.		New access to telecommuting tools grants employees remote access to the company network and intranet, email and documents, the Internet, phone service, web conferencing, remote collaboration, and Internet-based video cameras for face-to-face discussion.		

Current State Description	Future State Description
The current system for reporting employee hours, monitoring performance, and measuring efficiency is manually used with a limited number of employees.	All office-based employees are able to work from home offices, to securely access the company network and documents seamlessly, and to access the complete portfolio of telecommuting tools already in use from office locations.
	An online employee time reporting and measurement system to monitor employee efficiency and hours worked while telecommuting is in place.
Solution Type(s): Technology	*Solution Areas: Secure, Remote Access*
Proposed Approach to Fill Gap	

Enable telecommuting employees to access the company network and remote-collaboration technology tool suite from offsite locations by either high-speed or dial-up connections. Also enable online time reporting from offsite locations.

Timing Considerations

Completion of governance and training initiatives for telecommuters are prerequisites for employees to begin using this technology.

Opportunity Size: High Rationale	Ease of Implementation: High Rationale	Project Risk Level: Low Rationale
Fewer employees commuting to the office will reduce greenhouse gas emissions and provide substantial environmental benefits.	The solution involves relatively simple network access.	Funding is available and appropriate priority is expected.
The organization can achieve a longer-term cost-reduction benefit by reducing the amount of office space needed for the same number of employees.	The technical solution is available and mature.	Skilled resources are available, with the capacity to implement the initiative.
Having the choice to work from home offices part of the time will lead to higher employee retention and benefit employee morale and work-life balance.	The organization has the appropriate skills to implement the initiative.	

Table 4.6 Example Initiative-Definition Template Completed for One Initiative (continued)

Initiative Prioritization Criteria						Overall
Strategic Fit	Revenue Benefit	Cost Savings	Environmental Impact Improvement	Operations Risk Reduction & Compliance Contribution	Ease of Implemen- tation	
High	Low	High	High	High	High	High

The opportunity size should relate to the prioritization criteria associated with benefits (strategic fit, revenue benefit, cost savings, environmental impact improvement, and operations risk reduction and compliance contribution). These criteria should be well correlated to how their corresponding capabilities were rated for the same dimensions in a previous step. Ease of implementation, partly determined by implementation cost and the implementation resources needed and their availability, is high when the implementation isn't expected to be difficult. The low project-risk level indicates that organizational readiness is good, executives and managers are supportive, and priority for implementation resources and funding is high.

Other prioritization criteria to consider include the complexity of the initiative, the duration of the project and time to benefit, interdependencies with other initiatives, and potential options that the initiative provides for making follow-up improvements. At this step, it's possible to gather enough detail to make appropriate assumptions and calculate the net present value (NPV), internal rate of return (IRR), or return on investment (ROI) for each initiative.

With the elaborate planning environments in many businesses today, seldom does initiative prioritization, or project portfolio planning, result in a one-dimensional prioritized list of initiatives, with the ones below a certain score being cut from the plan. Figure 4.2 depicts a common prioritization framework and illustrates where the initiative described in Table 4.6 is positioned.

Initiatives that fall into Zones II and III typically make sense to launch and implement, but those in Zone I require additional focus to determine whether they should be pursued. Initiatives in Zone I often are assigned a later start date on the transformation roadmap, to allow more time for additional investigation and to raise the ease of implementation. Initiatives in Zone IV don't provide sufficient benefits, and the implementation difficulty is disproportionately high; those factors don't warrant making an implementation investment. In some cases, especially when business benefits depend on capturing market share and achieving revenue growth in a competitive environment, the implementation timing of an initiative can be the "critical path" to achieving projected results.

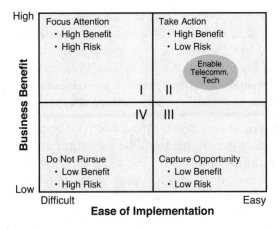

Figure 4.2   Prioritization framework

Now that a set of transformation initiatives has been defined with explicit traceability back to the strategic vision that they support, the next step is to establish a transformation roadmap.

4.7. Establish Transformation Roadmap and Future-State Blueprint

In Step 6 of this methodology, an organization creates a transformation roadmap and future-state blueprint to effectively manage the strategic vision implementation.

The organization has defined and prioritized the initiatives, quantified their costs and benefits, and defined the resources required to implement them. The transformation roadmap established in this step includes all the initiatives to be implemented and their timing, with approximate start and end dates, and considers interdependencies and constraints across initiatives. For example, if the capabilities enabled by one initiative are a prerequisite for beginning another initiative, the roadmap reflects this timing constraint for those two initiatives. Other typical constraints include funding limitations and scarcity of qualified resources.

Until this step is complete, the final portfolio of initiatives to be implemented is unknown. An organization should explore different roadmap alternatives before selecting the final one. Frequently considered roadmap alternatives include one in which spending is somewhat unconstrained and most initiatives are implemented, one with balanced investment in which low-priority initiatives are dropped, and one with limited investment in which even some high-value initiatives might be eliminated. Other dimensions to explore, in addition to investment and implementation cost, include the rate of value realized (quickly versus spread over a longer period of time), the business and technology risk level, and the amount of focus given to enterprise-level initiatives versus ones that benefit only a few business units. Comparing different alternatives across these dimensions makes clear which initiatives and associated benefits need to be dropped or delayed to meet the imposed constraints. Because complete traceability is still in place from each initiative back to the green strategy that they are intended to implement, it's also clear which aspects of the strategic vision must be compromised in different roadmap alternatives.

Although the time horizon of a transformation roadmap can extend five years or more, the initiatives associated with the telecommuting example from the case study can be implemented in one year. The roadmap for the case study, in Figure 4.3, reflects the timing of initiatives for the whole telecommuting program, and shows where initiatives might run concurrently to more rapidly achieve the overall objective.

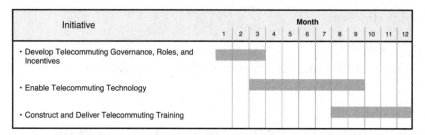

Figure 4.3   Transformation roadmap for telecommuting program

Some companies end their strategic-planning activity when they produce a final portfolio of initiatives and complete the transformation roadmap. However, the leading practice is to also establish the future-state blueprint so that a clear picture of the end state is created after all the initiatives are complete. A full blueprint includes a view of the end-state organization and the important changes, the end-state processes and how they will have changed, and the end-state information technology architecture and how it will have changed. These elements collectively represent a holistic view of the future-state business architecture.

Methods for articulating a holistic view of business architecture vary widely across different enterprises, depending on the level of complexity in the business and its operations. For example, some companies operate with decentralized technology functions without a complete view of their disparate systems, interfaces, and decentralized data. Other companies have clearly documented their applications, interfaces, data, and ownership governance so that identifying changes to the system architecture at an enterprise level is more straightforward. Similarly, companies with a relatively advanced business process management (BPM) structure in place typically have a straightforward task to articulate the future-state blueprint from a process perspective.

4.8. Manage Transformation, Measure Performance, and Sustain Improvements

The leading practices for transformation and change management apply to a green portfolio of initiatives in the same way they apply to most other business areas. Companies must manage the following activities:

- Project activities, for high-quality outcomes

- Staff and infrastructure, for high performance

- Scope and timeline, for cost-effectiveness

- Stakeholder relationships, for ongoing commitment

- Risks and mitigation options for smooth implementation

It's also important to verify that environmental, business, and organization benefits are realized as different projects are completed. Especially for quantified benefits, companies should establish a measurement and reporting system, measure baseline performance, set improvement targets, and monitor changes to the baseline to determine whether improvement targets are achieved. Where expected improvements don't materialize, the organization must analyze root causes and implement corrective actions.

For larger, complex programs that need to manage transformation efforts across business units or divisions, leading practices often call for a centralized program management organization (PMO) to manage multiple initiatives across different programs. A PMO can operate across initiatives to plan and monitor activities, communicate and report all aspects of transformation, manage and resolve escalated issues, and control changes to scope. The same PMO can manage contracts, finances, resources, documents, infrastructure, quality, and risk. An effective PMO can also manage and report benefits as they are demonstrated, and collect and communicate knowledge and lessons learned across initiatives.

Inevitably, new ideas for initiatives will spring from innovative thinking by all stakeholders, even after the initial transformation roadmap is developed. To respond to these new opportunities, an enterprise should have a streamlined process to evaluate new ideas and draft initiatives, prioritize them with the existing portfolio of initiatives, and place them on the transformation roadmap when applicable.

4.9. Refresh at Regular Intervals

Assuming that a transformation roadmap spans five years, the equivalent of at least one year should be refreshed annually. Even if the strategic vision and imperatives have not changed, some initiatives will be complete with their benefits in place, and the organization can define a new fifth year of activity. Changes to the strategic vision and imperatives, economic expansion or contraction, new legislative activity, changes in the competitive landscape, and availability of new technology and leading practices are additional reasons to refresh the transformation plan.

Refreshing the plan annually is most common, and it's usually coordinated with other business planning activities so that the organization can address interdependencies between initiatives for green strategy and other business initiatives.

Returning to our case study, consider the original set of enabling green business capabilities from Table 4.2. Capabilities 5 and 7—developing governance and policies for working with business partners, and enabling employees to proactively reduce their own carbon emissions—would likely gain significant traction and might be fully implemented in the first year of the transformation roadmap.

Capabilities 1, 3, and 4—retrofitting offices and manufacturing facilities, removing excess waste from business processes, and improving existing products—might start in the first year, but will likely extend into the second, third, and even fourth years of the roadmap. The timing of product-based benefits will depend on the length of the product development cycle, which varies widely across different industries.

Capabilities 2 and 6—constructing green facilities and identifying carbon emission–offset opportunities—will potentially be pursued vigorously in the second through fifth years of the transformation roadmap as the business grows into new markets and identifies new opportunities to meet the 2025 target. Capability 8 was eliminated, as too low-value, early in the process.

Chapter 6, "Applying Green Sigma to Optimize Carbon Emissions," describes an actual case in which facility improvements are made using the Green Sigma methodology and its technology toolset. The initiative described by that case is similar to the kind that would be expected from the enabling green capability that improves the efficiency of facilities.

4.10. Ten Critical Success Factors for Transformation

Analysts have identified the ten most critical success factors of initiatives that support environmental stewardship.

First, *committed leadership* is essential for achieving successful transformation in environmental stewardship. Unlike other business initiatives, those linked to a green strategy are always at risk of taking a back seat to other activities whose connection to traditional business performance is clearer. When leadership is visibly supportive and takes action to demonstrate commitment, the risk is mitigated. Expanding on the telecommuting illustration described earlier, committed leadership sponsors and commits to making appropriate investments, communicates the importance of the program for business and environmental benefits, and even participates in the program to reinforce the behavior in their employees. For environmental stewardship, commitment from leadership often must come from many different levels within the organization, not simply from executive management. For example, facilities managers are essential leaders who must be committed whenever a transformation initiative involves buildings and other facilities.

Second, establishing and maintaining a clear *focus on the environment* is an important factor for successful transformation. Just as a clear focus on the customer is needed for other business-driven initiatives, a focus on the environment ensures that affected processes are created from an environmental impact perspective. In the telecommuting program illustration, without a focus on the environment, an organization conceivably could develop a training class about telecommuting and deliver it through on-site training in a location where most participants would need to fly in to attend. Emissions from the flights alone could potentially cancel out any near-term environmental benefits from telecommuting and, depending on the flying distance and commuting time, other, longer-range benefits.

Third, *strategic alignment* is also critical so that initiatives support the green strategy, not just one department or individual's point of view. We've shown how organizations can formulate initiatives directly from a driving strategic vision with a clear line of traceability between the two. However, grassroots initiatives also need to be evaluated for their alignment with the strategy. Sometimes small pilot programs can demonstrate early success and then be replicated across larger areas of the business, or they can tap into specialized knowledge and high levels of personal interest from individuals who might otherwise never have been exposed to environmental improvement opportunities. In the telecommuting illustration, many companies first used telecommuting to improve the work/life balance for different scenarios, such as an alternative to extended maternity or paternity leave. By identifying how such programs align with a holistic strategic vision, they might be found to easily fit within the boundaries of environmental stewardship objectives as well as work/life balance ones. Occasionally, when exceptional ideas align poorly with a high-level strategic vision, the strategy itself can change and steer the business in a new direction.

Fourth, *full-time staffing and organization skill availability* are essential practical considerations for most large-scale initiatives, even those outside environmental stewardship. If full-time staffing isn't possible, the next-best alternative is to articulate clear priorities that support an established roadmap, a detailed project plan, and milestone targets for the team. Dedicated full-time contractors with specialized knowledge and skills can supplement such teams. As another illustration, consider that the initiative for environmental stewardship might be to replace utility-supplied electrical power with electricity from rooftop solar panels; the implementation schedule for this project could slip indefinitely without the business losing a single sale or dollar of revenue. This can occur when projects are staffed predominantly with resources that have other significant commitments outside the environmental-improvement initiative.

Fifth, the *business process framework* should encourage standardization and commonality wherever possible, especially in large multinational enterprises, to avoid duplicate efforts and establish models that are easily replicated and scalable. The telecommuting illustration is a good example where global processes likely apply, enabling technology can be shared around the world, and governance policies can be adapted regionally from globally common principles.

Sixth, the importance of having an *integrated approach to change* is difficult to overemphasize when it comes to environmental stewardship. Because a portfolio of initiatives that reduces the environmental impact of a business can potentially affect every functional area, a company must have an integrated view across those initiatives, more traditional business initiatives, and ongoing business operations. Identifying and managing interdependencies across initiatives and across the entire business is important, especially when resources and specialized skills might be in short supply. Training is one area for which integration across initiatives is sensible. For example, an organization can integrate telecommuting training with other awareness training, such as efficient equipment use or desktop computer shut-down policies during nonuse.

Seventh, conscious and explicit *benefit tracking* is another critical success factor. Benefit tracking usually is preceded by a quantified benefits case so that companies can identify expected benefits, measure key performance indicators, set targets, and report realized benefits when initiatives succeed. Benefit tracking also identifies whether the original assumptions of the benefit case have changed or whether expected value is not being realized. The organization then can identify root causes and implement corrective action. A benefits case also documents qualitative benefits that are difficult to measure but that can be qualitatively evaluated after an initiative is complete.

As more companies announce their intentions to reduce their carbon footprints and improve environmental stewardship in different ways, benefit tracking will grow in importance. To demonstrate that intentions have been achieved, benefit tracking will be important not just at an initiative or project level, but also at a program and enterprise level, where net benefits can be aggregated without "double-counting" them. The goodwill and business value companies generate from announcements on environmental-improvement targets will eventually need to be demonstrated back to customers and shareholders. Demonstrating conformance to potential regulatory requirements is also easier when companies are tracking and reporting benefits.

Eighth, effective *performance management* is another critical success factor. Companies need to implement appropriate incentives that motivate people to deliver environmentally sound improvements. The balanced scorecards that evaluate employee and team performance can include both environmental impacts and business results. Fortunately, the cultural change required to align environmental improvement results with incentives doesn't always need to be large. Because many initiatives for environmental stewardship lead to new products and revenue growth, or new efficiencies and cost reductions, environmental performance management often closely parallels business performance improvement. In the telecommuting illustration, an implementation project team could measure success by on-time delivery of the appropriate solution, employees could measure success by whether they use the program in an appropriate manner, managers could measure whether an appropriate percentage of their employees are telecommuting, and executives could measure ongoing benefits, such as reduced real-estate expenses from a smaller on-site workforce.

Ninth, *capability, learning, and knowledge management* are essential to an enterprise seeking to improve its environmental stewardship. Initiatives for environmental stewardship may start small, possibly focused on just one facility, site, or segment of a product portfolio. However, when the necessary skills are in place and a proven approach succeeds, the company can replicate such initiatives across more facilities or roll them out to a larger part of the organization. Without effective learning and knowledge management, each new initiative will essentially need to start from scratch, and the value of learning from similar projects will be minimal. Organizational skills and new subject matter expertise will also be needed. To strategically staff initiatives, an enterprise needs visibility into its existing capabilities and capability gaps and to have a clear path to fill those gaps.

Tenth, *deployment management* is the final critical success factor. Businesses must plan, govern, and coordinate initiatives and the portfolio of projects, to deliver the right outcomes. Deployment management can take many forms, depending on the level of autonomy with which various business units operate (command-and-control organizations versus decentralized, consensus-driven, or matrix organizations) and also the portfolio complexity of the initiatives in the roadmap. Strong and experienced project management is also a factor in success.

PART II

Apply Proven Transformation Methods

5

Transformation Methods and Green Sigma

5.1. Transformation Methods Facilitate Implementing Initiatives

New legislation, community pressure, or customer-safety concerns have historically spurred initiatives that benefited the environment. Section 1.1 in Chapter 1, "Driving Forces and Challenges That Organizations Face," provides examples of such improvements, and all stakeholders of society—from government lawmakers to corporate executives and consumer advocates—deserve the credit. In recent years, many companies have developed their own green strategies specifically to foster environmental stewardship, methodically identify new opportunities, and prioritize investment decisions to meet internally driven objectives and respond to external driving forces (described in Chapter 1, Section 1.3).

Chapter 2, "Formulate Green Strategy to Complement Traditional Strategy," and Chapter 3, "Green Strategy Supports Operational Improvements," describe how these strategies can foster a common culture of awareness and action, complement and strengthen traditional business strategy, drive operational decisions and transformation initiatives that improve the environment, and often offer attractive and cost-effective value propositions. They also help determine where to focus investments and resources for the greatest environmental improvement. To implement these strategies, applying the appropriate transformation methods and tools is just as important in the area of environmental stewardship as for any other business area.

Whether an enterprise explicitly develops a comprehensive green strategy and clear action plan or relies on more decentralized or grassroots efforts to pursue opportunities in environmental stewardship, effective transformation methods are ultimately needed to launch and execute improvement initiatives. Not surprisingly, methodologies designed to reduce waste are well suited to help companies that are working toward environmental-improvement objectives, such as reducing their carbon footprint and conserving natural resources.

Because of their focus on efficiency and waste reduction, organizations can readily adapt Lean practices, Six Sigma, and other mature business-transformation methodologies, and directly apply them to initiatives that improve the environment. Recent advances in regulations, technology, and standards make applying these methodologies to improve the environment even more compelling. Public and private enterprises have developed and applied such methodologies to support transformation for environmental stewardship.

In one example, the Office of the Federal Environmental Executive (OFEE) promotes the use of environmental management systems for planning and implementation tools to help federal agencies become better environmental stewards.[1] In another example, the Environmental Protection Agency (EPA) is working to improve state agency processes and environmental protection by adapting Lean and Six Sigma methods.[2] The Federal Highway Administration (FHWA) utilizes methods and tools, ranging from simple checklists to sophisticated online databases, to ensure that environmental commitments are implemented and results are tracked.[3]

Spanning a broad range of sectors and company sizes, private industry also applies well-adapted methodologies to support environmental stewardship. PepsiCo, the Fortune 100 snack and beverage company, minimizes the impact of its business on the environment "with methods that are socially responsible, scientifically based, and economically sound."[4] Burt's Bees, a smaller company that creates natural, Earth-friendly personal care products, has "sophisticated and measurable methods" to minimize environmental impact.[5] Ricoh, a $17 billion Japanese-based company that offers digital office solutions, utilizes a "sustainable environmental management evaluation method" to gain an understanding of the impact caused by all its businesses, using eco-balance and integrated environmental-impact evaluations. This method includes selecting measures for environmental accounting and evaluation of activity results.[6]

In addition to cost- and efficiency-focused methods, companies can adapt methodologies and tools that more directly support revenue-growth objectives. Innovation management methodologies can readily include new sources for "green" input in ideation; research and development–stage gate processes can include environmental stewardship factors as new product and service offerings are reviewed and tested; and product portfolio priorities, analyses, and tools can include green elements in addition to traditional ones. Other methods, such as those for customer segmentation and forecasting, should now consider trends of the green movement and even anticipated legislation in environmental stewardship that will change market dynamics. Companies can also adapt approaches to product lifecycle management (PLM) and other methods for managing products and services throughout their lifecycles, to align with environmental stewardship objectives. For example, companies can opt for "planned upgrading" or "planned refurbishment" for customers instead of "planned obsolescence" and products with short life spans. Companies can also recast methods for gathering and responding to market intelligence, to include a focus on environmental factors and preferences, such as methods for conducting surveys and leading customer focus groups with early adopters, the early majority, the late majority, and laggards. Although the rest of this chapter focuses primarily on a methodology to reduce waste, improve efficiency, and better manage natural resources for environmental stewardship, remember that enterprises use a portfolio of methods to achieve their business objectives, and most of these can be adapted to include factors for environmental stewardship in some way.

Green Sigma, developed by IBM, is one methodology that applies a proven process and incorporates newly developed analytic and technology solutions. It leverages the traditional Lean and Six Sigma methodologies and includes the necessary tools to identify, implement, and sustain improvements. The Green Sigma methodology is described in detail in this chapter and applied to an actual case in the next chapter; although many approaches exist, this book illustrates only one approach in detail. The leading practices of using a proven and repeatable transformation process, applying rigor in using the process, and leveraging a prescribed set of tools across a broad range of initiatives are relevant to many other methods that can also help enterprises reach their environmental stewardship goals.

The Green Sigma methodology incorporates lessons learned and leading practices from a long history of energy conservation and environmental stewardship within IBM and with its clients, dating back to the early 1970s. IBM was the first semiconductor manufacturer to establish a numeric goal for reducing perfluorocarbon (PFC) emissions in 1998. Between 1990 and 2007, the corporation conserved 4.6 billion kilowatt-hours (kWh) of electricity consumption and saved more than $310 million from annual energy-conservation efforts. During the same time period, IBM also avoided 3.1 million metric tons of carbon dioxide emissions.

IBM is also experienced in the strategic procurement of renewable energy. In 2001, the company purchased 11 million kWh of renewable energy and renewable energy credits (RECs). By 2007, that amount had increased to 455 million kWh, accounting for 8.5 percent of its total global electricity purchases.[7] The company also led the industry in reducing PFC emissions from semiconductor manufacturing by 55 percent.[8] IBM has well-established telecommuting and work-at-home programs, to help employees both balance work and life better and lower their carbon-footprint contribution from less commuting. Nearly 40 percent of its workforce is mobile.[9] These are only a few samples of the experience that has helped shape the Green Sigma methodology.

In 2008, IBM's plant in Poughkeepsie, New York, which develops and manufactures powerful and complex servers, mainframes, and supercomputers, was identified as one site for a Green Sigma initiative. In this example, the plant found it could reduce the environmental impact from end-to-end supply-chain operations, drive cost savings, and improve productivity through more efficient management of energy, materials, and natural resources while minimizing waste and emissions.[10] At facilities in Burlington,

Vermont, and Fishkill, New York, techniques such as the ones in this methodology have reduced water consumption by 27 percent, with savings of $3 million.[11]

This chapter explains the Green Sigma methodology, and the next chapter applies it to a manufacturing and warehouse facility in an actual case study. By following Green Sigma's five steps, applying analysis tools, and implementing a management dashboard system, IBM achieved energy savings of approximately 20 percent, as described in the case study.

Applying methodologies such as Green Sigma and implementing the associated technology tools represent an important milestone for an enterprise on the journey to intelligent information for environmental stewardship. Early activities focus on mining existing data and applying new analytics to capture "quick wins," reducing costs, and increasing efficiency in products, services, and infrastructure. Then an organization can focus on standardizing regionally, installing new sensors and information sources, and working toward integrating systems, sharing knowledge, and deploying leading practices worldwide. In medium- to long-term activities, an organization can leverage an intelligent information base to optimize greenhouse gas emissions and manage natural resources. Figure 5.1 illustrates how initial investments focus on environmental improvement with cost-driven business benefits. With the information-management structure in place, new opportunities make themselves available that might not otherwise have been possible.

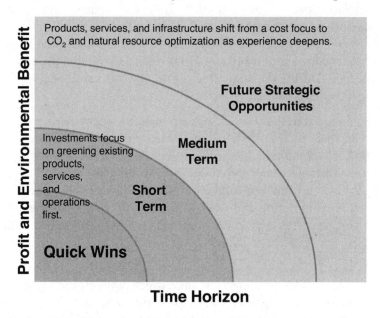

Figure 5.1   Focus evolves over time with the Green Sigma methodology

For context, it's helpful to understand some fundamentals of the traditional Lean and Six Sigma methodologies before describing Green Sigma in detail. The Lean methodology focuses on efficiency, waste reduction, and concepts of pull versus push on customer demand. Examples of Lean methodologies are the well-known "just-in-time" (JIT) approach to inventory management and the Toyota Product System (TPS). The traditional Six Sigma methodology focuses on process capabilities as they relate to quality, defects, and variation, to better meet customer requirements. The methodology incorporates business process management as a foundation to manage processes with data, and identify and select improvements to implement. It also enables the design of new processes, or Design for Six Sigma (DFSS), which addresses the prevention of defects. These practices use statistically based tool sets and have been responsible for driving significant savings and quality improvements across all major industries. Many companies have institutionalized Six Sigma coaches and mentors (called master black belts), project leads (black belts), and project members (green belts) as a core organizational competency. Many existing references describe the traditional Lean[12] and Six Sigma[13] methodologies in further detail.

Figure 5.2 shows the five steps of the Green Sigma methodology that align with proven practices from traditional Lean and Six Sigma. The first two steps involve defining key performance indicators and establishing a measurement system. The next two steps involve deploying a management dashboard system and optimizing processes. The fifth step involves controlling performance and establishing an environment of sustainable quality and continuous improvement.

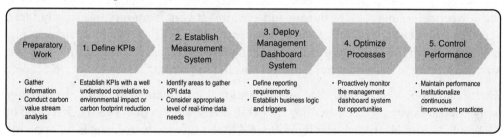

Figure 5.2 The Green Sigma methodology's five steps

Preparatory work is expected at the start of this methodology. Available data is collected, including any reports from existing carbon diagnostics, carbon modeling, or energy assessment and audit reviews. This data includes gas and electricity invoice history, and other energy and utility payment history, such as water usage. Relevant operational data is also collected, such as operating schedules, timing for when different building areas are occupied and vacant, and sources of energy loss, such as doors, windows, ducts, roof vents, and chimney stacks. Detailed data from established metering inside a facility is also collected and analyzed. For major systems, such as boilers, water heaters, and chilled water production, thermal analysis is performed to quantify energy losses in pipes. Depending on the application, data for raw material inputs, finished product outputs, and waste produced from business processes might also be gathered.

An inventory of processes and equipment that consume energy or use water and other natural resources is also created as part of the preparatory work. Energy and usage ratings for each item in the inventory are gathered, operating schedules are documented, and maintenance condition is captured. If this kind of information is unavailable, actual measurements might be necessary to characterize the energy consumed by different equipment in the inventory.

Organizational roles, policies, and governance that affect energy and natural resource usage are also investigated. Ownership of usage performance and responsibility for continuous-improvement projects are documented, clarity of equipment operating schedules is evaluated, and policies that govern conformance to those schedules are gathered. Security and safety policies might also be evaluated for dependencies with energy consumption, such as requirements for lighting in dark areas or after the normal workday ends. Governance and processes that control schedule deviations for equipment usage, and ensure that operations return to normal when the need for a deviation has ended, are also evaluated. Sometimes organizations can make relatively simple and inexpensive changes in these areas, without significant capital expenditure for new equipment, to yield significant short-term savings and a positive environmental impact.

If facilities are leased, the division of responsibility among all stakeholders needs to be clearly understood because the tenant might not have full authority to make improvements without consent from the owner. Ultimately, some improvement initiatives could include cooperation, input, resources, and even investment from multiple stakeholders, yet others might not be initially feasible because of contractual constraints. For example, one owner might be very interested in replacing old, inefficient heating, ventilating, and air-conditioning systems in a building, but another might not.

The organization can use the data and operational information from the preparatory work to create a voice of the environment (VOE) value-stream map (VSM), described in Section 5.5.1 and illustrated later by Figure 6.4 in the case study in Chapter 6, "Applying Green Sigma to Optimize Carbon Emissions." The VOE VSM is one tool that an organization can use to identify opportunities and define improvement initiatives. When the preparatory work is complete, the company has sufficient information on the use of energy and other natural resources to begin the first step of the Green Sigma methodology. The five steps of the methodology are each described next.

5.2. Step 1 Defines Key Performance Indicators

Establishing key performance indicators (KPIs) is an essential part of most business transformation initiatives. A business's capability to effectively manage and improve its processes for environmental stewardship often directly correlates to its capability to measure and analyze performance using tools such as trend analysis, root-cause analysis, and variation analysis. An organization should establish appropriate KPIs for three critical purposes.

First, KPIs are important for measuring the success of transformation initiatives and demonstrating that predicted benefits are actually realized. This is especially important for environmental-impact improvements because the concept of carbon credits is developing and maturing, along with emissions-trading scenarios, to mitigate global warming and associated climate change. An enterprise's capability to demonstrate future improvements in its carbon footprint could contribute to meeting financial, regulatory, and environmental goals and commitments. One survey by the Gartner Group[14] showed that the inability to determine benefits and the lack of a repeatable benefits-realization approach were companies' top two obstacles to justifying their investments. The same survey showed that companies can effectively use business process metrics as change agents to help secure the success of transformation initiatives.

Second, KPIs are important in monitoring process performance, assessing ongoing operations, and identifying new improvement opportunities. Without the appropriate measures for emissions and waste production in place, many companies have difficulty establishing their baseline performance. This makes it very difficult to set realistic improvement targets, and nearly impossible to know whether predicted benefits are ever achieved.

Third, KPIs are important for demonstrating adherence to standards or limits, such as regulatory standards, and managing breaches outside permissible limits. Automated triggers and alarm management is one growth area that is increasing operational efficiency across a broad range of applications in all industries, from oil refineries to pulp- and paper-manufacturing plants. These kinds of advancements, which require clearly defined performance measures, are helping companies reduce their risk of operating outside permissible limits.

With the trading market for carbon reaching $118 billion in 2008[15], after growing to $60 billion in 2007 (twice the market size of 2006)[16], it's clear that organizations must master the capability to establish relevant KPIs that correlate traditional operations performance with improved environmental stewardship. In addition to carbon management, areas that are growing in importance, with different KPIs, include the monitoring and management of water, other atmospheric emissions, liquid waste, solid waste, ground emissions, noise levels, air quality, and virtually any other raw material or natural resource.

Some companies have had KPI measurements in place for years. Examples include measurements related to recycled materials, water consumption, electricity consumption, fuel consumption, and raw-materials waste. However, most performance measures have traditionally been established at a relatively high level or are very specific in nature and intended to target a narrow area of waste. Enterprises are only now beginning to holistically characterize their operations based on environmental impact.

In the past, many companies measured and tracked gross energy use or even electric-bill charges, especially those with high energy-consuming manufacturing facilities. In the

---

future, more appropriate measurements could be based on real-time fluid temperatures, along with algorithms that automatically correlate different elements of a manufacturing process with waste. For example, chilled water and steam systems for air cooling and heating often measure and report temperature and flow rate at building entry and exit points, but they don't as often report data at points inside a building for insight into the highest consumption and waste areas. In this scenario, leaders can apply improved visibility and business logic to potentially identify problems and make adjustments even before unnecessary waste is produced.

The amount of recycled material, such as paper, metals, plastics, liquids, and gases, represents another area that many companies have been measuring. However, measuring these wastes more holistically can lead to improved performance. For example, measuring the amount of material consumed as value-added input to a manufacturing process, along with measuring the amount recycled, provides insightful information on the amount of waste that remains to be captured.

Other KPIs that draw a more holistic picture of waste production are being measured to support environmental stewardship and set business performance-improvement targets. In some businesses, the time to clean contaminated soil, the number of toxic spills on a global basis, or the number of injuries (both human and animal) from an accident or adverse event can all be part of a holistic picture.

To characterize an enterprise with respect to its environmental impact, one emerging and increasingly foundational practice is to correlate KPIs with their carbon-footprint impact. In many cases, organizations can correlate a positive environmental impact to a reduced carbon footprint. For example, automobile and factory emissions, forest products consumed and not renewed, and electricity use can all be correlated with a carbon footprint.

However, the realities of an imperfect world cannot be ignored. Global standards are not yet established for carbon footprint KPIs, although they are developing. The Carbon Trust offers one framework[17] in which KPIs can be grouped into six emission-type categories:

- Direct (such as on-site combustion of fuels)

- Indirect (such as off-site combustion of fuels for use on-site)

- Process (such as on-site emissions caused by processes)

- Energy export (such as on-site combustion of fuels for off-site use in electricity generation)

- Upstream (such as emissions caused by suppliers)

- Downstream (such as emissions caused by products during their lifecycle)

The Greenhouse Gas (GHG) Protocol[18] has developed another framework in which KPIs are grouped into three *scopes*. The first scope includes emissions that are directly produced from operating buildings, equipment, and vehicles. The second scope includes indirect emissions from purchased electricity, steam, or heat. The third scope includes indirect emissions from outsourced activities and business travel. The Green Sigma methodology establishes a set of measures and then maps them to these three scopes. Other efforts for standardization, beyond carbon emissions, are also developing. For example, the International Organization for Standardization (ISO) has developed requirements and guidance for use of ISO 14001:2004 that address environmental-management systems.[19] Companies such as Emerald Group Publishing[20] are getting certified for this standard to improve and demonstrate their competence in, and commitment to, environmental stewardship.

The initial challenge for most organizations is establishing the boundary conditions used for carbon-footprint reporting. When the boundary conditions are set, organizations can determine the appropriate KPIs and establish the measurement system. Although this chapter emphasizes carbon-footprint KPIs, it's easy to see how organizations can define KPIs for virtually any area that has an impact on the environment.

5.3. Step 2 Establishes a Measurement System

An organization must overcome unique challenges when establishing a measurement system that supports environmental stewardship. One challenge is that the processes for metering and monitoring KPIs are at various levels of maturity. For example, even the standards for carbon measurement and reporting are still in the early stages of development.

For most industries, especially the pharmaceutical, chemical, and other manufacturing-intensive industries, much of the metering and monitoring today is associated with air and ground emissions, such as waste water, organic and inorganic waste, and hazardous waste. These measures have been tightly controlled due to regulatory and legislative requirements across most geographic regions. Yet monitoring to meet regulatory compliance doesn't necessarily meet the monitoring needs for other purposes, such as waste reduction.

To illustrate this point, consider an industrial-manufacturing operation in which hazardous waste is measured for regulatory compliance purposes by counting the number of barrels or measuring the net liquid volume as an output of the facility. Using this measurement as an indicator of waste production provides little information on where, when, and how the waste is created. To improve the processes that generate hazardous waste, more detailed information is often needed about where in the process the waste comes from, what machinery is used and how it's maintained, chemical reactions involved, operating schedules, and other process-specific parameters. Inevitably, some measurements will be easier to take than others, technical challenges must be overcome, and legacy measurement infrastructure must be considered.

For some businesses, the most substantial challenge to metering deployment in their legacy environments relates to networking and communications. This challenge often involves solving the problem of how to effectively create networks for the existing metered infrastructure, especially when dispersed site locations are involved. Where meters are already deployed, processes are sometimes in place to take relatively infrequent, manual measurements that aren't very helpful in analyzing and reducing waste, and identifying problems early. In the example of metering to accurately capture water pollution, the dispersion can be spread along many miles of a river.

Although using wires for the installed metering network is perhaps the most reliable approach, it's also a costly and time-consuming solution. Using wireless technology is an alternative to consider for such challenges. Although standards have been developed for GSM/GPRS (Global System for Mobile Communications/General Packet Radio Service), Bluetooth, Zigbee, Wi-Fi, and WLAN (wireless local area network, IEEE 802.11 standard) technologies, not all are suitable for the challenges associated with difficult industrial environments, such as manufacturing facilities.

Solutions to the wireless challenge already exist in the marketplace, and the Green Sigma methodology offers a wireless metering solution that enables interface capability with most of the meters in the marketplace today. Other solutions have also been developed. "Smart wireless" from Emerson Process Management is one example that uses a self-organizing, smart-mesh network to reliably overcome harsh electric and magnetic field conditions.[21]

The steps in establishing a measurement system that supports environmental stewardship are similar to other metering solutions, in which multiple devices must be deployed and data must be relayed to a central data warehouse or to any number of synchronized databases. A spectrum of technology is available for metering that ranges from manual observation to fully wireless remote sensing, which can all fit into a straightforward conceptual technology architecture that companies can build. Existing legacy metering can also have a place in this architecture. Figure 5.3 illustrates such a conceptual architecture for a measurement system in which organizations can report information manually and initially capture it on spreadsheets, or fully automate it with wireless sensors.

In building such a measurement system, or extending the purpose of an existing one, an organization must consider a number of variables. First, the data sources themselves must meet certain levels of reliability, durability, accuracy, and maintainability. The data must adhere to standards that enable it to be aggregated and analyzed. Unreliable or nonstandard data will ultimately not be very useful; similarly, a network of sensing devices that is constantly under repair will not be beneficial. Fortunately, for the purpose of energy-use reporting, water use and consumption, and many other areas of environmental impact, sensing devices that have proven accurate and reliable are frequently available. An organization must consider the time interval for taking measurements (continuous, hourly, daily, and so on) in an automated sensing system.

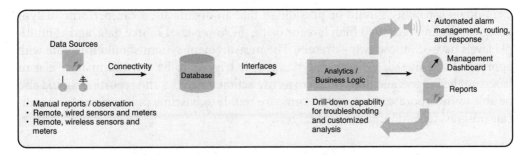

Figure 5.3 Conceptual technology architecture for the measurement system

Connectivity from the data sources, sensors, and meters to a database must be efficient and reliable. The same is true for interfaces between the data itself and software applications that analyze and report information. For example, if the method used includes manual observation of water use from a meter installed on a pipe and uses disparate spreadsheets to capture the data, appropriate governance also must be in place to ensure that the data is updated often enough that it's current and relevant when analyzed. The data should be collected into a central database or should be synchronized across databases so that an organization can easily aggregate and analyze it without errors.

The analytics and business logic should consider the business objectives of environmental stewardship and waste reduction. Business logic should have the capability to identify when parameters exceed certain limits so that alarms can be triggered and messages routed to someone who can initiate corrective action. Automated response might even be possible. For example, if building equipment continues to operate during evening hours when it should be shut off according to a standard schedule, alarm-management or automated-response functionality can be an effective way of correcting the situation before energy is wasted throughout the night. The management reporting and information visibility should be easily understood and interpreted, and should provide insight into problem areas and improvement opportunities. Figure 5.4 shows the management dashboard system, which is one solution that can provide such visibility and insight.

Leading practices for establishing effective measurement systems are also important to evaluate and can considerably reduce the ongoing operational cost if incorporated early on. Connectivity and interfaces in which data is communicated from one place to another should be automated as much as possible, especially when data is exchanged between different systems or altered. As with any other business process, such as order management, less manual intervention and rekeying of data reduces the opportunity to introduce errors and increases the reliability and efficiency of the whole system. An organization should evaluate trade-offs between cost and real-time data visibility so that information is accurate and timely, but not at the expense of being too costly.

Drill-down capability should be possible so that an organization can perform analysis using data at an aggregated high level or using the lower-level source data, and at multiple levels between those two extremes. The measurement system should integrate with appropriate business logic and analytics, enable triggers to be set, and manage alarms based on the triggers and prescribed corrective action. Analytics and reporting should also be able to incorporate benchmarks, compare trends to baseline performance, and indicate progress toward improvement targets.

5.3.1. Direct Measurement of Carbon Emissions

Direct metering has traditionally been limited to site or building entry-level metering for many industries. Utility companies often use direct metering for billing purposes installed during building construction, and then rarely make changes after construction is complete. As a result, existing KPIs in this area of direct measurement have typically not changed for many years. Natural gas and electricity companies typically include kilowatt-hours (kWh) monitored on a daily and cumulative usage basis, which can be converted to tons of carbon dioxide equivalent (tCO_2e) using established conversion criteria. The Carbon Trust[22] and a number of other sources discuss conversion criteria. Energy from more sustainable sources has correspondingly lower conversion factors.

Without measurement detail, many organizations lack a holistic understanding of their energy use and resultant carbon footprint. Four key reasons explain why this widespread lack of understanding has persisted. First, relatively inexpensive energy has been historically available without other drivers for improvement; therefore, most companies have not considered energy as a key cost driver. Projects that focused on energy conservation with long time horizons to achieve an attractive return on investment (ROI) were not viable, so companies didn't continue to invest in this area.

A second reason involves a lack of metering infrastructure. During the past 20 years, organizations have made little investment in energy-management infrastructure during the design and build phases of construction, except when energy consumption is especially high. As a result, most organizations with legacy infrastructure are now challenged with establishing an accurate position for energy management.

Third, legislative and regulatory drivers have been lacking, although improvements are being made. Section 1.3.3.3 in Chapter 1 described attempts to regulate carbon emissions, but no real external regulatory pressure is forcing organizations to optimize their carbon footprints. The emergence of the U.K. Climate Change Act might change this situation in the future. This legislation aims to drive changes in the U.K., but other countries will likely adopt and enforce similar legislation in the future.

Fourth, the accountability for energy use hasn't been well defined traditionally. Within most organizations, responsibility for energy management is often unclear or widely dispersed among many people, and often no single entity is incited, required, or empowered to make improvements.

Either implicitly or explicitly, many businesses have treated their planned "sustaining" and "transformation" roadmaps differently. The budget to support a transformation roadmap is often allocated and aligned to enable strategic imperatives with clear accountability for meeting key objectives as investments are made. However, the budget to support a sustaining roadmap is also needed for necessary maintenance and upkeep to "keep the lights on" for property, facilities, plants, equipment, and information-technology systems without any real connection to a strategic business imperative. With the strength of the green movement, businesses are now capturing opportunities to consider investments in their sustaining and transformation roadmaps in a more integrated way. Businesses can coordinate accountability for improvements and alignment with green strategic imperatives with necessary maintenance and "pay-the-bills" responsibility, to further improve environmental stewardship. Investment in measurement systems is one such area of opportunity.

Some industries have a significant opportunity to advance their state-of-the-art measurement systems in new ways. For example, companies in the transportation and logistics industry have the capability to collect direct mileage–metering data from their fleets using on-board truck and aircraft telemetry, and satellite-tracking technology.

Given the current legacy-metering infrastructure deficit that exists across most business sectors, the challenge now is for organizations to begin measuring, managing, and optimizing their energy use and to conserve other natural resources. To implement this quickly, companies need to design and implement nondisruptive metering solutions that they can integrate with the existing infrastructure.

5.3.1.1. Direct Measurement of Electrical Power

By deploying smarter metering technology, power utility companies around the world are helping raise awareness of electricity usage at the billing-meter level. However, a large gap remains between such top-level measurements and the need to understand the usage profiles for equipment that consumes significant energy inside facilities.

A few companies provide several well-established power-management solutions, such as monitoring and management capability for electrical power. Some example companies include Mitsubishi, Siemens, Ely, Schneider Electric, Omron, and Elutions. However, the challenges of deploying even these established solutions within a legacy environment can be quite substantial.

Particular problems arise in the deployment of power metering in a high-voltage (HV) or medium-voltage (MV) environment. To deploy a more granular level of sensing within MV distribution-board switch panels, planned power outages are invariably required for health and safety reasons. Arranging suitable times to carry out this work can be a lengthy process that is difficult to coordinate. To overcome this, companies are developing several innovative and minimally disruptive metering solutions at the MV level that reduce such delays in implementing new metering technology.

For companies and organizations whose operations require high availability both day and night, such as hospitals and manufacturing plants with multishift work schedules, arranging suitable change windows can be especially challenging. In one particular deployment at an industrial company in Europe, establishing power metering over a four-building site took nearly nine months, with only one outage per building allowed in each quarter.

Companies are more frequently changing their electrical energy mix supplied on-site or from utility companies by paying for electrical power generated from renewable energy sources. This is leading to a higher level of awareness and sophistication in carbon management. Not only is the price different for electrical power from renewable energy sources compared to traditional ones, but the conversion factors are also different in translating electricity consumption to equivalent carbon emissions. For example, the typical electricity power-conversion factor for carbon dioxide/kWh is 500–600g/kWh[23], but with the use of renewable energy or nuclear power averaged-in, this figure can fall to 400g/kWh or less. For electricity generated on-site with renewable energy sources, the conversion factor can drop to zero.[24] Some aspirations, such as the FIJI Water company, are actually aiming to achieve negative carbon-footprint commitments.[25] Chalet 1802, a family-run online skiing company based in the French Alps, has achieved a negative carbon footprint, partly from "purchasing all its electricity from renewable sources."[26] This practice can contribute to a company's objective of reducing the level of carbon dioxide it generates, even though universal standards for conversion-factor calculations are still being discussed. Perhaps when all the electricity is someday generated from renewable and sustainable sources, electrical power won't contribute to greenhouse gas emissions.

5.3.1.2. Direct Measurement of Natural Gas

Measurement of natural gas for most organizations involves building-level metering for utility-billing purposes. However, given the mechanical and often unsophisticated nature of these meters, most companies don't have automated-reporting capability. The exception is facilities with high gas usage, where automated uploads to the utility company through a General Packet Radio Service (GPRS) network link are often in place.

Except for the most basic gas meters, most offer some kind of output capability in the form of electrical pulses proportional to the actual gas flow. Organizations can convert and upload these pulses, often to a building management system (BMS). Buildings that consume natural gas, including offices, warehouses, stores, and manufacturing facilities, frequently use such meters.

Unlike electricity, which feeds a variety of machines, the gas supply is often a dedicated feed into a gas-boiler arrangement. As a result, building-level metering can be sufficient and the need to deploy additional submetering is low. However, several unique challenges exist for metering deployment with natural gas.

If the existing meters don't have information-uploading capability, a planned system outage might be required to deploy an appropriate inline gas-flow meter. However, several unobtrusive clamp-on ultrasonic gas-flow meters are available in the marketplace if no existing measurement system is available.

Because gas boilers are primarily used to generate hot water, another solution deploys unobtrusive secondary heat meters within high- or low-pressure hot-water systems. This deployment approach applies to situations in which an organization can use the heat energy measured within the hot water loops to determine the amount of gas consumed during the measurement period. This scenario eliminates the need for disruptive inline-meter deployment, and more rapid implementation and data reporting is possible.

5.3.2. Indirect Measurement of Carbon Emissions

Even less understood than direct measurement—and, therefore, potentially more challenging—is the capability to capture the relevant data for *indirect* measurement of carbon emissions. A few typical areas that require measurement to establish an organization's footprint include business travel, employee commuting, and inbound and outbound logistics associated with shipments of materials.

5.3.2.1. Indirect Measurement of Business Travel

For business travel, business leaders can obtain relevant KPI data from mining existing databases that already exist in most organizations. Information gained might include in-house business-expense claims data or travel requests. One relevant KPI is the combined tons of carbon dioxide equivalent (tCO_2e) emitted for the various modes of employee transport. Categorizing business travel by mode of transport and converting to tCO_2e based on known conversion factors can help an organization determine its carbon-footprint contribution. An illustration of this approach is provided later in Chapter 6, Section 6.2, with the case study.

5.3.2.2. Indirect Measurement of Employee Commuting

As in the approach for business travel, an organization can establish KPIs for emissions from employee commuting, and tons of carbon dioxide emissions saved by remote working in lieu of commuting, by querying telephony call-management systems and remote dial-in connection–reporting systems. Increased numbers of remote workers translate to lower emissions because of a decrease in employee commuting. An illustration of this approach is provided later in Chapter 6, Section 6.2, with the case study.

5.3.2.3. Indirect Measurement of Business Logistics

Organizations also need to measure and quantify carbon emissions associated with inbound and outbound logistics operations to establish a total carbon footprint. When attempting to assess the carbon-emissions equivalent from individual inbound and outbound shipments, each tracked through multiple carriers and multiple modes of transport, organizations realize the scale and complexity of the task. Dynamic reporting on a weekly, biweekly, or monthly basis increases the workload and adds complexity in the absence of automated technology tools. The KPIs established for tracking and reporting carbon emissions from logistics include equivalent tons of carbon per shipped ton (tCO_2e per shipped ton).

Solutions are available that enable organizations to model their carbon emissions produced by business logistics. For both inbound and outbound logistics, these solutions help a company understand its carbon footprint in a cost-effective way. In the future, modeling tools will enable organizations to test routing scenarios for carbon optimization. It will also be possible to adjust input variables (such as delivery times, shipment consolidation, and modes of transport) to estimate the smallest possible carbon footprint while still meeting customer requirements. The difference between optimal routes and actual routes represents an opportunity to reduce carbon emissions.

Tracking the ongoing difference between optimized routing and actual routing would be the ideal dashboard-level KPI to assess an organization's progress toward minimizing its carbon footprint from logistics operations. In the future, measurement of carbon emissions from logistics could be possible by using the technology of onboard telemetry with satellite tracking of delivery vehicles.

5.3.3. Direct and Indirect Measurement of Water and Other Natural Resources

Using many of the same techniques for measuring carbon, organizations can measure the use of water, air, metals, plastics, chemicals and gases, paper, and other natural resources at different points in a business process. In some cases, organizations can correlate known data with resource consumption indirectly; other times, direct measurements are necessary. For example, in an automobile-washing business, water use might easily be correlated with the number and type of vehicles serviced. Continuous, real-time measurement is often practical for liquid and gas usage or where continuous-flow processes are involved, such as with coal traveling along a conveyor belt. Discrete or batch-flow processes might measure weight or volume of materials at important points in the process. Although correlations to carbon emissions are established for energy, organizations can connect measurements of other natural resources to other environmental influences. For example, organizations can correlate water use to volume and availability, quality and pollution level, sanitation and health, and so forth.

An emerging leading practice in environmental stewardship is to deploy a portal-based management dashboard system that displays KPIs, metering data, and other critical information for making optimal business decisions.

5.4. Step 3 Deploys a Management Dashboard System

Displaying current KPI data on a single dashboard not only facilitates business reporting and accounting requirements: The dashboard can also serve as an active carbon-management and waste-monitoring tool. Organizations can use such a tool to monitor daily operations, optimization, and compliance with regulatory obligations.

Organizations make significant efforts to generate data to support the sustainability-performance section of many annual business reports. Such data-gathering efforts are often manual or static in nature and require significant costs to keep the data current.

Although many of the existing tools and carbon-footprint calculators are used to report some of the required footprint data, most aren't sufficiently accurate or adequate for revealing a full carbon position in three key areas. The first area involves defining clear boundary conditions for reporting. Second, the reported data is generally static and not comprehensive, primarily because of the significant effort involved in gathering such data. Finally, a high complexity and cost is associated with collecting even the baseline data, especially for the carbon position of inbound and outbound logistics.

As one of its core components, Green Sigma uses a portal-based dashboard to actively manage an environmental stewardship position. An organization can configure the dashboard to report on measures in any area of the business, including carbon, water, atmospheric emissions, liquid waste, solid waste, ground emissions, noise levels, and air quality. Figure 5.4 shows a sample dashboard. Note the flexible-reporting approach, which includes dials, graphs, and other chart formats that can display information from a variety of data sources, ranging from basic manual entry to real-time automated feeds. The figure also illustrates sample reports for several operational performance indicators that are related to areas such as electricity usage, gas usage (for three different buildings), logistics (inbound and outbound), and business mileage. It also illustrates weather-monitoring capability, alert-status reporting with current state and threshold limits, and summary-level carbon dioxide run-rates for normal, near-limit, and over-limit operating zones. Drop-down option menus enable a user to view these reports for different facilities, geographies, time horizons, formats, and units of measure.

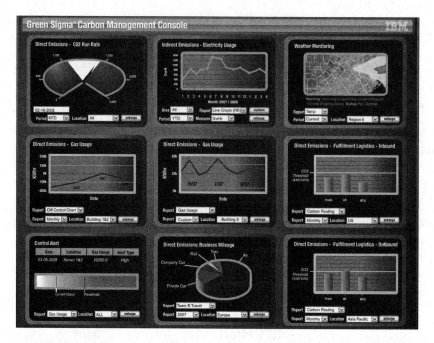

Figure 5.4   Active management dashboard system

Source: *IBM Journal of Research and Development*

Although it's sensible to focus on automating data feeds into such a dashboard, a well-designed system also offers the flexibility of manual data entry. This manual feed, with disparate spreadsheets and database report queries providing the data, is a possible short-term solution for many organizations. For carbon monitoring, companies should not overlook having manual-entry capability with the dashboard; it enables companies new to the carbon management space to quickly ascertain their carbon position without needing to immediately overcome all the measurement and networking challenges.

Green Sigma initially uses this portal-based tool as a solution for establishing an organization's baseline carbon footprint. That information is then applied to optimize carbon emissions. As organizations develop an understanding of their carbon position, the tool develops into more of a strategic-management system and provides active control capability.

Organizations achieve active carbon management by statistically modeling the business environment and linking the associated KPIs to actual process activities that contribute to different carbon sources. This approach is especially useful when KPI measurements come from gas, electricity, and water use because organizations can potentially take those measurements continuously and in real time. Having this level of visibility into process activities and corresponding resource consumption enables a company to actively manage and optimize its environmental impact through real-time alerts, alarm management, and automated responses.

Beyond the dashboard solution, enterprisewide environmental-management consoles can deliver complete enterprise-level reporting. Although it's useful for any company, enterprises with high carbon emissions, such as electrical power–generating utilities, might use this level of reporting. Organizations of this kind require greenhouse gas emissions to be measured at the chimney stack exit level, and the data must be aggregated and reported for the corporation to meet compliance requirements. At such an enterprise level, more real-time reporting capability can be used as a platform for revenue generating opportunities in the developing carbon credit–trading markets.

5.5. Step 4 Improves and Optimizes Processes

Green Sigma applies modified traditional manufacturing-type statistical- and waste-reduction techniques from Lean and Six Sigma, focused on environmental impact areas and more typical ones. The traditional "voice of the customer" (VOC) process that captures customer requirements is replaced by the "voice of the environment" (VOE). VOE addresses sustainability factors and the impact of processes on the environment.

By adapting the traditional VOC process to now identify VOE requirements, environmental impact areas are made more visible in analyses where they might have been ignored in the past. Some of the requirements from VOE might contradict those from VOC, to achieve a balance between the customer requirements and environmental requirements. As an illustration from the automotive industry, one VOC requirement might be rapid acceleration, but analogous VOE requirements might be fuel efficiency and engine noise level. In another illustration, a customer requirement for more powerful vehicle air-conditioning can be contrasted with environmental requirements for fuel efficiency and end-of-life refrigerant disposal.

By establishing KPIs and using the standard Lean methodology for data diagnostics, a company can identify, qualify, and capture target opportunities for process-focus areas. After the company fully develops the management dashboard system, analyzes the processes, and completes the necessary transformation actions with a continuous-improvement methodology, the final step is to standardize and replicate opportunities and process improvements across the enterprise. This further leverages the benefits of a Green Sigma or similar investment.

Two statistically based analysis techniques have been adapted for Green Sigma. The first is voice of the environment (VOE) value-stream mapping (VSM). The second is voice of the environment characterization and optimization through the application of statistical process control (SPC) and use of targeted design of experiments (DOE).

5.5.1. Voice of the Environment (VOE) Value Stream Mapping (VSM)

Starting with the traditional value stream mapping concept as a basis for identifying waste and implementing leaner process designs, it's possible to adapt the technique to improve environmental effects. This approach effectively defines the VOE factors for optimization within a targeted focus area.

Organizations can add information to the value-stream map for carbon emissions, managed water use, raw-materials consumption, and other environmental wastes. This not only improves the end-to-end view of a process, but it also enables companies to analyze high environmental-impact areas and identify opportunities for continuous improvement. Through various statistical techniques, organizations can optimize energy performance and waste production to simultaneously yield carbon-emission and waste reductions, cost reductions, and process improvements. For example, wasted natural gas energy and excessive carbon emissions from heating a building might introduce VOE factors, such as burning nonrenewable energy resources and the resulting carbon emissions.

In another example, the levels of waste from producing a jar of coffee might introduce VOE factors such as excessive water use, carbon emissions from manufacturing and transportation in the supply chain, and amounts of different wastes in landfills and hazardous waste dumps associated with the manufacturing process and discarded packaging.

VOE factors for selling a new refrigerator might include carbon emissions from transportation, ongoing in-use energy consumption measured by the energy rating of the product as a design feature, the excessive landfill requirement for packaging waste, and the eventual disposal needs for hazardous refrigerant.

5.5.2. Statistical Process Control (SPC) and Design of Experiments (DOE)

Applying standard SPC techniques using VOE KPIs is an effective method for optimizing and improving processes for environmental stewardship. The SPC technique establishes upper and lower control limits for parameters such as temperature or fuel consumption so that normal operation remains between these two limits. When normal operation is at risk of being outside these limits, organizations can take corrective action to prevent problems before they occur. Typical statistical tools include process-control charts, histograms, regression analysis, and DOE to model the chosen environment and select appropriate limits. Green Sigma can modify the traditional design for manufacture (DFM) and Design for Six Sigma (DFSS) principles and apply them to target design for the environment (DFE).

Organizations can realize substantial benefits by using these tools. As the case study in the next chapter demonstrates, applying these techniques can yield an energy savings of approximately 20 percent even before full-process optimization is complete.

5.6. Step 5 Controls Ongoing Performance

Institutionalizing behavioral changes in an organization and establishing effective continuous-improvement practices are essential elements in the overall effort to improve environmental impact on an ongoing basis. For most organizations, establishing performance measures, installing a measurement system, and providing effective reporting is just the beginning of the transformation journey.

The management dashboard system can report carbon emissions, environmental waste, water-management parameters, raw-materials consumption, and other areas critical to environmental impact. With such a sophisticated measurement and reporting system in place, organizations have the tools to better manage and improve performance on a sustained basis. Although this chapter is not intended to fully describe Lean and Six Sigma tools and techniques that support ongoing control and continuous improvement, you can read more about the key elements of waste elimination and process variability reduction in Step 5 of the case study in the next chapter (see Section 6.5).

6

Applying Green Sigma to Optimize Carbon Emissions

The Green Sigma approach has already demonstrated and quantified significant energy savings and corresponding greenhouse gas emission reductions. Organizations have also achieved improvements in water management and other key areas of environmental stewardship. This case study describes how an organization used the five-step Green Sigma methodology to improve carbon emissions by managing gas usage for environmental control inside a 200,000-square-foot electronics manufacturing and assembly facility in Europe. The case focuses on the warehouse portion of the facility, although actual data is also provided from the broader site to illustrate carbon measurement for business travel and employee commuting.

Readers can apply the findings and observations discussed in this chapter to virtually any reasonably large operation with a complex network of processes and equipment that consume energy or natural resources. This includes warehouses, manufacturing facilities, office buildings, retail sites, hotels and conference centers, theme parks, entertainment locations, and casinos.

6.1. Step 1 Defines Key Performance Indicators

The initial focus for a VOE (voice of the environment) key performance indicator (KPI) was daily cumulative kilograms of equivalent carbon dioxide emissions from warehouse operations. This was a straightforward calculation because it directly correlated to the measured kilowatt-hours (kWh) of gas use inside the building. However, analysis showed that this KPI was not sensitive enough to environmental factors, such as temperature, to provide a timely response to alarm triggers and for adequate investigation into out-of-control situations. One reason was the large scale and complex interactive nature of the energy-consuming equipment inside the building. An analysis yielded more than 100 pieces of energy-consuming equipment in the building.

Ultimately, analysts determined that an hourly reporting of peak gas flow in cubic meters per hour gave the optimum measurement to enable proactive business-process control. The analysts then correlated this flow rate to equipment operating schedules instead of environmental temperature, which fluctuated widely and was not a reliable predictor of alarm-triggering situations.

Analysts also identified and reported indirect measures for business travel and employee commuting associated with the broader site of multiple buildings. These were more straightforward to establish because they leveraged information in existing databases. For example, business-travel measures included air miles, company car miles, and car hire (taxi) miles. Employee commuting measures included data such as remote login information.

6.2. Step 2 Establishes a Measurement System

The onsite building management system (BMS) provided automated data feeds for gas use in the warehouse using the existing metering solutions described earlier.

Other measurements were done manually. The BMS was capable of controlling energy-consuming equipment with automated scheduling. However, when deviations to standard schedules were required, the system could not automatically return to normal at a pre-scribed point in time. Analysts tracked these deviations on paper and spreadsheets. For example, if the business required a temporary change in the BMS to accommodate a second shift of warehouse personnel for two days, the standard schedule would need to be manually changed in the system on the first day. Another manual system change was required later in the week to reestablish normal operating conditions.

Although not part of the initial focus on warehouse operations, analysts also measured and reported carbon emissions for the broader site from business travel and employee commuting. The following data and analyses are provided to illustrate a few possible findings.

6.2.1. Measurement System for Business Travel

Figure 6.1 provides one sample of actual data from the IBM facility in Europe. Analysts estimated air miles, company car miles, hired car (taxi) miles, and other travel miles from existing information, such as when employees report the necessary data for expense-reimbursement purposes. With the travel miles known, analysts used established conversion factors to calculate the equivalent carbon emissions. Such analyses are useful not only to better understand a company's carbon footprint, but also to identify high carbon-producing business activity that a company can target for improvement. In this illustration, air travel is one area in which a relatively small percentage improvement could have a significant positive impact, compared to the other transportation modes.

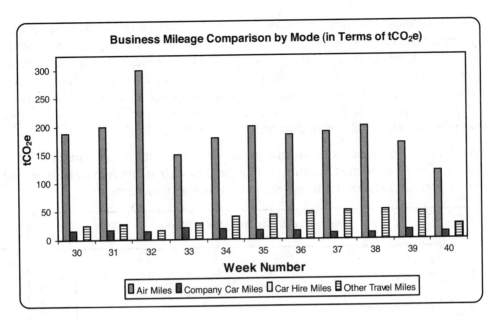

Figure 6.1 Indirect measurement of business travel

6.2.2. Measurement System for Employee Commuting

Figure 6.2 summarizes remote-login data from the same IBM facility in Europe. Analysts can also review videoconferencing and teleconferencing data. Analyses such as these are immediately useful in spotting trends and, with appropriate root-cause analysis, identifying opportunities to continue favorable trends and reverse unfavorable ones. Although the data is from actual operations, the following root-cause assessment is hypothetical, to highlight key benefits of the analysis.

Figure 6.2 suggests an unfavorable trend for environmental sustainability, in which fewer logins and a lower number of login hours are occurring over time. The simplest explanation could be that employees are commuting to the office more often, resulting in higher greenhouse gas emissions from commuting. After being validated, such a finding can lead to expanded training and new governance for telecommuting policies and procedures.

However, without the appropriate root-cause analysis and validation, data-driven hypotheses can be misleading. For example, if the number of logins in Figure 6.2 is decreasing because the company is improving the reliability of remote network access and users are experiencing fewer disconnects, the environmental impact would be essentially neutral. The company might also be enforcing auto-logoff software settings more rigorously during this time period by automatically logging off employees when they leave a computer unattended (such as overnight), thereby reducing the total number of login hours. In cases such as this, the conclusions are actually counterintuitive. Because network reliability is increasing, workforce efficiency will be higher even though the number of logins is decreasing. And because the total number of login hours is decreasing for hours that are not productive work hours, the environmental impact is favorable—since less computer power is used. A sensible next step in this scenario could be to train or communicate to employees that they should turn off their remote-office computers during nonworking hours, in addition to disconnecting from the network.

Without analyses such as these, the insights for environmental impact are difficult to hypothesize. More important, without visibility to data such as this, fully developing and testing hypotheses that lead to improvement ideas is even more difficult.

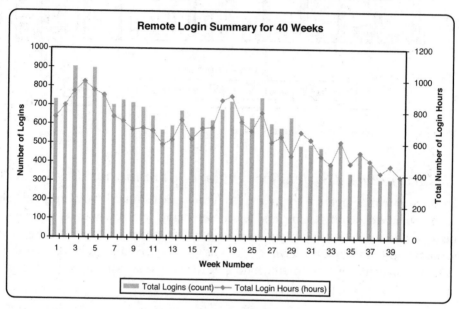

Figure 6.2   Indirect measurement of employee commuting

6.3. Step 3 Deploys the Management Dashboard System

The company automatically uploaded real-time reporting of cumulative gas-usage data to the management dashboard system shown in the last chapter in Figure 5.4. Analysts created an hourly control chart based on hourly gas flow in cubic meters per hour, similar to the one shown in Figure 6.5. Section 6.4.1 discusses this figure in greater detail.

6.4. Step 4 Improves and Optimizes Processes

With a data-gathering system in place and information automatically presented through the dashboard, the company could analyze and study hourly gas usage.

Analysis revealed a large number of factors that contributed to total gas use and its hourly variation. Using the building heating system equipment inventory, which included nearly 100 assets, analysts created a Sankey diagram to understand the significant energy users (SEUs) within the building. SEUs are pieces of equipment that consume a relatively large amount of energy. Sankey diagrams are drawn so that the width of the arrows is proportional to a particular KPI measurement, such as flow rate or energy use. To illustrate the level of complexity involved in this case, the system inventory included 3 domestic hot-water cylinders, 2 gas boilers, 7 air-handling units (AHUs), 40 small fan coil units (FCUs), and more than 40 space-heating radiators.

Figure 6.3 shows a Sankey diagram that's based on proportional estimates of gas consumption, using data from hot water flow rates for nearly 100 energy-consuming components. The diagram clearly identifies the SEUs because the width of each arrow is roughly proportional to the energy used by each component or group of components. Therefore, the SEUs are represented by the widest arrows. In analyzing the diagram, it is apparent that AHUs 4, 5, 6, and 7 consume 80 percent of the gas.

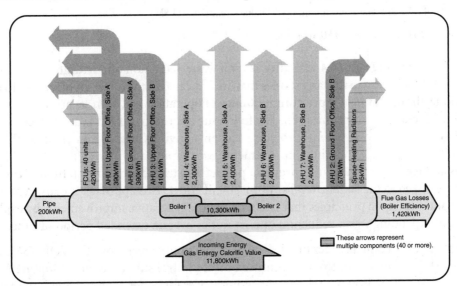

Figure 6.3 Gas-usage Sankey diagram

Source: *IBM Journal of Research and Development*

The next step involved developing an appropriate voice of the environment (VOE) value stream map (VSM) for the building to identify sources of waste and opportunity areas for improvement. For the heating-management process, carbon emissions related to lost heat generated from burning gas were the sources of waste, as shown in Figure 6.4. As in any building, some heat was lost through the building fabric, which includes the walls and ceiling; this is represented as a separate heat-loss arrow on the right side of the figure.

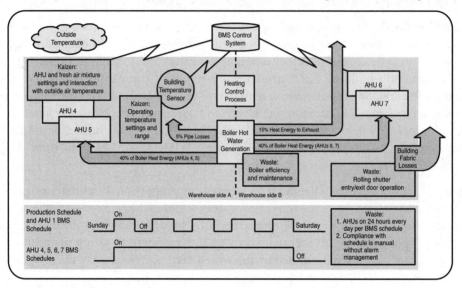

Figure 6.4 Voice of the environment (VOE) value stream map (VSM)

Source: *IBM Journal of Research and Development*

The VOE VSM in Figure 6.4 identified several waste-reduction opportunities for follow-up work, in addition to the largest ones that are indicated in the lower-right corner. In one example, the operating temperature and range of operation had been set arbitrarily without consideration for optimization. The follow-up approach utilized Lean "Kaizen" activities, or rapid-improvement projects. Kaizen activities are extremely effective in identifying and implementing improvements with rapid payoff, using a variety of Lean tools and templates. These improvement projects are tracked for both status and results, and are linked to the larger overall-improvement effort. This approach is consistent with Lean and Six Sigma principles that facilitate ongoing, iterative improvements by exploring and expanding waste-reduction opportunities over an extended period of time.

Ultimately, the company identified two key opportunity areas from the VOE VSM: utilizing AHU-schedule control to minimize out-of-control situations, and adopting AHU scheduling and environmental-control best practices for better alignment with the actual production schedule.

6.4.1. Control of AHU Scheduling

Managers usually set up and manage the AHU schedules from the building management system (BMS), based on environmental-control needs inside a building. Normally, these schedules should relate directly to production-timing requirements. However, facilities management might struggle to maintain schedule control when requests for deviation are received. The requests sometimes result in improvised changes to existing AHU schedules to accommodate temporary needs relating to maintenance, testing, or production shift changes. For example, when evening maintenance is required for production equipment repairs (to avoid daytime disruptions), managers can change the AHU schedules in the BMS to maintain a comfortable environment for work crews. However, failing to realign the schedules to their original settings can lead to significant energy waste because AHU equipment will continue to operate unnecessarily. This is a common problem in facilities that need to control hundreds of assets.

Figure 6.5 represents actual data that illustrates how poor AHU schedule control creates significant waste. The normal schedule shown in Figure 6.4 prescribes for AHUs 1, 4, 5, 6, and 7 to shut off during the weekend. However, they remained on during that time, consuming an estimated energy waste of 14,000kWh. Analysts made this estimate by calculating the difference between the gas volume consumed during the weekend with the AHUs turned on (the thick black line in Figure 6.5) and the volume consumed during a similar weekend time period when the AHUs operated with a more appropriate upper control limit (UCL) of 22 (the thin black line). Finally, the analysts converted the gas volume used to kWh of energy consumption.

Analysts established the control limits using the statistical process control (SPC) toolset introduced in Chapter 5, "Transformation Methods and Green Sigma," Section 5.5.2. By assessing process operations requirements and overlaying the standard AHU schedules in the management dashboard system, it was possible to statistically generate warning limits with respect to hourly gas usage. This enabled weekday operation to use an upper control limit (UCL) of 162, shown in Figure 6.5 by the upper dashed line; weekend operation used a significantly lower UCL of 22, shown by the lower dashed line.

Managers can use these limits to generate warnings and enable detection and correction of any significant AHU schedule out-of-profile event. This leads to significant ongoing energy and carbon emissions savings.

Assuming a conservative estimate of four to six detected events a year that would otherwise not be noticed, the expected savings would be nearly 2 percent annually. In energy terms, this corresponds to an annual reduction of more than 90mWh, with an equivalent carbon dioxide savings of nearly 20 tons for this building alone. By implementing real-time controls through the management dashboard system, the company could save more than 100 tons of carbon dioxide emissions across the entire five-building site.

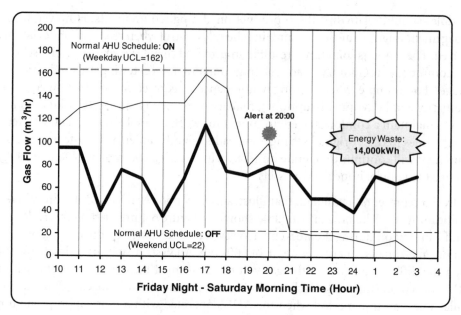

Figure 6.5   Energy consumption at beginning-of-weekend schedule

Source: *IBM Journal of Research and Development*

To trigger an alarm, managers established settings that required two nonconforming measurements, to reduce the likelihood of false alarms from anomalous or erratic data. But if a high level of reliability could be proven from just one nonconforming measurement, managers could save additional energy by triggering and responding to an alarm even more quickly. Further incremental environmental benefits might be possible by taking more frequent measurements.

Businesses must modify facilities-management procedures and work practices to ensure adequate responses to alarms, to improve schedule compliance checking, and to sustain improvements indefinitely.

6.4.2. Adoption of Environmental Control Best Practices

Optimizing energy use by adopting environmental control best practices was a major energy-saving opportunity, with a much higher environmental benefit than the 2 percent improvement described in the previous section. Within the same building, analyses such as Figure 6.6 showed that simply adopting AHU evening-hours shutdown procedures during the week would yield significant energy savings. The potential energy savings from this improvement is roughly 7,000kWh per day, achieved by shutting down the AHUs from 7 PM to 7 AM in the warehouse portion of the building (using the SEUs already identified in the Sankey diagram). This single schedule change yields up to an estimated 20 percent savings in annual gas usage, corresponding to an annual carbon dioxide emission reduction of nearly 260 tons per year. Considering that the entire site includes five similar buildings, applying this approach across the entire campus yields a much larger reduction in greenhouse gas emissions.

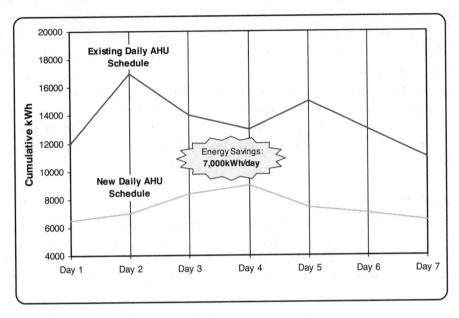

Figure 6.6 Energy consumption during off-hours

By facilitating the additional VOE Kaizens (rapid improvements) shown in Figure 6.4, the organization could challenge existing work practices and adopt more energy-efficient behavior without a negative effect on the work environment. The management dashboard system's capability to communicate real-time KPI information represents a powerful tool to help analyze and realize such benefits.

6.4.3. Use of Design of Experiments (DOE)

The organization can achieve further improvement by adopting Six Sigma design of experiments (DOE) principles to characterize the environmental control heating process. The objective of such an exercise is to realize efficiency gains from the SEU assets, identified in the Sankey diagram in Figure 6.3 as AHU 4, 5, 6, and 7, and the duty standby gas boilers 1 and 2.

Using DOE, which can include factors for different AHUs, boiler types, and key hardware settings, the organization can identify hardware-optimization opportunities that yield further gains of 10–15 percent of total energy use. This corresponds to a further annual carbon dioxide reduction of 100–150 tons.

6.5. Step 5 Controls Ongoing Performance

By applying DOE principles and having an enhanced understanding of the sources of variation and waste, organizations can sustain and improve their ongoing control of energy consumption. Predictive-modeling capability from real-time visibility to gas usage enables organizations to accurately forecast expected carbon-emission levels, which could form the basis for a powerful decision engine and carbon-trading platform in the future.

By controlling ongoing performance and enabling continuous improvement for the warehouse operation, business travel, employee commuting, and all other business areas, organizations can follow a standard approach to further eliminate waste and reduce variability. Eliminating waste and reducing variability are two foundational principles from Lean practices and Six Sigma methods; next we describe frameworks that adapt them to environmental stewardship.

6.5.1. Eliminating Waste

Lean practices help eliminate waste, increase efficiency, and reduce lead time for process execution. Organizations can adapt Lean practices to target specific types of waste, sometimes referred to as "muda," that have a direct impact on the environment and the organization's carbon footprint. Eight typical areas of process-driven waste adversely impact the environment.

Overproduction clearly leads to increased carbon emissions from unnecessary manufacturing processes, larger requirements for warehousing facilities, and increased scrap from obsolescence that ultimately increases disposal and landfill needs. Similarly, *waiting* takes on many forms, from underutilized human resources to machinery that waits for work in process before adding value. In all cases, waiting leads to underutilized capacity and added facility requirements. This increases heating, lighting, water, and other utility consumption. *Inventory* that is either excessive or not stored at the optimal location also leads to added facility requirements, along with increased heating, lighting, water, and other utility consumption.

Reducing *motion* and *transportation* also reduces greenhouse gas emissions. Less motion and shorter transportation distances result in less energy usage and decreased total emissions. Motion refers to the movement that typically takes place within a facility, and transportation refers to distances traveled to move product or people between locations.

Rework refers to activities undertaken to revise a product or implement a fix, which clearly contributes to emissions and waste that adversely impact the environment. Similarly, *overprocessing* represents processing that doesn't add value and could be eliminated from a process with the appropriate configuration changes. Eliminating overprocessing decreases energy and materials consumption, producing a positive impact on the environment.

Improper utilization of intellect is another form of waste that indirectly has an adverse impact on the environment. Not matching the right skills and tools to perform operations can clearly slow processes, cause rework, increase energy consumption, and waste natural resources.

The management dashboard system and the capability to assess the underlying data with statistical analyses are tools to help identify waste in all these areas. Identifying the root cause of waste enables organizations to take corrective action quickly and to define and launch longer-term improvement initiatives. When standardized data becomes available from multiple processes, companies, and entire industries, benchmarking becomes another valuable tool to determine whether current performance, defined by various KPIs, is adequate and where opportunities for improvement might exist.

6.5.2. Reducing Variability

Six Sigma practices help reduce process variability, making the valued outcomes more predictable and consistent. With process baseline performance known and understood, organizations can apply root-cause analysis when unwanted deviations occur. Two analytical tools adapted from Six Sigma can help organizations accomplish this for environmental sustainability.

First, statistical process control (SPC) with control limits (introduced in Chapter 5, Section 5.5.2) can help reduce variability. This analytical tool is also leveraged in the earlier optimization step, with upper and lower control limits statistically derived based on process-performance information. Organizations can use control limits in the management dashboard system for ongoing monitoring and control. As control factors deviate from their normal operating values toward the upper or lower limits, organizations can identify and take corrective action before problems occur. Process improvements or environmental changes might prompt organizations to change control limits and adjust alerts. For example, wide temperature variations from annual season changes can lead to required control-limit adjustments, especially when heating, ventilating, and air-conditioning (HVAC) systems are involved.

Second, design of experiments (DOE) uses controlled experiments to identify causes of variation within a process and to improve ongoing control. By designing and running a series of controlled experiments on a target process, DOE helps develop a greater understanding of the critical controllable input factors and their interactions. This understanding can reveal opportunities to reduce process variation. Because the "control ongoing performance" step is iterative, it's normal for organizations to statistically adjust process control limits after conducting and learning from experiments.

6.6. Case Study Summary

Decreasing the level of facility or process operations reduces energy consumption. However, for large facilities, such as the one in this case study, organizations initially do not know the amount of energy they can save. Organizations must manage hundreds of components simultaneously without knowing which ones are the significant energy users (SEUs), and without clear responsibility for energy waste reduction. In this kind of complex environment, methodologies such as Green Sigma can help clearly identify the highest-priority opportunities to pursue, supply the information to quantify benefits, and provide the analysis and reporting tools to optimize operations, sustain benefits, and institutionalize continuous process improvement.

Establishing KPIs and associated measurement systems plays an important role in enabling enterprises to better manage and improve operations, reduce waste, reduce emissions, and better manage natural resources. The management dashboard system is one tool that has been shown to help companies achieve and sustain their environmental-stewardship aspirations. More broadly, the fully developed and proven practices from Lean and Six Sigma are well suited to support transformation and continuous-improvement programs whose objectives are to foster environmental conservation while reducing cost and waste.

It's important to recognize that the same tools supporting data analysis and information visibility from Green Sigma, such as the management dashboard system, can also be effective drivers of behavioral and cultural change in an organization. Communicating environmental impact success stories through quantified operational improvements, and granting individuals access to process performance information that they can personally affect, enables companies to dramatically increase employee interest in and responsibility for improving the environment.

Organizations sometimes leave energy-consuming equipment operating during times of nonoperation, such as weekends, evenings, and nights, simply because the waste is perceived to be small, although it might actually be quite large. This is especially true for heating, ventilating, and air-conditioning (HVAC) systems that are often centrally managed, as well as desktop computers and supporting devices, lighting, and a myriad of other daily-use equipment and machinery that is typically managed in a decentralized way. For example, many companies today don't have specific policies and awareness training for turning off computers or using "sleep mode" during off-business hours because business leaders themselves are unaware of the quantified opportunity that exists. For one employee, the effect is small; for a facility with thousands of employees, the impact can be significant. Even fewer companies communicate guidance on home office energy-conserving policies in which little or no visibility to conformance exists, even though the trend toward telecommuting is steadily growing.

Many businesses have already benefited from initiatives that align with their strategy to improve environmental stewardship. Carbon strategy is fast becoming a competitive issue among corporate boardrooms.[1] As a greater number of businesses adopt more holistic approaches to improving the environment, effectively applying methodologies such as Green Sigma will become increasingly important.

PART III

Technology Innovations and Solutions

7

Instrumenting the Planet for an Intelligent, Sustainable World

7.1. Benefits from Instrumenting Our Planet Are Enormous

"Instrumenting the planet" is an important part of realizing the full potential of an increasingly intelligent world, just as environmental stewardship can be an integral part of an organization's social responsibility program.

Organizations can construct and deploy instrumentation technology (such as sensors), imaging technology (such as video cameras), and information technology (such as integrated systems) to monitor resources and better manage their end-to-end lifecycles. Such systems enable organizations to measure the state of different resources at key points throughout their lifecycles, from extraction to reuse. This describes an *instrumented world*. Implementation of such systems is referred to as *instrumenting the planet*. Organizations can analyze real-time or continuous data streams to enable quantitative decision making and to optimize use of constrained resources. Organizations can apply the concept of an instrumented world at any level, including the department or site level, the enterprise or city level, and the country or planet level.

In creating an instrumented world, enterprises can capture many business benefits. Products, services, and new infrastructure requirements of an instrumented world offer revenue-growth opportunities to companies that are well positioned to develop and supply them. Instrumented world systems will also greatly enhance how enterprises manage and use natural resources, such as energy and water, and construct infrastructure to lower costs. Environmental benefits are equally significant from lower water and natural-resource waste, and reduced greenhouse gas emissions.

The Climate Group's 2008 report "SMART 2020: Enabling the Low-Carbon Economy in the Information Age," concludes that smarter technology use could reduce global emissions by 15 percent and save global industry $800 billion in annual energy costs by 2020. This represents a reduction of 7.8 gigatons of carbon dioxide equivalent ($gtCO_2e$). This work has been called the first comprehensive global study of the information and communication technology (ICT) sector's growing significance for the world's climate.

Although this industry sector's carbon footprint represents only 2 percent of global emissions, its importance in enabling all industries to reduce greenhouse gas emissions is substantial.[1] In a speech to the Council on Foreign Relations in 2008, Sam Palmissano, IBM's chairman and CEO, stated that a smarter planet is being made possible because the world is becoming more instrumented, the world is becoming interconnected, and "all things are becoming intelligent."[2]

More than 50 years ago, instrumentation and widespread measurement systems for monitoring the environment were already beginning to emerge from efforts to better understand the planet. Activities in 1957 and 1958 associated with the "International Geophysical Year" actually spanned the globe with participation from scientists. One primary focus was on making Earth measurements, such as measuring ice depths, and the effort represented advancements not only in technology, but also in process and global cooperation.[3]

The means for collecting data on human activity and the many transactions we experience has also been developing higher degrees of sophistication during the past several decades. By 2008, Earth supported three billion mobile telephones[4] and several million radio frequency identification (RFID) sensors[5] and Global Positioning System (GPS) receivers.[6] According to iSuppli, a market-research firm, the shift from radio frequency–delivered video to Internet Protocol (IP) cameras that use IP for data transport will increase the number of video-surveillance units from 30 million in 2006 to 66 million in 2011.[7] These devices represent only a handful of those whose widespread use has delivered conveniences and efficiencies, but they can also serve as useful infrastructure in an instrumented world.

Significant growth is also occurring for the number of water meters[8] and sensor networks that monitor natural environments, such as forests[9] and other habitats,[10] rivers, oceans,[11] and glaciers.[12] Sensor networks that monitor human-made infrastructures are growing in size and number to measure such things as electricity grids, traffic patterns, and managed water supplies. Organizations can measure other activities through electronic payment systems, mobile telephone calls and text messages, e-mail traffic, and navigation systems that all create detailed record trails. Technologists have also launched weather and imaging satellites, and installed weather radar systems and dense networks of weather stations around the world. Instrumentation for hydrology is less common, but interest is rising for large-scale sensor deployments that monitor rivers and oceans.[13] Widely available wireless and wired networks can now connect sensors to inexpensive data storage and computing facilities to gather and process vast streams of data, and to ultimately improve our understanding and management of the Earth's natural resources.

We are surrounded by a virtual cloud of real-world data representing people's behavior and the Earth's environment. With computing capabilities and analytical modeling techniques sufficiently advanced, it's now possible to extract "real-time" insights from available information to support better decision making and improved environmental stewardship. "Real-time," as it's used here, refers to situations in which operational deadlines (for a system response to the occurrence of an event) are established. In contrast, a non–real-time system has no deadline. Therefore, real-time intervals can vary widely for different systems. For example, deadlines for a system response when monitoring electricity usage on a power grid might be very short and possibly measured in fractions of a second; however, a system that monitors pollution levels or water-flow rates in a network of rivers might require measurements to be reported only every hour, day, or week. The systems for capturing data streams, analyzing them to gain insights, and applying those insights to drive operational efficiency represent a new form of computing that is essential for an instrumented world. Without these capabilities, much of the potential value from insights that support better business decisions and improved management of critical natural resources would be lost.

Figure 7.1 shows the conceptual flow of data and information for a system in an instrumented world. The system begins with real-world data and ends with insight that drives decision making. On the left side of the figure, the flow begins with the capture of raw, unprocessed data from sensors and other devices, such as intelligent electric meters, and possibly from the output of other systems. The raw data is transported over various access networks to the processing system that converts it into information streams that are standardized by the type of industry application being supported. The processing system might combine the streams from different types of input in predefined ways for processing. Then the processing system communicates the standard streams to an analytical or modeling framework that is again standardized according to the type of industry application. The purpose of this analytical or modeling framework is to identify insights from real-world events or features in the information streams that are relevant to decision making. Data from real-world sensors can enable time-dependent decision making for improved process efficiency and management of natural resources. Businesses might implement these systems for their own use, such as improving operations in a chemical plant. In other cases, the sensors might be part of a public infrastructure, such as a highway system, and authorities can share the insights as a service to multiple organizations. This "information utility" concept at the top of Figure 7.1 indicates that multiple processing steps and data-visibility levels can exist for the various insights that the system produces.

In one example of an information utility, Cisco is partnering with NASA, the United Nations, multilateral development banks, businesses, international government agencies, universities, think-tank organizations, nongovernmental agencies, and foundations to develop the "planetary skin" that captures, collects, analyzes, and reports data on environmental conditions around the world. The concept is to create an online collaborative platform to capture and analyze data from satellite-, airborne-, sea-, and land-based sensors across the globe. This data would be made available for the general public, governments, and businesses to measure, report, and verify environmental information in near-real-time to help detect and adapt to global climate change.[14]

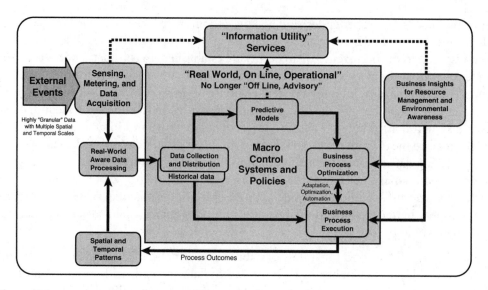

Figure 7.1 Data and information flow in an instrumented-world system

Source: IBM

The figure uses the term "real-world" to represent data from systems in the physical environment, such as weather and traffic, which is different than data from systems in virtual environments, such as e-commerce and online banking systems. This leads to the concept of *real world–aware (RWA) computing,* an essential component of an instrumented world. This chapter provides examples of several existing systems that support the concept of an instrumented world and examples of others that are in development and emerging. It also describes distinctive features of an instrumented world.

New forms of environmental data and modern high-performance computing systems during the late twentieth century have established a solid foundation for instrumenting the planet and have helped develop real-world models. Organizations can now apply such models to gain an understanding of and formulate a response to global climate change. Processing large streams of time-dependent data places different requirements on computing infrastructures than mainstream transaction-oriented systems that businesses are most familiar with.

Humankind's capability to instrument the planet is growing at a time when several factors compel us to address the increasing challenges of climate change and the scarcity of many important natural resources (such as fossil fuels, clean water, and air) and constructed resources (such as roadways and utility networks). At a time when businesses are identifying ways to improve their role as environmental stewards, understanding the contribution that instrumenting the planet offers toward addressing environmental challenges is especially relevant.

7.2. Growing Demand and Increased Scarcity of Resources

Much of the world's supply of constrained natural resources can easily be transported anywhere around the globe. Effective management and efficient use of these resources increasingly requires insight from an instrumented world. In 1970, the Club of Rome sponsored a body of work that was published with the title *Limits to Growth*.[15] This work reviewed the effect of a number of parameters upon the planet's resources, including exponential population growth. The researchers built a model that explained the effect of these parameters upon the long-term growth and material economy of the world. They also presented a number of scenarios in which the world could exist in a sustainable state, and other scenarios in which humanity could use resources in such a way that they would not be replaced. A recent update[16] reviewed this and subsequent works and presents a number of scenarios, ranging from the dire to the benign.

In 1999, Wackernagel and colleagues studied the world's capacity to sustain its population and determined that the "regenerative capacity of the biosphere" was exceeded in 1980.[17] That is, the population was using resources at a rate that exceeded the planet's capability to replace them. More recently, the 2007 United Nations Environment Program (UNEP) "Global Environment Outlook 4 Report"[18] showed that insufficient arable land exists on the planet to extend Western lifestyles to the global population. A growing body of credible work shows that demands from society for the Earth's resources will outstrip supplies without making changes in how those resources are managed and used.

Since the early 1950s, the global population has grown from 2.5 billion to approximately 6.7 billion people,[19] and it is projected to reach 9.3 billion by the middle of the twenty-first century.[20] During this span of time, worldwide oil production[21] has grown from approximately 4 billion barrels of oil per year to 24 billion, and global grain production has risen from about 500 million tons to 3 billion tons.[22]

Historically, supplies of petroleum and basic agricultural crops, such as corn, grain, and soy, have been relatively unconstrained. Today global demand approaches supply so closely that even small variations in availability can disrupt markets, increase prices, and invite speculation. The use of agricultural crops to produce "clean" energy and other environmentally friendly products has also led to food price increases[23] as their original destinations for animal and human consumption are diverted to other areas, such as ethanol and biodiesel production. To add to evidence that risk is growing, the prices for many commodities have at least doubled[24] and fluctuated widely with economic cycles during the last several years as demand—driven by emerging economies and rising living standards—has increased. In general, scarcity invites speculation, and speculation tends to widen price fluctuations and decrease price stability, ultimately leading to increased risk for business operations across industries. Yet compelling evidence exists that industries can improve supply constraints if they manage resources more effectively. For example, it's estimated that up to 30 percent of food is wasted in developed countries because of a host of inefficiencies that come from such areas as the supply chain and how consumers use food.[25]

Unwanted variation in the supply of increasingly constrained natural resources, and the business risk from potential price variability, points to a more general concern. The constrained availability of many natural resources requires a better understanding and efficient management of their use. Economics will continue to play a major role in maintaining the balance between supply and demand for constrained resources, but changes in the behavior of governments, enterprises, and individuals will produce much of the necessary operational restructuring. These behavioral changes will emerge, at least in part, as price signals and other triggers corresponding to resources that were formerly considered low-cost become recognized as financially significant or contributors to other global distress. Price, availability, societal distress, or climate change from global warming might be the trigger. An appropriate global response then is imperative when the implications of the scarcity or distress become known.

For example, the European Commission, backed by government regulations, has established a cap-and-trade program[26] and market-based dynamics to reduce carbon dioxide emissions and other greenhouse gases to mitigate global warming and associated climate and weather change. Experiments by electrical utilities to optimize consumer demand while giving consumers the choice to reduce power or maximize comfort[27] have shown that overall demand can be reduced with little actual change in comfort for the consumer. Also in the utility sector, IBM launched a pilot project with Consumer Energy to test a smart-metering program.[28] In another example, IBM teams[29] working with the Singapore government are developing traffic models that enable the government to predict vehicle volumes and more efficiently manage the road infrastructure.

It's clear that the twenty-first century will require improved methods for managing the use of natural resources and constructed infrastructure. Information technology and analytics, such as mathematical modeling, will play critical roles in stimulating behavioral change. Through the design and implementation of effective models that utilize real-world information, businesses can make better decisions to improve price, reduce greenhouse gas emissions, and effectively manage scarce resources.

7.3. Growth of Real-World Sensing

In a world that has been instrumented, business leaders and policy makers can use information technology and analytics to make use of data to develop insights about strategic decisions, effective planning, and tactical operations. Organizations have deployed large numbers of sensors in recent years for monitoring various aspects of the planet, collectively producing vast streams of data from both the ecosphere and human activity. The scope of in situ (on-site) sensing is vast, covering such areas as water quality and quantity, air quality and atmospheric information, camera and video images for traffic management and facilities safety, and global positioning of vehicles and containers.

For many decades, remote sensing from afar has provided communication and monitoring services for commercial and military purposes, using technology such as aircraft and satellites. Modern satellites in both low-Earth and geostationary orbits can facilitate scientific observation of the universe and collection of meteorological, remote-sensing, geodetic, atmospheric, and navigation data.[30] According to a NASA Goddard report,[31] more than 4,000 satellites have already been launched, and several hundred remain in orbit today. Some satellites[32] generate terabytes of data each day.

One notable U.S. scientific program focuses on the measurement of atmospheric carbon dioxide gas. The Orbiting Carbon Observatory[33] was expected to make 8 million carbon-dioxide measurements every 16 days and identify greenhouse-gas sources from around the planet. However, the program experienced a setback in 2009 when the satellite failed to launch successfully.[34] A Japanese satellite program, the Greenhouse Gases Observing Satellite (GOSAT), is capable of measuring carbon dioxide, water, methane, and ozone in the atmosphere.[35] This satellite successfully launched in 2009.[36] Satellites are only one source that provide information both synchronously and in various processed formats to many different industries for their use and benefit.

In a comparable way, the approximately three billion mobile telephones[37] currently in use provide a valuable network of sensors to measure many aspects of human behavior. This sensor network is already being leveraged in social-network applications and related marketing programs. The technology to triangulate the location of mobile devices continues to improve. These technologies include *Path Intelligence*,[38] which can locate a user's phone within 1–2m inside a retail store; *Cellint*,[39] which monitors vehicle traffic movement through cellphone triangulation; and *INRIX*,[40] which uses Bayesian statistical-analysis models integrated with vehicle traffic information and other parameters to predict traffic conditions. Clearly, organizations can use this information to analyze all types of traffic and to predict patterns in urban travel.

Organizations are using information from accelerometers in laptop computers, normally used to protect hard disks from sudden jolts, for environmental monitoring to detect earthquakes. Project Quake Catcher Network (QCN), with about 1,500 laptops connected in a network, has detected seismic activity that ranges from tremors to a magnitude-5.4 earthquake in Los Angeles.[41]

Video-surveillance cameras are another nearly ubiquitous source of sensor data that is beginning to permeate most developed cities. Central London has deployed 500,000 cameras, and Shenzhen, China, plans to install two million cameras during the next few years.[42]

These kinds of sensor networks and others, such as those facilitated by radio frequency identification (RFID) sensors and Global Positioning System (GPS) technology, will provide increasingly detailed information as companies add more functionality to devices and techniques to extract insight from sensor data improve. Although they provide valuable environmental and societal data, such sensors also raise difficult questions with respect to privacy and human rights. The importance of resolving privacy and human rights issues is difficult to understate as the use of information from personal technology devices, individual activity and transactions, and video imaging expands. Data-security technology and privacy policy is certain to play a central role as such issues are identified and resolved.

The sensor-network systems being deployed today lead to the accumulation of large databases that reflect real-world phenomena, such as the detailed flow of vehicles in an urban area for technology applications such as Cellint and INRIX. From these networks and technology applications, organizations can use mathematical modeling and analysis to capture insights for more effective decision making.[43] The rapid growth in computing power and data-storage capacity also enables more efficient implementations and effective use of mathematical models.

Integrating data from the growing sets of distributed sensors enables organizations to apply a broad range of information technology and analytics-based services to manage resources within agriculture, land management, engineering and construction, weather related emergencies, defense management, environmental management, mineral and oil management, electrical-power management, water management, and other areas. Dramatic cost reductions in semiconductor manufacturing have made these sensors more affordable for large-scale deployments. Similarly, the commercial adoption of the Internet Protocol and the emergence of pervasive IP networks since 1995 provide an enabling layer of connectivity. Finally, flexible integration methods, such as service-oriented architecture (SOA), enable rapid experimentation with various sensor networks. By applying information technology, organizations are making better business decisions and managing natural resources more efficiently.

7.4. Models for Managing Real-World Systems

Mathematical models and simulation are an essential component in a world that has been instrumented, providing the "intelligence" behind the design and control of its systems. These models aim to optimize multivariable systems in ways that haven't been possible in the past, such as optimizing greenhouse gas emissions during daily supply-chain operations or using appropriate business logic in manufacturing execution systems (MES) software. In such systems, mathematical models might fill one or more of the roles described in Table 7.1, subject to appropriate constraints.

Table 7.1 Roles of Mathematical Models in an Instrumented World

Role of Models	Illustration
Provide approximate representations of a real-world system using mathematical functions and expressions	Estimating water flow in a river system subject to rainfall, evaporation, and agricultural consumption
Characterize collected data in an insightful manner	Traffic volume and average speed in a transportation system
Predict values of "missing" data	Midpoint river flow rate and water temperature, knowing upstream and downstream values
Predict future outcomes and quantify their probability of occurrence	Weather forecasting or traffic congestion
Estimate the impact of system inputs on system outputs	Levee failure impacts on surrounding communities
Prescribe policies or actions that will result in optimal system behavior	Dynamic pricing to relieve traffic congestion in transportation systems[44]

A variety of mathematical-modeling approaches exist for performing these roles. For example, organizations can use statistical and data-mining techniques to discover interesting and insightful patterns in a data set, and to predict the values of missing data and future outcomes. Table 7.2 describes some of the most frequently used techniques.

Table 7.2 Mathematical-Modeling Techniques

Modeling Technique	Illustration
Classification that determines class intervals and class boundaries, often to construct color-graduated maps	Maps with isotherms to show temperature patterns
Clustering that partitions data into subsets that share a common trait	Ocean water measurements associated with either high-tide or low-tide conditions
Interpolation that calculates values between points where actual data is available	Water-pollution level at an unmeasured point that lies between two or more measured ones
Extrapolation that calculates values outside the domain where actual data is available	Water-pollution level downstream in a river where only upstream values are measured

Table 7.2   Mathematical-Modeling Techniques (continued)

Modeling Technique	Illustration
Times-series analysis that aims to understand a sequence of data points, often successively in time and uniformly spaced	Ocean temperature data collected over time to determine when high and low values occur, and to study temperature variations
Analysis of variance, in which the observed variance is segmented into different components based on explanatory variables	The effect of different fuel additives on automobile greenhouse gas emissions

Organizations can also use simulation techniques to predict future outcomes and to perform a variety of analyses for testing sensitivities to different initial conditions. Table 7.3 describes three of these techniques.

Table 7.3   Computer Simulation Techniques

Simulation Technique	Illustration
Discrete-event methods in which a chronological sequence of events represents systems	Intelligent transportation systems with virtual sensors that represent a combination of physical sensors and data processing and interpretation software[45]
System-dynamics methods in which complex systems are simulated over time, with feedback loops and a strong capability to capture nonlinear system behavior	Dynamically complex systems in water-resource management to provide foresight for how to maximize a system's adaptive capacity to changes from resource exploitation, development pressures, population growth, and climate change[46]
Numerical simulation that aims to create a virtual (computer) model of a target system	Weather and climate simulation to create a high-resolution profile of the atmosphere that shows such activity as rainfall and cyclone paths[47]

Organizations can use optimization techniques to identify an optimal action or set of actions, and then establish a set that is realistically acceptable, particularly in the presence of multiple real-world constraints. Organizations measure the optimal actions against a given objective, such as minimizing cost or carbon emissions, or maximizing revenue or fresh-water flow. These actions might facilitate improvements to the systems that sensor networks are monitoring, or even influence the design of the sensor networks themselves. Table 7.4 describes four common optimization techniques.

Table 7.4 Optimization Techniques

Modeling Technique	Illustration
Stochastic dynamic programming for handling uncertainty in which a feasible solution is sought for all possible scenarios but might be optimal for only a few of them	Determining optimal strategies and designing cost-effective policies that meet greenhouse gas emission–reduction targets in the presence of uncertain technological change and economic growth[48]
Linear programming that seeks to find the best outcome for a system that is represented by linear equations	Using a model of the Chinese economy to simulate alternative strategies to stabilize carbon dioxide emissions at 20 percent below a prescribed baseline level[49]
Mixed-integer programming, in which some of the variables must be integers	Determining the optimal portfolio of fuels to encourage power plants to cofire biomass and refuse-derived fuel with coal, minimize operating cost with respect to possible fuel combinations, reduce sulfur dioxide emissions, and maintain the same level of electricity generation[50]
Nonlinear programming, in which a model's objective function or some of the constraints are nonlinear	Using a hybrid fuel cell-power plant system that produces cleaner, efficient, more cost-effective, and greener electricity in which the objective of the model is to obtain designs with minimal environmental impacts and superior performance[51]

Ensemble models that combine results from different models to achieve a better prediction are also relevant to the area of environmental stewardship. Organizations can use several approaches to create ensemble models. The ensemble modeling method of "bagging" seeks to reduce the variability of predictive models, "stacking" seeks to decrease the predictive bias in addition to reducing variance, and "boosting" aims to transform the results from a collection of weak models into one strong model through such techniques as weighting. Ensemble models are used in areas such as forecasting, in which combining forecast results can provide a better result than simply trying to choose the best model.[52]

An instrumented world will support broader types of systems models[53] that consist of assemblies of models representing heterogeneous systems. National power-grid models that are assembled from many local models are one example. The data required to support such complex system models will come from multiple data sources and sensor networks. The capability to combine data from different domains and use that data for a common objective is a challenge that remains to be overcome, but it's within the reach of existing science and technology. Although it's for a relatively small population of approximately 400,000 people, one project aims to develop a national "smart-utility" system for the Mediterranean island nation of Malta that will digitize the country's electricity grid and water system.[54]

High-quality, reliable, real-world data is essential for the development of mathematical models that represent actual systems. Such models and the data they analyze must account for the definition and validation of model assumptions and the calibration of model parameters. Organizations shouldn't underestimate the need to validate models because inadequate validation can inhibit model acceptance. After mathematical models have been developed and deployed, high-quality data is again essential for providing input to the model and for adapting the model to potential changes in the real system environment. Instrumenting the planet makes it possible to provide large volumes of high-quality, current data for the development, implementation, and ongoing use of mathematical models.

Beyond the underlying science and technology of modeling, a gap often remains between the scientists who develop the models and the business practitioners who use their results. Most companies that develop or use mathematical models struggle with the issue of making knowledge and insight developed by highly focused mathematicians, environmentalists, and other scientists available and useful to business line managers, who are often generalists. Peter Williams, IBM's chief technology officer (CTO) for Big Green Innovations, has commented that to close this gap, "We have to democratize the models that will run different aspects of our lives" so that the scientists developing models, the practitioners making decisions, and the public at large whose surroundings might be affected all have a voice and understand how the management of their environment is transforming.[55]

7.5. Applications of Models in an Instrumented World

Several examples of applications already exist in which mathematical models are providing the "intelligence" that is essential to an instrumented world. Such intelligence enables better decision making, more effective real-world system design, and improved resource management. Enterprises must consider and overcome some of the potential challenges that they might encounter during the course of instrumenting the planet. The rest of this chapter discusses several important examples of existing applications.

7.5.1. Electric Power Supply Management

A combination of environmental and behavioral factors drives electricity consumption. Two environmental factors include temperature, which influences heating and air-conditioning usage, and natural sunlight intensity, which influences lighting use. Behavioral factors include the level of "conservation culture" achieved, the discretionary budget that is made available for electricity usage, and the usage response to price fluctuations. Information on consumption patterns and trends is a critical input to mathematical models for electric-utility production planning, capacity planning, and demand management, with the objective to match supply and demand. In an instrumented world, organizations can combine environmental information, such as weather data and forecasts, with time-series data collected from utility meters at customer locations to better predict consumption patterns using simulation or statistical models. Continual data streams from sensors that monitor the capacity of the power-generation network are also valuable inputs to these models.

A 2006 report by the Department of Energy (DOE)[56] recognized a need to develop improved optimization models for solving the optimal power-flow problem. Solving this problem is to optimize the production cost of energy, subject to numerous operating constraints. According to this report, "a next-generation optimal power-flow problem solution needs to perform time-dependent, full-system calculations for location-dependent, marginal prices" that reflect the value of energy at a specific location and time of delivery, subject to an accurate representation of current bids from customers and offers from the provider. Clearly, mathematical models that address this problem would benefit from time-dependent data feeds of marginal prices by location, hourly fluctuations in bids and offers, and the state of the power grid for plant-production capacities. All these data elements would ideally be available in an instrumented world. Integrating alternative energy supplies into a conventional grid is also a key part of solving the power-flow problem.

Dynamic pricing is a form of demand management that organizations can use to optimally match supply and demand under changing conditions. Organizations can use mathematical models to develop effective mechanisms for implementing dynamic pricing. Dynamic electricity pricing for household consumers is not widely practiced today, beyond a number of experiments. A pilot study implementing dynamic electricity pricing for certain household consumers was conducted in Denmark and Norway.[57] In the U.S., the Electric Power Research Institute (EPRI) has contemplated reducing peak consumption by building a dynamic energy infrastructure that supports a "prices-to-devices" concept that delivers hourly power prices to the homes of end users using smart devices.[58] These smart devices could conceivably make use of optimization models that determine the best time to operate household appliances, subject to constraints specified by the resident.

7.5.2. Water Management

As global climate change redistributes fresh water supplies, industrialization places more stress on existing sources; as growing populations consume more water, effective water management is becoming critical to global sustainability. In fact, several areas associated with water management have already deployed instrumentation as a means to better manage supplies.

7.5.2.1. Reservoir Management

Managing the water in a reservoir or network of reservoirs generally involves controlling the volume of water in the reservoir, to limit the risk of flooding, while maximizing the storage of water for future consumption, navigation, and recreation. Reservoir management might also involve optimally coordinating hydroelectric power-generation needs with other demands for reservoir water.

Organizations can use mathematical models to help optimize reservoir-management decisions.[59, 60] Important inputs to reservoir-management models include rainfall, evaporation rates, runoff and infiltration rates, water composition and quality, and the rate at which consumers and businesses use water. Research work by Westphal, et al.[61]; Rasmussen, et al.[62]; Georgakakos, et al.[63]; and the Maryland Department of Natural Resources[64] made attempts to combine climate and hydrology forecasts with reservoir-management models. In an instrumented world, environmental data for variables such as rainfall and evaporation rate could be provided on a continuous basis to reservoir-management models.

7.5.2.2. Water Quality Prediction

The quality of the water in Earth's rivers and streams is important for sustaining wildlife and supporting human activities, such as agriculture and fishing. Although water quality–monitoring networks do exist,[65] gaps in coverage are unavoidable. Organizations can use various spatiotemporal-statistical methods to estimate the quality of the water in unmonitored regions, using input factors such as chemical and sediment composition and temperature. In one example, the Kriging[66] method produces an estimator that is a weighted sum of observations at measurement sites, with the weights depending on the correlation structure of the underlying spatial process. However, spatiotemporal models that are based on regression analysis might be more useful for predicting water quality in unmonitored locations because they account for root causes of contamination.[67]

Supported by the insights generated from statistical models, organizations can use optimization techniques to determine the optimal position of water-monitoring sensors that generate the most accurate predictions of water quality for a given sensor-network investment. Bandwidth constraints can impact routing data from a network of wireless sensors. Therefore, it might be desirable to determine the most efficient way of aggregating and routing data within the network without a loss in the quality of the insights gained from information retrieved.[68] Using models for optimizing sensor positions, aggregating sensor data, and routing is also relevant in non-water-related sensor-network applications.

7.5.2.3. Water-Supply and Demand Management

Brandt and Lauria developed goal-programming optimization models for implementing water-supply rationing rules. They point out the need for greater dependence on optimization and simulation when implementing such rules, as opposed to the current practice of relying heavily on experience and judgment.[69] As an alternative to rationing, southeastern Australia, Chile, and the U.S. are using market trading of water to manage consumption.[70] In market-driven environments, businesses might begin to view water pricing similar to carbon-trading activities,[71] in which a business's right to use water above its quota must be offset by purchasing unused quotas from other businesses. In such an environment, market participants can use mathematical models that forecast future water prices to guide their decisions. In a nonmarket setting, organizations can use optimization models to design effective pricing schemes for improving the alignment between the supply and demand for water.

7.5.3. Traffic and Public Transportation Management

Given the limited amount of road and highway infrastructure available to growing volumes of traffic in urban areas, an increasing number of cities are considering measures to implement controls for traffic volume during peak hours. For example, the Singapore government recognizes the need to not only discourage driving into the most congested parts of the island during certain hours (using methods such as congestion pricing), but also to encourage greater use of public transportation systems. The success of such approaches depends on the capability to accurately predict traffic patterns. Min, et al.,[72] successfully developed a prototype for a statistical traffic-prediction tool for Singapore's central business district using time-dependent data feeds of traffic volume and speed. Because transportation networks might not be fully monitored, gaps can exist in the data for certain links in the transportation network, such as missing information for volume and speed. Organizations can use statistical models to estimate traffic flow along unmonitored links, and then use the results from these models as input to optimization models that would recommend the most effective locations for additional sensors, to improve the accuracy of the estimations on unmonitored links.

Accurate and continuous predictions of traffic patterns would enable congestion-pricing policies to become more dynamic, with prices changing not only by time of day, but also in reaction to developing traffic conditions. Predictive models would also enable public transportation systems to run more effectively. For example, monitors at bus stops could display bus arrival times, or mobile devices could convey arrival times to commuters so they can better plan their journeys, perhaps with the aid of an optimization model.

7.5.4. Wind Farm, Solar-Electric, and Solar-Thermal Power Management

The energy yield from wind farms is highly uncertain because it depends on wind speed and direction. Simulation models to investigate the performance of wind farms have been developed that evaluate power production under varying wind conditions and turbine availability.[73, 74] Organizations could combine these models with weather and atmospheric models that predict wind speed and direction[75] to forecast wind farm electricity production. Organizations could use these forecasts to support demand-management models for dynamic pricing, or production models for optimally coordinating the amount of electricity generated by wind in contrast to electricity generated by hydroelectric dams. Delerue, Luickx, and D'haeseleer use a combination of simulation and mixed-integer optimization models to investigate the potential cost and carbon dioxide emission savings from wind power.[76, 77] They also study the impact of wind-forecast accuracy on the reliability of power generation.

Solar electricity generation from photovoltaic technology and solar-thermal power generation, often from generating steam, share a similar trait to wind farms: Electricity production levels depend partly on weather conditions. Instead of modeling wind, organizations can model and predict factors such as cloud cover. Organizations can include other factors in mathematical models, such as sunlight intensity variation throughout the day and through seasonal changes, the angle at which power-generating equipment is set, potential dust on protective equipment covering, and other equipment-performance parameters, such as efficiency as a function of age. If fragile equipment, such as mirrors, is involved, organizations could use models to predict high wind, hail, and storm conditions to mitigate the risk of damage and predict associated power outages when protective action is necessary.

7.5.5. Intelligent Levee Management

Systems that use sensors based on Brillouin optical time domain reflectometry (BOTDR) have been demonstrated to provide early detection of the deformation of river embankments.[78] BOTDR technology measures the elapsed time and intensity of light reflected on optical fiber, and has already been applied to measure strain in the ground and in buildings and bridges.[79] This technology can also monitor the movement and subsidence of levee structures, which might be precursors to levee failure. Using the data from this monitoring technology, along with weather forecasts and data produced by flow meters in the water, hydrological simulation models can estimate the probability of structural failure in levees and the subsequent flooding probability and severity. If such monitoring and modeling is done continually, results could be used as input to stochastic-optimization models to compute the optimal trade-offs between the risk of flooding and the cost of alternative mitigation strategies. In the case of extreme deformations, the sensor data might help alert local authorities of an impending disaster. One project in the Netherlands is working to understand what an instrumented levee will "look and feel like" as it breaks, evaluate the effectiveness of different sensor types and their application to levee management, evaluate the applicability of numerical models, and predict storm impacts and responses.[80]

7.5.6. Data-Centric Modeling of the Environment

Current approaches to climate modeling typically involve explicitly simulating physical and social processes to identify and understand key contributors to climate change. Such simulations have limitations. For example, it's computationally intensive to model all potentially significant physical and behavioral processes pertaining to the climate.[81]

Researchers at the IBM T. J. Watson Research Center are studying the potential use for a data-centric, as opposed to physics-based, approach to modeling the climate. Given the vast amount of spatiotemporal climate data that is publicly available (such as surface and atmospheric data; snow, ice, and frozen-ground observations; and oceanic-climate, sea-level, and atmospheric-constituent measurements) and the spatiotemporal data that might explain climate change (such as data related to land cover, land use, carbon dioxide, methane, aerosols, ozone emissions, solar irradiance, and volcanic activity), they aim to develop new mathematical modeling approaches for effectively generating insights about climate change. By using sophisticated data-modeling approaches, researchers hope to quantify the impact of various factors on climate change more efficiently than relying purely on simulations. This type of approach has also been applied with some success in the field of computational biology.[82] More tractable methods for modeling causal relationships would also improve subsequent optimization models that use these relationships.

Researchers can apply the systems of an instrumented world to a vast number of ecosystems. However, without the technology to support instrumenting the planet and optimizing resource management, many imagined benefits would be impossible to achieve. The next chapter describes important elements of this enabling technology.

8

Technology That Supports Instrumenting the Planet

8.1. Challenges on the Path to an Instrumented World

The potential challenges associated with instrumenting the planet require numerous nontrivial needs to be met. Achieving strategic change, operational change, and cultural change in organizations is undoubtedly as much a challenge in this area as any other where significant transformation occurs, as discussed earlier in Section 2.2 of Chapter 2, "Formulate Green Strategy to Complement Traditional Strategy." However, because technology plays such a central role in an instrumented world, its challenges are particularly important for enterprises to understand and address.

Among the technical challenges is the integration of disparate models and data sources. Establishing metadata and data standards, data-filtering methods, erratic data-detection and correction processes, sensor network maintenance processes and procedures, model aggregation rules, standard interfaces, autocalibration and recalibration mechanisms, and fail-safe system designs are only a few of the needs that must be met.

8.1.1. Meeting the Need for Standard Interfaces to Support Mathematical Models

Computer models are frequently customized for a specific user before they are implemented, although examples also exist of simulation software that is widely shared. Customization often limits the capability to share or jointly develop models across different users. The need for a standardized modeling adapter, or translator, that includes a standard data model and requirements for each domain is an important one. A standard technology architecture for storing and extracting the data; standard processes for collecting, testing, and "cleansing" the data (that is, filtering the data to remove inappropriate elements); and standard methods for preparing the data for use by the models are also needed. Although the task of achieving such convergence is far from trivial, some industries have made similar advancements. For example, researchers resolved many differences in various standards associated with genomics research in the early 1990s, greatly facilitating the work of scientists in that field. Similarly, widespread adoption of Universal

Product Code (UPC) numbers and associated bar codes in the retail industry has made countless processes more efficient over the last few decades.

One example of a modeling system that provides some of the functionality from such an adapter is the Spatiotemporal Epidemiological Modeler (STEM),[1] developed at IBM Research. STEM provides a standard modeling interface for epidemiological models and facilitates the development of advanced mathematical models for epidemiology. Although the domain is different from those in environmental stewardship, the principles are similar.

Another example that supports environmental stewardship comes from the Geophysical Fluid Dynamics Laboratory at Princeton University: Researchers there developed the Flexible Modeling System,[2] a software framework for the efficient development, construction, execution, and scientific interpretation of atmospheric, oceanic, and climate system models. An alternative framework is the Earth System Modeling Framework,[3, 4], jointly funded by the United States Department of Defense, the National Aeronautics and Space Administration (NASA), the National Science Foundation, and the National Oceanic and Atmospheric Administration (NOAA). Some progress has clearly been made in this area, but more work is needed.

8.1.2. Establishing Consistency Among Fragmented Data Sources

To study interactions between systems (such as between weather and power grid systems, or between atmospheric and hydrological systems), data sources from different fields of research must be combined. However, data from different sources are often inconsistent. For example, inconsistencies might exist in the frequency and density of the data, or in the definition and precision of the data itself.

To illustrate this need in one area, Xu, et al.,[5] anticipate that, in the near future, studies in which both climatologists and hydrologists address the same problem at the same time will lead to significantly improved predictions. The implication is that greater interdisciplinary dialogue and collaboration are needed to integrate disparate models and data that supports the models.

8.1.3. Sharing Data and Using Distributed Collaboration Tools

In a world where people are increasingly aware of the benefits associated with shared information and knowledge, a natural advancement is collecting and assembling information provided by many different individuals and enterprises to achieve a "network effect." This shared data can provide value far beyond the value of private information available to any of the individual contributing entities themselves. For example, in the financial services industry, Moody's ratings[6] on bonds became sufficiently established to be required for any financial services offering. An instrumented world could face similarly important pressures for gathering data on, for example, carbon or water efficiency, to ensure that the information reaches a public utility where it can become a resource for others to use and compare. Even some business models, such as that of YouTube.com, are founded on the principle that value can come from sharing data from a wide range of disparate sources while conforming to certain standards. The Carbon Rating Agency (CRA) and Bloomberg already provide uniform information about the carbon market and integrate that data with analytic tools to help organizations make informed decisions about carbon offset trading. Information is made available across a range of carbon-reduction projects[7]. The Climate Disclosure Project (CDP) is another organization that maintains a database of corporate climate change information and provides primary climate-change data to the global marketplace.

Researchers might also require a means of visualizing data supplied from various groups or individuals. IBM Many Eyes has explored one approach, derived from social-networking methods and applied to data analysis[8]. This work allows people to share and analyze data, with collaboration adding value to insights from the data.

An instrumented world not only provides the technology needed to collect, store, and disseminate data from sensor networks, but also enables the analytic capability to generate solutions that decision makers and policy makers can use to improve the efficiency with which they manage constrained resources. Mathematical models are already being applied in many ways to provide the analytical capabilities needed. Still, some important challenges remain in creating an instrumented world.

8.2. Real World–Aware Systems and Interactive Models

Real world–aware (RWA) computing provides the bridge that captures the state of the actual world and extracts insights for decision making to enable an instrumented world. Three important drivers for instrumenting the planet that we have already discussed are the availability of detailed sensing data in real time, the need to manage and optimize the use of scarce natural resources, and the availability of advanced modeling techniques that offer guidance on how to more efficiently use scarce resources and provide advance warning of shortages.

A fourth enabling driver is the emergence and growing use of real world–aware information technologies for adaptive, automated control of manufacturing, mining, transport, distribution, and other processes that integrate with enterprise business information records, policies, and processing systems. Real world–aware processing builds on optimization and control modeling and might also incorporate simulation. It is relevant to many of the application areas discussed previously, particularly in demand-driven electricity and water resource management, as well as optimal traffic and public transportation management.

Well-established business information systems focus on the reliable, transactional processing and storage of business information, such as requests to transfer funds, make travel reservations, and order goods. Real world–aware systems in an instrumented world extend this type of functionality by tightly coupling traditional business information processing with the current state of the world. They also use stream (continuous) processing to link the real world and the business processing functions. This capability enables leaders to make more informed business decisions and enables optimization based on current information instead of static, historical reporting. Business operations benefit from enterprisewide optimization, policy guidance, and analytics that use information from such networked devices as automated sensors, actuators, and RFID systems.

Figure 8.1 shows the topology of a real world–aware system. It is organized into an edge domain, a stream-processing domain, and a transactional and business-processing domain.

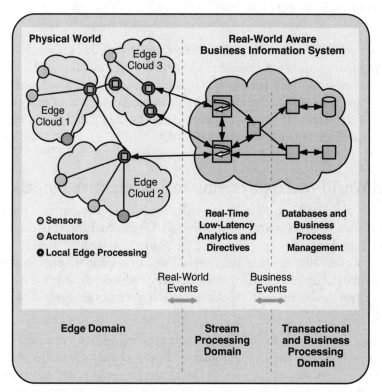

Figure 8.1 Topology of real world–aware systems

Source: *IBM Journal of Research and Development*

8.2.1. Edge Domain of a Real World–Aware System

The edge domain at the left of Figure 8.1 shows potentially numerous deployments of sensors gathering real-world data and actuators taking action, such as opening and closing valves or doors, in response to feedback controls. The edge domain is organized into edge clouds. The edge clouds each represent a physically contiguous, or connected, group of sensor and actuator devices, with some level of local processing close to them. Local processing in a particular edge cloud is useful for initially screening or filtering sensor data; first-level feedback for the control of actuators in that cloud is based only on local-state information. For example, in a real world–aware system designed to represent many rivers on a continent, one edge cloud might be associated with each river, with each edge cloud including data processing to filter out anomalous information and activate local irrigation systems.

8.2.2. Transactional and Business-Processing Domain of a Real World–Aware System

The transactional and business-processing domain at the right of Figure 8.1 includes the processes and databases necessary for reliable and robust business request handling. This domain incorporates an enterprise's awareness of the state of its business and, thus, resembles a conventional business IT system, such as an enterprise resource planning (ERP) application. The domain accepts and handles direct requests for specific business actions from end users. It also receives and reacts to business events and insights derived from analytics in the stream-processing domain in the central part of the figure.

8.2.3. Stream-Processing Domain of a Real World–Aware System

The stream-processing domain includes functionality to continuously analyze information that arrives from multiple edge clouds, and processing to combine this information with business events and requests for real-world action (which are received from the adjacent business processing domain). The stream-processing domain can receive large amounts of continuously arriving data from many edge clouds, and it applies low-latency analytics and correlation analysis to extract insights in real time. This domain interacts with edge clouds by receiving information related to the physical world and passing directives and actuation guidance back to the clouds. The stream-processing domain interacts with the transactional and business-processing domain by exchanging business events and real-world information.

The net effect of this three-domain approach is twofold. It enables business processes to use current-state information, and it optimizes operational actions associated with distributed resources. These actions are guided and potentially automated based on both time-dependent analytics and enterprisewide business information.

Several emerging technological advances are being combined to make this new approach to real world–aware systems more feasible and economically attractive. These include advances in stream-processing systems, in sensor networks and analytics for sensed data, and for component-based assemblies of distributed and responsive systems.

Although the technology involved is becoming increasingly complex, some of the most advanced stream-processing systems are being designed to achieve a number of objectives that are important to any enterprise that uses them. First, the software capabilities focus on high performance, enable parallel processing, and scale over a range of hardware configurations. This leverages legacy (existing) infrastructure. Second, rapid and automated reconfiguration of the stream-processing system is possible in response to changing user objectives, available data, and the variability of system resources. For example, if computing capacity becomes constrained, data-processing actions can be prioritized to avoid neglecting the most important insights. Third, incremental tasking in the face of rapidly changing data forms and types is possible. For example, if a new edge cloud is added to an edge domain that includes new data types and requires new tasks in the stream-processing domain, the necessary system changes are only incremental. Finally, the systems are secure and privacy-compliant, and can be audited.[9]

Stream-processing systems enable low-latency, continuous analysis of potentially large amounts of information arriving from sensor networks or other real-world streams from such sources as the Internet, wired networks, and wireless "sensor fields." The stream-processing programming model facilitates the construction of an analytic flow network in which simple processing elements can be connected and combined to provide an incrementally extensible system with multiple inputs and outputs.

The system can be optimized to use virtually all available processing capacity, while high bandwidth and reliable connectivity facilitate the support of large quantities of streamed data. In some contexts, the stream-processing results must connect to a storage system, to retain insight and data features or replay historical streams. The stream-processing approach enables subject matter experts to easily develop flexible, time-dependent, real-time analytics. Insights derived from the analytics can offer high business value, and the system can be easily scaled to receive and respond to large volumes of real-world data as it arrives.

8.2.4. Advantages and Illustrations of Real World–Aware Systems

One advantage of a typical real world–aware solution is that it addresses multiple levels of responsiveness. That is, some events require detection and response within milliseconds, others assume human response times of hundreds of milliseconds or longer, and yet others afford processing windows of seconds or minutes. For example, in a system that senses vehicles and charges different amounts for road use based on traffic density, data can be analyzed in the field for immediate action and subsequently can be reused to optimize traffic behavior, this time with relaxed constraints on time dependency.

In the past, when real-time data and the insights from it were not available, business managers sometimes had difficulty initially determining what to do with them. In the area of water management, for example, to make real-time visibility of water quality most valuable, new processes might be needed, such as direct communication channels and new delegation of authority to rapidly respond to adverse changes before problems occur. As an example, such processes could immediately shut off water flow from contaminated sources once detected.

A second critical area of advantage and recent progress for real world–aware systems involves sensor networks and sensor-based analytics. Technology is becoming available for self-organizing sensor networks[10] to use wireless devices, to decrease the cost of gathering basic information from the environment. Progress is also being made in extracting and analyzing significant metadata features from sensed data sources such as video images[11]. The combination of inexpensive digital cameras, wireless functionality to deliver video streams to processing locations, automated feature extraction, and low-cost intelligent storage has led to a significant cost reduction for the deployment of, for example, a video-based safety system. Casinos, airports, and city governments are all beginning to deploy systems with thousands of cameras on a scale that would have been prohibitively expensive a few years ago.

A third advantage and emerging technological advance that is critical to the widespread use of real world–aware systems is in component-based middleware that connects software components or applications with messaging for assembling time-dependent distributed solutions. Service Oriented Architecture (SOA) and its associated infrastructure technologies can support precise specifications for the functional properties of each element (shown in Figure 8.2) needed to assemble the information-processing solutions. The lifecycle cost of a solution, such as analytics-based operations in an intelligent electrical utility network, will be prohibitive if performance reengineering (around such parameters as latency or expected fault tolerances) is required each time a subnetwork is deployed or a new household is attached. This will be true even though each household and subnetwork comes with its own individual topology, attached devices, processing hardware, and usage patterns.

8.2.5. The Application Layers and Technical Architecture of Interactive Models

Figure 8.2 illustrates five application layers of an interactive modeling framework. As information moves from one layer to the next, the level of analysis and insight from the sensed data increases. At the lowest levels, multiple sensors can generate and relay data to a real-world model through streaming middleware, as in the stream-processing system described earlier. The modeling layer provides for data transformation, metadata management, and different modeling components and compositions. It also supports calibration and execution. Models then form the basis for running simulations and generating insight from both sensed data and related business data. Finally, insights are communicated so that improved business decisions can be made at the top layer.

The application layers in Figure 8.2 are generalized and can apply conceptually to many areas in support of environmental stewardship, including intelligent transportation systems; intelligent utility networks; advanced water management; enterprise and supply chain carbon management; energy and water management for smart buildings and cities; management and planning of weather-sensitive operations; industrial process management at refineries and chemical plants; recyclable content management; resource demand forecasting for energy, water, or minerals; alternative energy production management, such as wind or photovoltaic power; and regional climate impact modeling.

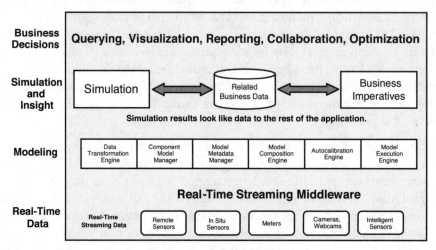

Figure 8.2 Application layers of an interactive modeling framework

Source: IBM

The generalized reference architecture in Figure 8.3 illustrates sample technology elements that are relevant at the enterprise level, the operational level, and the sensor level. This figure illustrates the level of complexity that can be involved, with a diverse portfolio of functional requirements, hardware and data needs, and significant integration effort.

Success of the enabling technologies described here is measured by the extent to which the technologies help subject matter experts assemble solutions that combine high performance computing (HPC)–based models using time-dependent sensor data with analytics. An instrumented world is a better place to live in only if the additional information helps people manage scarce resources better and consume them more efficiently and safely. Real world–aware solutions, made feasible by the technologies summarized here, provide a natural approach to combining the best available analytics and modeling of resources, and integrating that insight with business information–processing systems to improve the management of intelligent transportation, manufacturing and energy, or other scarce resources.

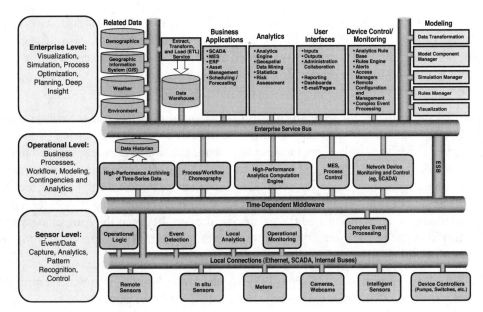

Figure 8.3 Reference architecture to support an interactive modeling framework

Source: IBM

Many of the business processes in both private and public enterprises have traditionally operated within the boundaries of an organization and its extended ecosystem, and have had little intelligent interaction with events in the real world. However, these processes will increasingly need to be aware of the state of the real world, to achieve optimal use of scarce or expensive resources.

8.3. Examples of Instrumented World Systems

Examples of these new systems are beginning to deliver benefits to the enterprises that use them. In 2007, the Pacific Northwest National Laboratory (PNNL) conducted a pilot project for distributed energy resource management in northwest Washington State on behalf of the U.S. Department of Energy. The pilot was known as the GridWise Olympic Peninsula Project.[12] One purpose of the project was to explore time-dependent pricing for electric power, essentially in real time, to enable the local utility to control residential demand for power. In the time-dependent pricing part of the project, residential customers used a personal computer connected to the Internet to establish a range of prices they would be willing to pay to maintain the temperature of their homes within a zone of comfort. These price preferences were converted into bids that were submitted to a shadow energy market (defined shortly) that was "cleared" every five minutes. The term *clearance* refers to the fact that, every few minutes, the "buy bids" from the customers were matched to the "sell bids" from the utility, and the process began again. If a given consumer's monetary bid for energy is accepted in the market (that is, accepted by the utility company providing the energy as a service), the air-conditioning or heating system would run at the residence.

Figure 8.4 shows the major elements of this project and the central role the energy market played in regulating consumer demand. The left side of the figure, labeled "Residential Home," shows the kinds of appliances and systems that were actively controlled in the pilot, including clothes dryers and heating systems. Networking devices from Invensys, one of the partners for the project, remotely controlled appliances. In the figure, a grid-friendly appliance (GFA) implies that an electrical utility is controlling the device. Load control modules (LCM) indicated the particular interface between the control logic and the controlled device. Domestic demand was communicated through personal computers, and domestic load was controlled via a "home gateway."

The central part of Figure 8.4, labeled "Port Angeles Water Supply," represents a municipal water supply district that used electric motors to drive water pumps. Again, a control or application computer connected to the network served as the means for the utilities to control the pumps. The term "Additional DR" refers to additional pieces of equipment that were controlled as part of managing the demand response. The right part of Figure 8.4 shows a power generator at the PNNL, together with various energy consumers at the laboratory, including a heating system.

Information on available generating capacity and domestic demand were collected and matched through the shadow "energy market." The top part of Figure 8.4 shows the shadow energy market operated by PNNL, which matched and cleared bids submitted on behalf of energy consumers and energy providers. The term *shadow market* indicates that this market was shadowing (that is, tracking) wholesale energy costs in the western interconnection power grid. Finally, the various technology elements in the figure were integrated through the event-based programming environment shown in the center of the figure.

Although the pilot study was relatively small in scale, with 112 residences total, it demonstrated the potential use of auctions in making operational decisions in close to real time. The energy market mechanism permitted the utility to express the true marginal cost of power as demand started to rise, and the rising price smoothed the demand curve. This enabled the utility to optimize the available energy-generating capacity. In some cases, in which demand peaks would ordinarily drive some subnetworks in the distribution system to their operational limits, the utility delivered more total energy over the course of the day.

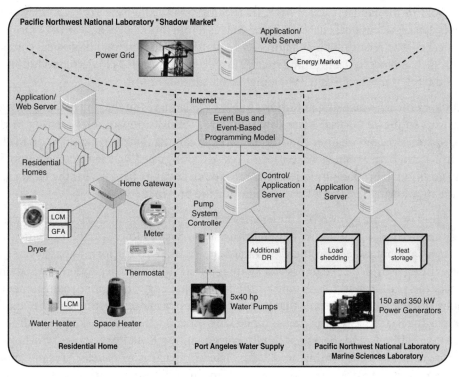

Figure 8.4 Schematic diagram of key elements in the GridWise project

Source: *IBM Journal of Research and Development*

In another industry, more information is needed about water supplies to improve how water systems work and to enable more efficient use of this increasingly scarce resource. With IBM's participation, the Great Rivers Partnership of the Nature Conservancy,[13] now called Water for Tomorrow, is using information from several of the most important rivers in the world and from the surrounding land to enable fact-based decision making for water and land use. One objective of the project is to better understand the impact of land-use decisions on different aspects of the river basin ecosystem, such as water quantity, water quality, crop production, and biodiversity. This project's initial focus is the Mississippi River basin in the U.S., Brazil's Paraguay–Paraná River system, and China's Yangtze River.[14]

Another effort monitors progress for one of the largest American flood plain-restoration projects, at Emiquon, in central Illinois. This project uses sensors from YSI, Inc., that detect water quality. The technology that monitors this wetland uses wireless links to send time-dependent data to a web-based visualization system.[15] Similarly, the Beacon Institute is establishing a River and Estuary Observatory Network (REON)[16] to collect, analyze, and visualize time-dependent data from hundreds—and, eventually, thousands—

of sensors in the Hudson River from the headwaters to the New York City bay. These devices can sense physical characteristics such as temperature, depth, flow rate, turbidity; chemical characteristics such as acidity and pollution; and potential biological contamination such as bacteria. Combining such data will enable scientists to detect pollution earlier and track it to its source within a matter of minutes or hours.

In 2005, in the province of Canterbury in New Zealand, researchers installed a network of sensors in the Te Ngawai River catchment[17] to measure variables relating to river flow, water usage, and weather conditions. Farmers can use the information to decide how to extract and better manage water resources without exceeding their agreed-upon limits. In addition to producing environmental and productivity benefits for the farmers, the remote monitoring resulted in cost savings for the province.

The U.S.-based Consortium of Universities for the Advancement of Hydrologic Science has announced plans for a Hydrologic Information System to create the first integrated data-management system for the U.S. water supply.[18] This platform is based on federating existing hydrological databases, so it does not include time-dependent data streams. Instead, the platform addresses one of the major challenges for water management, to simply provide access and tools that help analyze and visualize existing data. In another example, the Bear River Commission, along with other partners, is working to address the multiple pollutants and diverse pollutant sources in the Bear River Basin, which covers large areas in Idaho, Wyoming, and Utah. The approach is to develop a water-quality trading program that allows point and nonpoint pollutant sources to trade water-quality credits. Along with such a trading program, a water-quality trading model is being developed that can analyze potential water quality–monitoring scenarios.[19] According to the U.S. Environmental Protection Agency, more than a dozen states have some form of water-quality trading framework in place or under development; statewide water-quality trading frameworks exist in Oregon, Idaho, Colorado, Michigan, Ohio, Pennsylvania, and Vermont. Pollutants that can potentially be measured and traded include phosphorus, nitrogen, heavy metals, selenium, copper, temperature, sediment, and flow.[20]

Following the 2004 tsunami off the coast of Sumatra, Indonesia, many countries around the Pacific Ocean have deployed or strengthened their tsunami warning systems. For example, in 2008, the Tsunami Program of the National Oceanic and Atmospheric Administration deployed 39 Deep-Ocean Assessment and Reporting of Tsunamis (DART) sensors[21] around the Pacific Rim and in the Atlantic Ocean. The stations monitor hydrostatic pressure at the ocean floor and search for changes in the apparent sea surface height. The system is adaptive, normally reporting on a 15-minute schedule, but it can shift to burst mode and provide 15-second averages immediately following an apparent tsunami danger. Next, the system provides one-minute reporting. The tsunami system collects data from all sensors via a wireless network. Its detection algorithm continuously predicts the next sample of apparent sea surface height from preceding samples and raises an alarm when the difference exceeds 3cm.

False warnings from tsunami alarm systems are extremely disruptive and expensive, and they can cause personnel to not take warnings seriously. Thus, considerable intelligence is required to avoid false warnings. The U.S. National Oceanic and Atmospheric Administration (NOAA) emphasizes the need to reduce false-positive alarms by combining this kind of sensing with other sources of information, such as that from seismic instruments. More precise insights arise from combinations of data streams from varied sources, and combination is a key characteristic of systems in an instrumented world.

The Singapore Land Transport Authority introduced an Electronic Road-Pricing[22] scheme in 1998 and continues to improve it as a means of regulating congestion by moderating road usage during peak hours. The Singapore system works by detecting an RFID device mounted in each vehicle. The driver inserts a cash card into the RFID device, and the value of the card is decremented by a back-end transaction system whenever the vehicle is detected. A similar system was tested in Stockholm in 2005 and brought into full production in 2007. The Stockholm system, which relies on license-plate recognition from video cameras, produced a reduction in traffic of nearly 25 percent, a 14 percent reduction in emissions from traffic in the inner city, and a 6 percent increase in the use of public transportation.[23]

The transaction rates in such traffic systems can be quite high: Large numbers of vehicles are viewed perhaps hundreds of times per day in a city with a dense networks of cameras. However, the transactions are independent, so it is easy to provide highly scalable platforms. Although these are relatively simple transaction systems, they create a platform of spatiotemporal data on which more sophisticated traffic-prediction systems can be developed to deliver a hierarchy of insights both for the operating agency and for commuters and transportation companies.

Masdar, a planned city in Abu Dhabi, in the United Arab Emirates, is another example in which technology and environmental stewardship go hand-in-hand. The city plans to rely entirely on solar energy and other renewable sources, with a zero-carbon, zero-waste environmental impact. Although some compromises are being made to meet these objectives (such as importing electricity from traditional sources during the night and exporting solar generated electricity during the day, and not allowing energy-intensive industries), the model is an impressive environmental marvel. A carbon-management unit monetizes greenhouse gas emission reductions and identifies greenhouse gas emission–improvement projects to achieve benefits, consistent with the Kyoto Protocol provisions.[24] One of the anchor partners, General Electric, will have an ecomagination center there that, among other things, will support the development of energy-efficient products in the region and raise awareness of energy conservation among the Masdar City community.[25]

These are just a few examples of innovative technology solutions that provide an early glimpse into the potential of an instrumented world. Although the technology underlying these systems has been emerging for some time, it is being more widely applied and becoming more visible, as a result of pressures from climate change, natural resource constraints, and limitations in our constructed infrastructure. This evolution is beginning in the public domain but is moving toward the private sector as well. In a world of constrained resources (whether through speculation or real shortages), the new approach to resource management described here can enable enterprises, governments, and individuals to be significantly more efficient and can mitigate the volatile costs and risks associated with scarce resources.

8.4. Leading Toward the Future in an Instrumented World

An increasingly instrumented world will affect businesses across all industries. In the twenty-first century, humanity faces new challenges, with information technology and analytics, as embodied in an instrumented world, playing important roles. Growing populations and rising living standards are leading to scarcity in basic resources such as clean water, energy, food, and minerals, all of which directly influence the global economy. The expected result is price volatility and increased business risk related to the availability of these scarce resources. Responses to the scarcity of resources are constrained by the need to minimize greenhouse gas emissions. Hence, the efficient use and management of resources has become increasingly desirable, even though it has never been unimportant in the past.

A promising approach to managing these resources better is to apply mathematical optimization and other quantitative operations-research methods, which depend highly on the availability of data describing the environment. Fortunately, a large deployment of various sensor types is producing potentially valuable data about social and environmental phenomena. Moreover, the pervasive global deployment of wireless and wired digital network systems offers the capability to capture streams of real-world sensor data. Still, some key areas, notably hydrology, are seriously underprovisioned.

Only a few years ago, the cost of such systems restricted their use mostly to academic research. Computing technology has now become inexpensive and powerful enough that enterprises can readily afford to apply it to capture, manage, process, and store data for commercial and social purposes. In parallel, the improved affordability of computing power and access to various sources of data have led researchers to implement increasingly sophisticated mathematical modeling techniques that generate insights from these streams of real-world data and offer optimal decisions. Leaders can use these insights and decisions to drive organizational and individual activity to optimize resource management.

Thanks to the combination of increased amounts of accessible real-world data over pervasive networks and affordable computing platforms for implementing innovative modeling techniques, we can implement systems to improve our efficiency in managing scarce resources. Partnerships will become increasingly important in an instrumented world, and all industries will be affected—and all will potentially benefit. These include well-established businesses, such as those that depend on and provide communications and networking infrastructure, agricultural resources, engineering skills, geotechnical skills, transportation, water infrastructure, buildings and facilities, appliances, energy infrastructure, sensors and meters, enterprise and specialized software, and specialty hardware. Some new business models are also possible and could emerge in areas such as carbon trading, advanced optimization and modeling of scarce resources and emissions, sensor network deployment, and outsourcing of ongoing monitoring and maintenance.

Instrumenting the planet is feasible and increasingly viable, and it can help address some of the challenges the world faces. Certainly, technology alone cannot serve as a panacea, yet we can expect that the form of computing associated with an instrumented world can play a key role in addressing the challenges of climate change, the scarcity of basic resources, and limited transportation and utility infrastructures.

Already, some business leaders are moving away from managing their operations based on historical reports and are managing based on real-time intelligence from the environment. Companies are realizing opportunities to optimize waste, better manage natural resources, and improve environmental stewardship, but much work remains to be done. In the future, business leaders will increasingly manage in "future time" instead of real time, anticipating and even avoiding future consequences before they occur. In some cases, the management time shift from historical, to real time, and then to future time will occur gradually as sensor networks and technology solutions advance; in other cases, business leaders should expect and be looking for rapid step-changes. Best-in-class businesses have been viewed for some time as having proactive operations instead of reactive ones, and that view is now working its way into how businesses manage their activities for environmental stewardship.

Companies will not realize all the business benefits overnight, even though important steps have already been taken on the journey toward an instrumented world. Green supply-chain optimization, business event–processing software, traffic management and integration, water management, intelligent utility demand management, and intelligent meter management and integration are all areas currently being explored; in most cases, at least proof-of-concept pilot projects exist. Further out in time, but still within the foreseeable future, are opportunities in areas such as carbon-trading services, advanced predictive water management, smart-grid operations, and condition-based asset management. Even further in time are information utility services based on smart planet knowledge, total city integration and management, water management with total system integration, and utility integration.

9

Business Considerations for Technology Solutions

9.1. Many Solutions Are Available or Developing

Solutions that apply to all businesses, and others that are industry-specific, are growing in number, maturing, and becoming easier to implement for many companies. Some solutions that have significant potential to directly improve the environment have been reasonably available for many decades. In most cases, performance has improved over that time as the underlying technology has advanced. Some of these now traditional and well-known solutions are also enjoying renewed visibility, as many businesses are successfully using them to generate energy or transform operations to become more efficient. Examples span a broad range that covers everything from the proper use of programmable thermostats, to efficient and alternative energy production.

In a 2009 interview, David Cote, the chairman and CEO of Honeywell, commented that technologies his company alone already has "could reduce the U.S. energy bill by 20 percent" if aggressively used.[1] One study from the Rocky Mountain Institute found that, simply by closing efficiency gaps in electricity production across all the U.S., the country would save 30 percent of its energy, or the equivalent of reducing coal-fired electrical power generation by 62 percent.[2]

Some sources of alternative and renewable energy have been providing environmentally clean power for decades. Hydroelectric power from dams and "water wheels" has been a source of reliable electricity for more than a century. Wind-generated electricity has been growing in importance for many years as well, and more recent "wind farms" are growing in prominence as they supply more power to locations around the world. Photovoltaic (solar) electricity is also well established and has been used for many purposes over the years; it also represents one area in which significant advancements in technology are still being made as the capability to efficiently convert sunlight to electricity increases. Even though these solutions are already available, the business considerations for their adoption are not as widely understood.

Other solutions that generate renewable power have been developed and continue to evolve. Hydroelectric power from wave and tidal motion, power from geothermal energy, and fuels such as ethanol, biofuels, and methane from "methane digesters" are all in use today. Developing solutions consume traditional fossil fuels more efficiently, such as through cleaner-coal technology and fuel cells.

Solutions that generate renewable or environmentally clean power are not the only ones to consider for environmental stewardship. Information technology solutions, such as those associated with Green Sigma and different approaches for instrumenting the planet, are being deployed to proactively manage and analyze information so that business leaders can make better decisions. Technology solutions are also emerging to improve the impact on the environment from supply chain operations, such as those that optimize inbound and outbound logistics activities. Other solutions that are diagnostic in nature, such as carbon calculators, maturity models, and facility-efficiency assessments, are playing increasingly important roles to guide enterprises in their decisions.

Beyond information management, diagnostic solutions, and transformation methodologies are a host of point solutions that solve one particular problem. Some of these are already fully developed and available; others are being offered and tested in the marketplace. For example, green building practices are well developed, along with passive and active heating and cooling mechanisms for air and water from solar heaters and thermal cooling devices. Solar lighting can be part of green building designs or can be integrated into an existing facility to make it more energy efficient. Point solutions also come from a growing portfolio of innovative green product technologies, such as green computing and green data centers, energy-efficient appliances and electronics, and hybrid and electric vehicles. Still other solutions that are becoming important include those that improve water handling, waste-water reclamation, and recycling capabilities.

Each of these solutions offers opportunities for individual businesses to consider. A solution that makes sense for one enterprise or in one location might not make sense for another in a different location. Section 2.3.2 of Chapter 2, "Formulate Green Strategy to Complement Traditional Strategy," introduced many of these solutions in a strategic context, and some are described further here in their operational context. More solutions exist than this book can describe, but collectively they comprise a landscape of available technology to support business operations that any enterprise leader can understand. Figure 9.1 shows one view of this landscape.

The next section offers a brief overview of these solutions that support environmental sustainability. We identify a number of high-level issues that make sense for businesses to consider as they make decisions to improve their environmental stewardship.

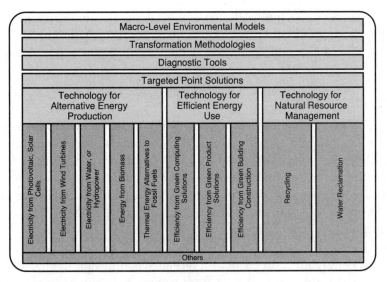

Figure 9.1 Solutions landscape that supports business operations

9.2. Macro-Level Environmental Models

Collaboration and government intervention will speed the adoption of certain large-scale models. The instrumented, interconnected, intelligent Smart Planet vision from IBM[3] is one model that takes advantage of sensing and metering to better understand and control business and human activity. This new paradigm for using information technology to improve business process performance across an enterprise, country, or industry is emerging at different rates in different sectors. Based on a sensor-derived "real-world awareness," advanced optimization techniques, and business process modeling, the instrumented, smart-planet concepts link real-world awareness directly with business decisions and processes. Organizations can apply the approach to numerous business areas, improving the management of carbon emissions, optimizing transportation systems, creating intelligent utility and energy networks, and creating advanced water-management systems, to name a few. Chapters 7, "Instrumenting the Planet for an Intelligent, Sustainable World," and 8, "Technology That Supports Instrumenting the Planet," explained these solutions in more detail.

9.3. Transformation Methodologies

Advanced transformation methodologies to help companies implement initiatives that improve environmental stewardship are already available. These proven, repeatable methodologies are accompanied by supporting technology, tools, training, and services to effectively capture opportunities for an organization. They are springing up in every industry, from both public and private enterprises. Section 5.1 in Chapter 5, "Transformation Methods and Green Sigma," illustrated several of these methodologies.

9.4. Diagnostic Tools

Diagnostic tools are making the steps toward environmental stewardship easier for businesses to take. For example, carbon calculators are helping businesses quickly assess their operations, to first define a carbon footprint and then identify opportunities for improvement. One example, the Carbon Tradeoff Modeler from IBM, calculates carbon emissions for all parts of a company and determines the overall environmental impact of its operations.[4] Businesses also can access free online carbon calculators from TerraPass,[5] Carbon Footprint,[6] EcoForests.org,[7] CarbonTrust, [8] The Carbon Neutral Company,[9] and Carbon UK[10]. Other tools help diagnose the management of specific natural resources. For example, the Center for Sustainable Innovation offers the Corporate Water Gauge as "a turnkey solution for measuring the sustainability of organizational water use" using a five-step approach.[11] The sophisticated web-based tool GreenCert, from C-Lock Technology, IBM, Enterprise Information Management, and Foxconn, can accurately measure and manage greenhouse gas information with a scalability dimension for both worldwide and large enterprise applications in various industries. The GreenCert system helps companies accurately establish a baseline for emissions, quantify improvements, and output the measurements as Certified Carbon Emissions Reduction Credits (CCERS), which are potentially valuable in various trading markets and registries.[12]

Diagnostic tools such as carbon calculators have powerful potential to give both businesses and individuals insight into their carbon emissions, but the current state of their development is still not mature. One study, whose focus was primarily Internet-based carbon calculators for personal use, concluded that significant improvements are still possible, to give users more accurate and consistent results across different models, provide more meaningful feedback and guidance to help users improve their energy use, and better connect users with a network of others working toward similar goals.[13] Another study that rated 11 calculators for emissions level accuracy from air travel found that only 4 of them performed "very good" or better.[14] Yet another work proposes six different methods for calculating the greenhouse gas emissions from consumer products over their lifetime,[15] each with a different expected level of accuracy. Clearly, before an enterprise chooses to rely on the results of a carbon calculator to make more informed business decisions, it must evaluate the strengths and weaknesses of different alternatives for attributes such as overall modeling approach, model complexity and rigor in capturing details, transparency of calculations, scope of emissions covered, visual appeal and ease of use, and accuracy and organization of results.

Maturity models are also emerging that enable companies to assess their progress toward environmental sustainability and improved environmental stewardship. The Carbon-View offering from Supply Chain Consulting (SCC)[16] (with IBM as the preferred implementation partner[17]) offers one maturity model that includes five phases to maturity: basics, company level, process level, product level, and optimized level. IBM's House of Carbon is one model whose objective is to assess the different components that make up a firm's carbon-reduction strategy and map how they impact one another.[18] The Results Group (TRG) is another company that has developed a Green Enterprise Maturity Model designed to help companies establish a roadmap to increase revenue, lower cost, and reduce their carbon footprint.[19] This model includes four maturity levels that include compliers, dabblers, consistent improvers, and enterprise optimizers.[20] The IT Capability Maturity Framework (IT-CMF), from the Innovation Value Institute (IVI) at National University of Ireland Maynooth, provides another toolset that categorizes core business processes into high-level management groupings that cover all the activities in an IT department. Assessments based on those processes help highlight where a company can both fill gaps in efficiency and identify new opportunities to gain extra value from the IT department.[21] In yet another example, the Accenture Green Technology Suite includes a green maturity model to assess a firm's environmental efficiency based on 300 questions across five key areas.[22]

9.5. Targeted Point Solutions for Alternative Energy Production

Targeted point solutions represent a broad class of devices that solve specific environmental stewardship issues. These solutions can be very simple products or can involve highly complex machinery and computing equipment. They can be designed to target virtually any environmental issue, from alternative energy production, to energy efficiency and natural resource management. Often deep subject matter expertise is required to design and implement the more sophisticated solutions in this category. Even though it would be impractical to cover every targeted point solution here, several key illustrations are relevant to most industries.

Renewable-energy technologies such as electricity from photovoltaic solar cells, electricity from wind turbines and "wind farms," electricity from hydropower, energy from biomass, solar thermal energy, and geothermal energy are now proven solutions whose value propositions and payback time horizons can be calculated with relative ease. As fuel prices remain volatile and risky by traditional standards (and predictions include a high level of uncertainty), the value propositions become more attractive, and the time to break even on an investment in renewable energy sources becomes shorter. Even tax incentives for making these investments are relatively easy to factor into a value proposition.

9.5.1. Electricity from Photovoltaic, Solar Cells

Solar cells are devices that convert sunlight directly into electricity. These devices will play a prominent role for many businesses as they improve their environmental impact. By some estimates, solar cells could be generating almost 14 percent of the world's electricity in the foreseeable future. Installations have been growing at an average annual rate of 35 percent since 1998, and historical growth over the past several years has exceeded the levels predicted. In 2007, the photovoltaic industry in Germany alone employed 42,000 people; by 2030, the solar power industry could create ten million full-time jobs, half in the area of systems installation and marketing.[23] Solar cells currently available have efficiencies in the range of 12–18 percent, which is a measure of how much energy from sunlight is converted to electricity. Looking to the future, efficiencies as high as 42 percent have been demonstrated.[24]

Today solar cells are being integrated into rooftops, building facades, roadways,[25] and a variety of other constructed surfaces that traditionally remained unused for environmental-improvement purposes.

One significant business consideration for the use of solar cells is the relatively high initial cost for materials and installation. The actual time to break even varies depending on installation and maintenance labor rates, environmental factors such as sunlight intensity and cloud cover, financial incentives available, and cost of supply from traditional sources. The energy payback time is the time it takes for a solar cell or array of solar panels to generate the amount of energy that was consumed during production. In 2000, the energy payback time was estimated at 8 to 11 years;[26] by 2006, technical progress and production efficiencies reduced the time to between 1.5 and 2 years.[27] With a useful lifespan of at least 20 years, photovoltaic systems have increasingly attractive value propositions.

Another broad measure of financial attractiveness for solar cells is the point at which grid parity is reached. This is the point at which photovoltaic electricity is equal to or cheaper than grid power. Grid parity is achieved first in areas with abundant sunlight and relatively high grid electricity prices, such as California and Japan. In fact, Japan is already close to achieving grid parity.[28] The U.S. has established a goal of reaching grid parity by 2015.[29]

Financial value is only one measure of benefit from solar cells. The financial trade-offs between using photovoltaic technology and using other sources of electricity from burning fossil fuels are already well understood, but we should not overlook other dimensions of environmental benefit. For environmental sustainability, organizations also should consider the carbon emissions benefit. For example, a company can assess trade-offs between installing a rooftop-mounted solar array and building a "green rooftop" that absorbs carbon from the atmosphere. Similarly, a power station that replaces a grass field or part of a forest area with photovoltaic arrays very likely has a positive net benefit to the environment, but that benefit is fractionally smaller when accounting for the lost photo-synthesis from removing plant life.

Solar cells are a scalable technology that can be expanded after an initial investment. Individual solar cells can be wired together into solar panels, and solar panels can be combined into a system, or array, of panels. In this way, investments can be made incrementally over a period of time, and the concept of "self-funding" can be adopted: Savings from an initial investment can fund further electricity production. Solar cells can also be installed locally, close to where the electricity generated is actually consumed, thus avoiding at least some transmission losses (which can average more than 7 percent).[30]

Solar cells are also convenient and can be considered for the supply of electrical power anywhere electricity is needed. Residential and commercial rooftops are obvious places to consider installing solar panels, but remote, rural locations are also good candidates because grid power might be unavailable there. Solar cells can be found in applications that range everywhere from power stations that supply large amounts of electricity to the grid, to small, stand-alone devices such as emergency telephones, novelty items (perhaps battery-free calculators), and toys. Early applications that still exist today include space-craft: Renewable and perpetual energy sources are critical over the lifespan of a mission that could last many years.

Businesses can also scan the legislative environment for incentives that might lower the cost of adopting solar technology for electricity generation. Countries that are further ahead in adopting this technology are also the ones with aggressive incentives, such as Germany and Japan.

Although they are not completely free of maintenance requirements, solar panels and arrays have relatively low ongoing operating costs. Of course, surfaces need to be cleaned periodically so that maximum sunlight can reach the solar cells, and the usual maintenance of other electricity delivery systems applies as well. Another advantage, in addition to a decades-long lifespan, is that a solar array is highly recyclable, so nearly all materials can be reused.[31]

Photovoltaic technology is one of the most widely applied renewable energy sources for electrical power, and it can be used across a broad range of applications. However, it is not the only source of electricity from environmentally friendly, renewable sources.

9.5.2. Electricity from Wind Turbines

Wind turbines convert energy from the wind directly into electricity. Power from wind energy can be harnessed from solutions that vary in scale from large wind farms to small operations that power modest appliances or charge batteries. Unlike sunlight, however, electricity from wind turbines can operate around the clock and during times of significant cloud cover. Still, wind is an intermittent resource in most locations that requires a combination of favorable weather patterns, geography, and topology.

An enterprise must consider many factors in evaluating energy production from wind turbines over other renewable sources. For example, businesses that own and operate large areas of land, such as ranches, farms, or oil fields, are good candidates if construction of a wind farm would not impede other operations. Regardless of the type of business, determining whether electricity can be effectively generated from the wind involves the speed of the wind and available space to deploy wind turbines.

Another consideration is aesthetics. In one example, the Cape Wind project in Massachusetts was delayed for years primarily because of aesthetic concerns.[32] Acres of wind turbines lack the high-tech look of photovoltaic, solar cells, and wind turbine operation is not completely silent. In fact, some claim that the noise, consisting of both audible and inaudible low frequencies, can make people physically ill.[33]

Adverse environmental impact from wind turbines is another consideration that businesses must account for. The danger to birds is one of the main complaints against wind turbines. One study from 2005 concluded that wind farms could damage the populations of some bird species if they are not carefully located.[34] Still, a consensus has developed that wind farm and ornithological interests can coexist as long as relatively simple steps are taken, such as mapping and avoiding migratory and feeding paths.[35] In fact, methods have been devised to monitor wind turbines for bird and bat collisions.[36]

The British Wind Energy Association claims that the average wind farm pays back the energy used in its manufacture within three to five months of operation.[37] This is a remarkably short period of time, given that the lifespan of a wind farm is measured in decades. Some payback time estimates are longer, at about 1.1 years.[38]

Clearly, electricity generated by harnessing wind energy using turbines is a clean, renewable source that can provide an alternative to burning fossil fuel. After the useful life of a wind farm has been reached, the land can easily be returned to its original state by removing the turbines, and material from the turbines themselves can be recycled.

9.5.3. Electricity from Water, or Hydropower

Hydroelectric power uses the kinetic energy from moving water to turn turbines and generate electricity. Hydraulic power has served many purposes throughout history in such applications as irrigating land and operating machinery (including watermills, textile machines, sawmills, grain mills, dock cranes, and domestic lifts). It accounts for approximately 19 percent of worldwide electricity production today,[39] although at the turn of the century, that percentage was much higher, at more than 40 percent.[40]

Unlike photovoltaic technology and wind turbines, whose technology is basically the same for large- and small-scale electricity production, hydroelectric power uses different technologies, depending on the scale of energy production and the environment available. The different technologies include dam and reservoir systems, water wheels for smaller scales, tidal power, wave power, and ocean current power, among others.

One common technology is the dam and reservoir system, which usually requires a carefully chosen site, takes up a large land mass, and stores significant water volume. For businesses that own and operate such systems, one advantage of dams is that water can be released through the turbines at certain times to manage demand with supply. But in the U.S., where hydroelectric power accounts for about 10 percent of the total supply, most of the good sites to locate large hydro plants (at least, with dam and reservoir systems) have already been taken.[41] Another familiar technology is the water wheel, which can be used in smaller-scale electricity generation and can effectively deliver power to remote locations where water reliably flows.

Although hydroelectric power already supplies part of the planet's electricity, the potential for businesses to independently pursue initiatives that develop power in this way is limited to where waterway access is possible and where communities allow water to be used for this purpose.

Other means of extracting power from moving water exist, and some are still developing. For example, researchers are exploring ways to generate electricity from the water movement in ocean tides,[42] waves,[43] and currents,[44] but solutions such as these are not yet widely available commercially.

9.5.4. Energy from Biomass

Energy from biomass comes from converting biological material, such as plants or waste, into usable energy such as ethanol. Energy from biomass can be developed into solid, liquid, or gas fuel that can, in turn, be used to operate machinery, heat facilities or cook food, or generate steam and electricity in the same way fossil fuel does. Fuel can be produced from virtually any kind of agricultural crop, especially those high in starch or sugar, such as sugar cane. Crops can be converted to ethanol through fermentation processes. Crops that have high vegetable oil content can be processed into energy sources such as biodiesel. Even wood can be processed into fuel such as methanol. Methane digestion processes can be applied to biomass and biowaste such as compost to produce ethane and fertilizer. Fuel can also be produced from biowaste through processes such as landfill off-gassing. The Disneyland Resort has railroad train and riverboat attractions powered with biodiesel derived from cooking oil that is harvested throughout the complex.[45]

Clearly, many methods are available for converting biomass to usable fuel, but not all are suitable for any business—or even economically practical today. For example, businesses in rural locations that generate moderate amounts of organic waste can use methane digesters to generate biogas and fertilizer, both of which likely will have local demand either on-site or from other businesses. Methane digesters are a relatively simple technology solution that consists of a container that holds organic waste in a manner that allows natural bacterial digestion to occur in the absence of oxygen.[46] Some businesses have made significant capital investments in solutions that generate biofuel on a large scale, often with government support or legislation. For example, Brazil's economy includes business operations that convert a portion of the country's sugar cane crop into ethanol, to reduce its requirement for fossil fuels.

One consideration that impacts a broad group of businesses is that, as the availability of biofuels grows, products that consume fossil fuels can be converted to run on biofuel. Virtually any engine, machinery, or heating device that currently burns fossil fuel can be converted or redesigned, with varying degrees of configuration change, to consume biofuel instead. As supply increases, machinery and products are converted, and demand for biofuels rises, distribution systems will adapt and adjust to the change. Brazil's government created legislation years ago to facilitate the transformation of automobile service stations so that they can accommodate both fossil and biofuel distribution.

9.5.5. Thermal Energy Alternatives to Fossil Fuels

Thermal energy from the sun or geothermal activity can serve as an alternative to traditional forms of energy. Solutions already take advantage of thermal energy, and some of these have been in use for decades or even longer. These include both passive and active solar heating devices.

One of these devices includes solar collectors for heating water, with circulation established by natural convection or forced pumping. This approach runs water through pipes that are built into a solar collector plate, heated by sunlight. It can be used on a small or large scale, with solar collectors installed in arrays to heat larger volumes of water. Some of the more advanced collectors will focus or concentrate sunlight to achieve higher water temperatures.

In fact, a 5mW power plant constructed in only seven months was successfully tested in Nevada; a series of mirrors focuses sunlight to heat water and generate electricity. Solar thermal power plants such as this one concentrate sunlight to heat water and drive electricity-generating turbines. The technology for solar thermal electricity plants has existed for many years and was tested on a large scale in California's Mojave Desert in 1981, where 1,800 mirrors concentrated sunlight into one area and generated steam to drive a turbine.[47]

Methods to heat buildings using solar energy are often divided into passive and active systems. Passive systems are sometimes not considered technology solutions: For example, a properly placed tree provides shade or a well-positioned window provides sunlight at the appropriate time of day, to allow for passive temperature control. The passive use of thermal energy from sunlight is low cost, and many building designs already incorporate it. Active systems are more complex. They can use heated water from solar collectors, or use dense material such as rocks to store heat until it is needed for environmental temperature control. Active systems require an initial investment and ongoing maintenance as well. One key consideration for businesses in this area relates to the trade-offs between solar heating systems, whether for water or environmental control inside facilities, and other options, such as photovoltaic electricity generation, to operate traditional heating, ventilation, and air-conditioning equipment.

Geothermal energy from heat stored in the earth is not widely used in most areas because it is economical only where appropriate geological activity is present and communities allow it to be developed as useful energy. For example, much of the thermal activity at Yellowstone National Park in Wyoming is protected and cannot be exploited for business purposes. California, however, is home to one of the largest networks of geothermal power plants, generating enough electricity to power a city the size of San Francisco.[48] Supplying less than half a percent of the world's energy,[49] geothermal solutions are ones that businesses can exploit only when the opportunity is available.

Technologies that supply renewable energy, reduce carbon emissions, and support environmental stewardship are only one part of the portfolio of point solutions available to businesses as they identify opportunities to improve their operations. A second group of solutions focuses not on energy generation, but on efficiency.

9.6. Targeted Point Solutions for Efficiency and Resource Management

Among the targeted point solutions available is a broad range of energy-efficient equipment that includes green building construction solutions and a myriad of other environmentally friendly products. Some of these products include hybrid and electric vehicles, energy-efficient appliances, and cleaner coal–burning technology. Green computing and data centers are one example of technology advancements that reduce energy consumption. Other targeted solutions include software tools that can monitor, evaluate, and optimize the performance of business processes to improve environmental stewardship. For example, IBM[50] and Microsoft[51] have both developed solutions for environmental stewardship that include dashboard views to summarize business environments and optimize process performance. Accenture has developed a green technology suite to help organizations use information technology (IT) to assess and improve their green agendas.[52] Recycling and water-reclamation solutions are also available for businesses that decide to improve their environmental impact with them.

9.6.1. Efficiency from Green Computing Solutions

Green computing improves environmental stewardship by increasing energy efficiency, improving information management, and providing appropriate analytical capability. Long before there was consensus that global climate change was a worldwide problem and the green movement was firmly underway, technology companies were already working to make computers of all kinds more efficient and consume less energy. For laptop computers and hand-held devices, the primary driver to reduce energy consumption was to make batteries last longer between recharges. For large data centers that serve the needs of an enterprise, less energy consumption translates to lower cooling requirements and lower operating costs.

Holistic perspectives on Green Data Centers that support enterprise IT needs are driving new advances. For example, one framework from IBM describes the Green Data Center concept with five key principles. The first principle is to begin by understanding energy use and diagnosing a company's technology landscape, to identify opportunities for improvement so that transformation actions are soundly based on the current state. Another principle, when the opportunity exists, is to plan, build, and upgrade to energy-efficient data centers. This can involve significant investments in new hardware and potentially even new computing facilities because data center overhauls are not always possible. Migrating to an improved solution over time is often more feasible. Next, innovative solutions that aim to increase efficiency should provide cooling. Companies can also implement virtualization to improve resource utilization and information availability. Finally, companies should manage and measure performance with energy-management software[53] so that they can achieve further efficiency over time.

Although the technology of green computing and green data centers is advanced and its benefits are well understood, the business objectives for transforming from legacy technology to efficient computing platforms that improve environmental stewardship should be clear. In a 2008 study by The Enterprise Strategy Group, Inc., nearly half of senior business executives indicated that their organization had a green initiative or program underway in the area of data centers, IT power, and cooling. A larger number, 70 percent, indicated that cost reduction from reduced energy consumption was a metric closely tracked to measure success of green initiatives. Thus, there is still a significant potential for green computing to move higher on business leadership agendas as these percentages rise.[54]

Beyond green computing and green data center technology, a new portfolio of green product technology is emerging that can help businesses across all industries improve their environmental stewardship.

9.6.2. Efficiency from Green Product Solutions

Green product solutions improve environmental stewardship partly by increasing energy efficiency. Green products that are more efficient than the ones they replace hold a unique place for environmental stewards. On one hand, the companies and consumers that purchase and use such products in their daily activities improve their positions as environmental stewards by reducing energy consumption or waste, making their carbon footprints smaller and benefiting the environment as a result. On the other hand, the companies that manufacture and supply these products are acting as responsible environmental stewards because they make it possible to reduce the energy consumption or waste across the entire lifecycle of a product.

For example, when compared to traditional automobiles that consume fossil fuels, the manufacture and delivery of a hybrid or electric automobile might consume a similar amount of energy. However, because these vehicles partly consume ethanol or electricity that potentially comes from renewable energy sources, the individuals and companies that use them have a net positive impact on the environment. The circumstances are similar for energy-efficient appliances and electronics. When ice cream company Ben & Jerry's started testing more environmentally clean freezers in 2008,[55] the company improved its position as an environmental steward and reduced its carbon footprint. In another example, when Avis offered hybrid vehicles in its rental car fleet and advertised "For a green time call[el],"[56] it improved its position as an environmental steward, as did the customers who rented and drove those automobiles. Other products enable existing devices to be retrofitted so that they are more efficient. PowerDown software, a free download designed at the University of Liverpool, is one example that allows computer "retrofits" so that they power down and conserve energy after a period of nonuse. An average PC can be left on 24 hours a day but generally is used only 40 hours a week, so savings can be significant.[57]

Telecommuting and "in lieu of travel" solutions that help companies more efficiently use (or even eliminate) energy for travel include traditional ones as well as emerging technologies. One solution from IBM enables people to meet, communicate, and collaborate in three-dimensional, virtual environments that simulate actual in-person experiences.[58] An enormous number of product technology advancements have been made to improve environmental stewardship in recent years. The newly developed and other enhanced products directly improve environmental impact, and their use will continue to grow as procurement practices adopt environmental considerations in decision making. Enterprises should consider the portfolio of available product solutions that improve environmental impact as they evaluate their inventory of energy-consuming equipment, machinery, and appliances. Moreover, after identifying opportunities, companies can accomplish the necessary transformation over a deliberate period of time using a roadmap with key milestones. In some cases, the most sensible action might be to continue using existing equipment until its useful life ends, but then replace that equipment with its higher-efficiency counterpart at an economically feasible time.

9.6.3. Efficiency from Green Building Construction

Green buildings improve environmental stewardship partly by consuming less energy while they operate. Principles for green buildings and other facilities are well developed but are not always applied to the greatest extent possible. As companies design new facilities, renovate existing ones, or seek to lease property, they must increasingly recognize energy-efficient designs and compare them to other designs whose environmental considerations are not emphasized. In fact, where facilities are occupied under long-term lease agreements and building modifications are necessary (such as installing company signage and configuring inside office space), companies could negotiate environmentally friendly improvements, such as allowing the installation of rooftop photovoltaic arrays.

Of course, green buildings should incorporate environmentally conscientious construction supplies and should be constructed with energy efficiency in mind. Energy efficiency includes optimal use of insulation, heating, ventilation and air-conditioning equipment, and water-conserving technology. Green building designs recognize that natural lighting is highly efficient wherever it is possible, using such devices as skylights and even mirrors to direct sunlight into appropriate areas.

A robust body of work already describes green building solutions and approaches to increasing efficiency and reducing environmental impact. C. Lockwood points out, "A substantial body of experience and a set of tested standards have made 'green' a realistic choice for most building projects."[59] Many of the books available are both prescriptive, to explain methods and tools that support improved environmental stewardship, and descriptive, to illustrate examples from existing buildings that have achieved meaningful results. These works emphasize how to take action in tactical ways. Some of these focused works include such books as Kibert's *Sustainable Construction: Green Building Design and Delivery*[60] and Werthmann's *Green Roof—A Case Study.*[61]

9.6.4. Environmental Stewardship through Recycling and Water Reclamation

Water reclamation and recycling of other natural resources improve environmental stewardship by reducing waste. Many large businesses and residential complexes, where operations and employees use a significant amount of water on a daily basis, often have an opportunity to reuse or reclaim some of the water that would otherwise be wasted through municipal sewage systems. In developing countries, the concept of reusing water is well established, but in nations where people consider water plentiful (such as the U.S.), water is most often used once and thrown away.[62] Some of the most easily reclaimed water is so-called "gray water," the wastewater that drains out of washing machines, sinks, bathtubs, and showers. Gray water can be easily recycled locally where it is initially used and can even be recycled as irrigation for vegetation on the business site. For example, Epuramat's Box4Water product "can treat very dirty wastewater all the way up to drinking water quality" for approximately 200 residents.[63]

Previously in Chapter 3, "Green Strategy Supports Operational Improvements," Section 3.1.1, we discussed that companies are extending their influence throughout the lifecycle chain by creating innovative recycling programs that help retain customer loyalty while also improving the environment. We also showed that legislative action is playing a role in recycling through take-back programs. Numerous recycling solutions have already been developed to process materials such as glass, plastic, metals of all kinds, rubber, paper products, and used oil. Some recycling solutions reprocess materials by melting and reforming metals and glass so that new products can be manufactured with little or no noticeable difference from products made with virgin materials. Other solutions cleanse and grind recyclable materials so that they can be formed into products such as insulation, surfboards, or flooring for playgrounds and athletic facilities.

The combination triangle/number labeling now found on many products and their packaging is well understood and has made recycling efforts more effective as a result. Some recycling solutions are not as widely known, though. The IST Energy Corporation offers a mobile Green Energy Machine (GEM) that converts waste into energy and can process up to 3 tons of trash a day,[64] while producing enough energy to power and heat a 200,000-square-foot building housing more than 500 people. Other solutions include plasma arc gasification devices that "vaporize" waste, generate combustible gas as part of the process, and produce byproducts that are useful in such areas as roads and construction.[65]

The solutions and approaches to recycling are too numerous to mention here, as are the products made from recycled materials. However, all businesses should identify sources of waste generated across the enterprise and seek to not only reduce those wastes, but also find ways to turn the waste back into useful resources. Some business models actually take on recycling responsibility for many organizations and gain better economies of scale. For example, TerraCycle, Inc., places bins for collecting recyclable materials at companies such as Petco, OfficeMax, Home Depot, and Best Buy, with hopes to ultimately cover 10,000 locations.[66] Another consideration for businesses to proactively explore is to understand how products can be manufactured so that they are ultimately easier to recycle or can include more recycled raw material content. This consideration turns traditional "design for manufacturability" (DFM) into "design for recycling" (DFR). For example, the U.S. Tile Company earned the Cradle to Cradle (C2C) certification for healthy and sustainable product design from MBDC for its line of clay roofing-tile products produced in the U.S.[67]

Of course, not all the solutions being developed and offered are equally proven in the marketplace, and cautious business judgment is still appropriate for emerging solutions. Companies can mitigate risk through a number of familiar approaches: launching small-scale pilot projects, sharing financial risk and reward with business partners, and testing different solutions on a small scale before making larger decisions on where to invest. Organizations should also decide how close they want to be on the innovation frontier in different areas: to be fast followers or to be late adopters of developing green solutions. For example, no standard, agreed-upon way exists for measuring the carbon footprint of products across industry boundaries, nor are universal standards available to measure optimal water management for different industries. Yet many businesses are making investments in targeted point solutions in these areas and are clearly becoming better environmental stewards.

PART IV

Conclusions

10

Critical Trends Shaping the Future

10.1. The Imperative for Change Will Continue and Strengthen

In many parts of the world, environmental stewardship has already grown in importance. It has enabled some businesses to demonstrate their capability to lead and innovate within their industry, compelled others to reevaluate their business processes and how they impact the environment, and driven still others to begin considering what an appropriate competitive response should be as their performance falls behind that of their peers.

Unlike fleeting trends that have influenced business management, environmental stewardship has many self-sustaining characteristics of other important, and even common, elements of business and operations strategies. Some familiar improvement themes are tied to names such as total quality management (TQM), design for manufacture (DFM), concurrent engineering, and shared services. Since these ideas were first introduced decades ago, they have had a significant impact on businesses and how they operate. They eliminated duplication of effort; significantly shortened cycle times for many business processes; increased quality and avoided scrap and rework; and significantly improved manufacturing cost through efforts to standardize parts, simplify product assemblies, and focus on process outcomes rather than activities. Relentless global forces supported such broad-based transformation: Entire industries became more efficient and learned to compete more effectively, and barriers to global trade continued to fall at the same time. Even today, concepts of hypercompetition, globalization, ever-shortening product lifecycles, and rapidly changing consumer preferences continue to drive businesses to be more cost-competitive, more quality conscious, more responsive, and faster to market.

Environmental stewardship ties businesses and their whole industries to common global imperatives, just as these other themes and concepts have in the past. Now, however, the driving forces are even more compelling to continue growth in the green movement.

Irreversible damage to the planet from greenhouse gas emissions and global climate change, uncontrollable risk from energy and raw material price fluctuations, water stress, and sophisticated expectations from environmentally aware consumers are external factors that will continue to drive businesses to improve their impact on the environment. Until the effects of global climate change show signs of a new global equilibrium that the world's population is content to live with, the imperative to reduce greenhouse gas emissions will remain important for all enterprises. And with some carbon emission reduction targets set to be achieved as far out as 2050,[1] the longevity of this global imperative is clear. Population growth and industrialization only make the imperative more pressing.

Although no natural resources are in danger of immediate global depletion, their supply is limited. By some estimates, such as one from BP's Statistical Review of World Energy published in 2008,[2] the world has as many as 1,238 billion barrels of oil in proved reserves. This equates to about 40 years of uninterrupted oil supply (excluding sources such as the Canadian oil sands). Forty years might look like an immeasurably long time when most businesses construct detailed plans and allocate funding for initiatives over a time horizon that ranges from 1 to 5 years. Even detailed strategic planning rarely considers a horizon of 40 years for most industries, except for scenario envisioning–type planning[3] and large capital investments that can be amortized over many years. However, considering that many large businesses routinely formulate strategic objectives and construct roadmaps for high-level planning purposes that extend 3 to 10 years into the future—and some businesses even articulate strategic visions that extend 20 years—40 years starts to appear much shorter indeed.

One resource in shorter supply is our ability to burn fossil fuels without causing further, irreversible global warming and the associated unwanted climate and weather change. Perhaps as the global economy moves toward a higher use of renewable energy and away from fossil fuel consumption, estimates for the supply of oil might change from decades to centuries, and modern society's dependence on fossil fuel will decrease. Between now and that time, businesses that improve their energy efficiency and find ways to transition to sustainable energy sources will benefit from more reliable energy supplies and more stable prices.

With copper, lead, mercury, nickel, gallium, tin, zinc,[4] and phosphorous [5] due to run out (albeit arguably) within 50 years, by some estimates, oil clearly is not the only natural resource that faces depletion within our—or our children's—lifetime. Substitute materials for some of these resources are difficult to find, especially for certain applications. The fact that these minerals are projected to reach depletion within ten years of the depletion timing for oil points to potentially significant supply chain constraints ahead unless enterprises continue to improve their role as environmental stewards. When all businesses work toward the common objective of conserving and recycling natural resources that are headed for depletion, their global availability will increase. Also, businesses that explore alternative materials and find different approaches to meet customer needs by using abundant resources will inevitably benefit from a continued, unconstrained supply chain and a more stable cost structure.

By the time enterprises find alternatives to using scarce natural resources, convert their energy supply to renewable sources, and learn to optimally manage water where supplies are scarce, consumers will also have learned to more fully recognize value from companies that innovate to protect the environment. Sometimes consumer behavior will be driven by positive reinforcement led by businesses—for example, products are increasingly favored when the environmental impact is communicated through advertising- or standards-based labeling. Other times, negative consumer behavior such as protests and boycotts will redirect certain business activity. Inevitably, both proactive positive reinforcement and reactive negative redirection toward improved environmental stewardship will be reflected in shareholder and stakeholder value.

Many discussions of corporate social responsibility already focus as much attention on environmental stewardship as they do on ethics, human rights, and financial transparency. This new importance of environmental stewardship won't likely diminish. It may still be a challenge to see a chief green officer (CGO) or chief sustainability officer (CSO) sitting at the table with every company's CEO, CFO, CIO, and COO, but it's not entirely an alien concept either, as businesses increasingly assign green responsibilities at higher management levels.

Only a handful of companies have actually designated a CSO who has a direct reporting relationship to the CEO, but that fact itself can be misleading when assessing the trend. Most major corporations with a global presence already have green, or sustainability, executives at senior or middle management levels.[6] Georgia-Pacific is one company that created such a role in its organization when it announced a new CSO in 2007. This role has responsibility for overall efforts internally to develop and implement sustainability strategies, goals, measurement, and reporting. The CSO also represents the company in external sustainability discussions with customers and other external groups.[7]

Numerous other companies have appointed leadership in a CSO or similar role across all the major industries. A few of these companies include Google, Dow Chemical, DuPont, Owens Corning, Home Depot, HSBC Group, General Electric, and SAP. The CSO role is also becoming more common in companies that want to profit from going green and consciously guard and even grow the value of their brand. The rise in popularity of the CSO role in so many large enterprises is a clear indication that companies realize that sustainability and efficiency go hand in hand.[8] Peter Williams, IBM's CTO for Big Green Innovations, has noted, "There are still opportunities to improve the integration of priorities for these emerging leadership positions with existing business priorities so that there is more direct responsibility and authority to change manufacturing activity, supply chain operations, and product content. Chief sustainability officers today rarely have direct operational responsibility for things like the supply chain and manufacturing, which is where some of the biggest impacts can be made, so it's vital that the CSO is able to work effectively with senior executives in those areas."[9]

10.2. The Role of Government Will Grow and Align Globally

Independent, voluntary activity from proactive initiatives led by many enterprises, both public and private, has already achieved impressive results. Regardless of the prevailing economic conditions, environmental stewardship is visible in the daily news, frequent press releases, and numerous policy announcements. Still, as environmentally related standards mature, labeling becomes common and bolder claims are made for significant environmental impact improvements, the burden of proof and level of oversight will increase. Still, with roughly three-quarters of the largest 100 U.S. companies reporting sustainability data in 2008,[10] gaps still must be filled. Although it will take time for corporate sustainability reports to be required and audited as financial reports are today, it is easy to envision that a higher level of oversight and standardized reporting will be expected in the not-too-distant future. One offering from Underwriters Laboratories, which provides product safety testing services, now has an environmental claims–verification service to "help companies and the public make sense of green claims and provide manufacturers with transparency and credibility in the marketplace."[11]

Government has the power to incite businesses to follow long-range plans that they might not otherwise devise themselves. The automobile industry has a history of legislated efficiency and emissions requirements that have been credited with pollution control, reduced smog in urban areas, and lower incidences of acid rain. In a similar way, government incentives are accelerating the development, launch, and consumer acceptance of more environmentally friendly automobiles that consume hybrid fuels, alternative energy, and electricity. Creative examples include laws that allow environmentally friendly vehicles access to commuter lanes without multiple passengers onboard.[12] Electric automobiles consume energy that can originate from numerous sources, including "clean coal technology," nuclear power, solar power, wind power, or hydroelectric power. The automobile industry is only one example of where government intervention is helping to make progress along with market forces.

Legislation is also making environmental stewardship easier for other businesses around the world. Examples include electronics companies, with "take-back" recycling programs; the real estate industry, through efficiency and energy-consumption proposals; electric utilities, by setting targets for supply percentages from renewable sources; and food producers, with well-established beverage-container recycling programs.

Carbon credit trading may also require more government regulation, cross-border cooperation, and global standards for enforcement. As different countries begin to participate in such programs, with efficient enterprises able to "sell" their carbon credits to those with higher greenhouse gas emissions, government enforcement and penalties could become an issue. In an alternative scenario, enterprises could reduce their emissions and approach "carbon neutrality" more quickly, with carbon credits ultimately losing their economic value. Such programs then would be less prominent than many people currently expect.

For now, though, carbon credit trading programs represent a clear and growing trend. For all European Union countries, the approach the Kyoto Protocol laid out has been adopted for CO_2 trading under the European Trading Scheme (EU ETS). In the United States, the California Air Resources Board in 2008 adopted the most comprehensive global warming plan in the country, outlining how individuals and businesses would meet a 2006 law that made the state a leader for global climate change. The plan requires California's utilities, refineries, and large factories to transform their operations and cut greenhouse gas emissions. At the heart of the plan is a carbon credit market that gives major polluters potentially less expensive ways to cut the amount of their emissions.[13] The U.S.'s Chicago Climate Exchange (CCX) operates as a cap-and-trade system for all six greenhouse gases, supporting emissions registry and reduction. Here members make a voluntary but legally binding commitment to meet reduction targets. When an organization exceeds reduction targets, it can sell or keep the surplus; when targets are not met, the company must purchase contracts.[14] In 2009, the Environmental Defense Fund identified and mapped 1,200 companies in key manufacturing states that are poised to benefit from U.S. legislation that limits, or caps, global warming pollution.[15]

In his 2008 campaign, U.S. President Barack Obama made energy independence and efficiency one of his key platforms. President Obama's plan, even before taking office, included such measures as investing $150 billion over ten years to create five million "green collar" jobs, and ensuring that 25 percent of the nation's electricity comes from renewable sources by 2025.[16] After taking office in the midst of a global recession, his administration continued with an agenda that addresses environmental issues in ways that past administrations have not. More pervasive policies that are less cavalier toward dependence on fossil fuels should be anticipated as a result.

Examples do exist in which government has already played a role to ensure that long-term trends stay on course, some with quite remarkable outcomes. In some cases, macro-level models designed to encourage and achieve environmental sustainability have proven successful. Brazil's transition from using fossil fuels to using renewable energy is one such example. In the 1970s, Brazil was importing roughly 80 percent of its oil. By incrementally increasing the amount of ethanol into the economy between 1975 and 2006, Brazilian President Lula de Silva was able to declare energy independence in 2006. Because Brazil achieved energy independence by replacing fossil fuels with renewable sources, the country significantly lessened its global carbon footprint contribution as well. Of course, government intervention played an important role in the transformation: The Proalcool Program ordered sugar companies to increase production and required the state-run oil company, Petrobas, to make ethanol available at its fuel stations.[17] The feasibility of adopting a similar model in other countries remains a valid question, but notable sources such as *The Washington Post* have suggested Brazil as a model for the "road to energy independence" in the United States.[18] Brazil is not the only country that uses renewable resources to meet a significant amount of its energy needs. As of 2007, Iceland has supplied more than 82 percent of its primary energy needs from geothermal and hydropower sources.[19]

The seeds for similarly ambitious goals are already being sown elsewhere. Google's philanthropic arm has offered a $4 trillion program (the Clean Energy 2030 plan) to significantly reduce dependence on fossil fuels in the United States by 2030.[20] Separately, the Institute for 21st Century Energy, an affiliate of the U.S. Chamber of Commerce, offers a "Blueprint for Securing America's Energy Future" that makes more than 75 policy recommendations.[21] Perhaps aspiring to adopt an economic model that relies on more renewable resources is worthy of debate after all and could strengthen a long-term trend that is already important to businesses worldwide.

Over the long-term horizon of 50 years or more, different natural resources will certainly become scarce at different points in time. The models to address those shortages will no doubt depend on prevailing circumstances. Supply shortages will inevitably be resolved by discovering ways to use resources more efficiently and identifying more abundant alternatives that allow for a similar customer experience. In some cases, the world will learn to live without some resources and the products that are produced from them. As these scenarios unfold, governments, industries, and companies will need to identify new ways of working together toward collaborative solutions. Without informed and deliberate collaboration, other scenarios that might emerge would involve significant yet transient economic power shifts to regions where scarce commodities are mined, legislated protectionism, and the potential to socialize private assets for a higher degree of government control and price stability.

10.3. Environmental Intelligence Will Integrate with Traditional Operations

On a planet that is becoming increasingly instrumented, interconnected, and intelligent, the information and insight gained from widespread sensor networks inevitably will influence many aspects of business operations.

A 2008 survey of automotive industry leaders found general agreement that, by 2020, vehicles will have the capability to communicate with their environment in multiple ways: vehicle to vehicle, vehicle to transportation infrastructure, and vehicle to homes and businesses.[22] Vehicle-to-vehicle communication is actually not difficult to imagine: Some existing designs already allow vehicles to detect nearby hazards with sensors, and rear-mounted video surveillance makes moving a vehicle in reverse safer. Hypothetically, a system might allow one vehicle to analyze the route plan of another and statistically predict the potential for its driver to "swerve" across lanes to exit a highway at the appropriate off-ramp. Vehicle–to–transportation infrastructure communication is also easy to imagine: Vehicles could detect road and driving conditions, such as snow and rain; traffic conditions, such as congestion and construction; other obstacles, such as accidents; and availability of commuter lanes. With this information from the infrastructure environment, onboard computing could propose alternative routes and minimize time, fuel consumption, and greenhouse gas emissions. Vehicle-to-home and business communication is also easily envisioned: Onboard systems might some day be capable of identifying the closest service station with the lowest fuel price; they already can identify nearby restaurants, retail stores, and entertainment locations while driving.

The possibility of more deliberately and creatively managed demand for resources such as electricity and water is also foreseeable when considering existing technology, instrumentation around the world, and expected scarcity. Parts of the United States have already experienced forced "rolling blackouts" in urban areas such as Southern California in recent years.[23] Some argue that such events can be avoided with improved power management and related policy changes. Public announcements in some urban areas routinely ask energy consumers to help "smooth electricity demand" by using household appliances in the evening instead of during peak business hours. In the future, messages to consumers could be focused differently to drive alternative behavior, with incentives put in place to encourage more use during daytime hours, when solar power generation is the highest.

Food is another resource whose associated transportation consumes energy, with inefficient distribution and use leading to waste. As pointed out in Section 7.2 of Chapter 7, "Instrumenting the Planet for an Intelligent, Sustainable World," up to 30 percent of the food in developed countries simply goes to waste—in the United States alone, that amounts to $48 billion annually. In another illustration, 75 percent of the apples sold in New York City come from the West Coast or overseas, even though the state produces more apples than city residents consume.[24] Reducing waste such as this is clearly not a one-dimensional issue; it must include not only information technology advances, but also innovative collaboration approaches across companies and geographic borders, government action, and consumer preference changes.

Chapters 5, "Transformation Methods and Green Sigma," and 6, "Applying Green Sigma to Optimize Carbon Emissions," showed how a relatively small set of sensors can provide input into a management dashboard to control and improve environmental performance. Using Green Sigma or other approaches, companies can improve greenhouse gas emissions, better manage water, and reduce raw materials waste. Chapters 7, "Instrumenting the Planet for an Intelligent, Sustainable World," and 8, "Technology That Supports Instrumenting the Planet," showed that vast networks of environmental sensors and instrumentation can be networked together to provide necessary input into intelligent computer models; companies can then use those insights to improve environmental impact in virtually any industry. A few examples include transportation management, electricity management, water management, and wind farm management.

In a 2008 speech, titled "A Smart Planet: The Next Leadership Agenda," to the Council on Foreign Relations in New York City, Sam Palmisano, IBM's chief executive, observed that all things are becoming intelligent as "the digital and physical infrastructures of the world are converging." He outlined a world transformed by the impact of rising globalization and sees an era of increasing connectivity in which more systems and objects will "speak" to each another.[25] Saul Berman, IBM's global lead partner for the strategy and change services consulting practice, reinforced this theme in a 2008 interview, noting that as the world becomes more interconnected, new risks and opportunities will arise. Competitive implications accompany this fact. Berman commented, "There's a viral spread of information, which creates a widening gap between those who apply the information correctly and those who do not have the same information."[26]

10.4. Businesses That Master Green Strategy Will Win in the Marketplace

Businesses that have developed and implemented green strategies are offering innovative products and services to the marketplace that are driving revenue growth, making their operations more efficient in environmentally important ways, reducing costs, and identifying opportunities across the lifecycle chain that are possible now that the green movement is underway and gaining momentum. In the future, virtually all businesses likely will have some form of environmental stewardship position and established guiding principles.

Many companies are already recognizing long-term trends and making appropriate investments to respond and win in the marketplace. In one trend, Australia has announced that it will ban incandescent light bulbs in favor of compact fluorescent light (CFL) and light emitting diode (LED) technology; Venezuela and Cuba are working to phase them out as well. California is taking similar steps, along with others. This trend has prompted General Electric to invent the covered GE Energy Smart CFL bulb, protected with more than a dozen U.S. patent applications, whose profile is virtually identical to that of a standard incandescent light bulb.[27] This kind of product innovation not only helps solve the light fixture retrofit problem, but also gives the manufacturers of light fixtures the flexibility to preserve existing designs or develop new ones that accommodate either old or new bulb profiles—or both. In fact, with some countries and states working to eliminate incandescent light bulbs altogether, this type of invention has ready-made markets where legacy light fixtures cannot conveniently accommodate existing CFLs because of their nontraditional profiles. Other businesses are responding to this "here to stay" trend. Some hotels that have retrofitted the lighting in their guest rooms to be more efficient also tether the new, more expensive CFLs to the lamp, to discourage theft.

In the hotel industry, one survey of more than 700 people conducted by A Closer Look, Inc., [28] in 2007 found that 75 percent of respondents chose the hotel where they stay partly based on whether it follows "green practices."[29] Another survey of best practices from the Coalition for Environmentally Responsible Economies,[30] allows companies to "communicate their environmental preferences to the hotel industry."[31] This kind of market intelligence is becoming available in virtually every industry. Combining this with industry best practices, companies that are well positioned with respect to environmental stewardship can identify and take advantage of opportunities to build better, differentiated brands.

Even before the green movement started, hotels in some countries, such as Cambodia, interfaced the electricity in each room with the room key so that no electricity can be consumed when guests are not in the hotel. The room key essentially becomes not only a security device for the door lock, but also a protection device that prohibits energy waste. In developed countries, an analogous approach in which motion-sensitive light switches limit energy waste is becoming more common.

In the electronics industry, numerous examples can point to companies developing consumer products that improve their environmental stewardship and help them compete more effectively. Motorola's fully recyclable MOTO W233 Renew mobile phone, partly manufactured from recycled water bottles, is the "world's first carbon-neutral mobile phone," certified as such by Carbonfund.org after an "extensive product lifecycle assessment."[32] This product comes from a company that is a leading environmental steward. Motorola has previously been among the Citizen's Advisors top ten Corporate Citizens in Environmental Stewardship.[33] Its recyclable phone fits nicely with Motorola's existing recycling program, discussed earlier in Chapter 3, "Green Strategy Supports Operational Improvements" (Section 3.1.1). Electronics companies are also differentiating themselves by setting—and, in some cases, already achieving—aggressive carbon-neutral and emissions-reduction targets at the enterprise level.

According to a 2008 IBM survey of 125 executives from the automotive industry in 15 countries, fuel efficiency and eco-friendliness will represent the two largest changes in vehicle-buying criteria by 2020. The survey also found that, by 2020, automobile fuel will likely be 65 percent sourced from fossil fuel (compared with 95 percent in 2008) and that 88 percent of materials that make up an automobile will be recyclable. This aligns well with the finding that, in 2020, every vehicle is expected to have some level of hybridization and that lithium-ion batteries will dominate.[34] As in other industries, the automotive industry will undergo significant change over a long time horizon, to improve the environmental impact from its processes and products. The dominant automotive companies are already positioning themselves with product innovations, process-efficiency improvements, and branded awareness campaigns to compete effectively.

Leading in environmental stewardship will help companies win in the marketplace not only because customers can more easily accept their products and services, but also because the companies can be more cost-competitive and can reduce excessive waste that they might have needlessly consumed for decades. The list of companies taking action to improve operational efficiency grows steadily; those that have already achieved benefits are often taking further steps to make additional improvements. For example, Raytheon strives to integrate environmentally friendly behavior into daily practice. As a result, it has reduced hazardous waste by 85 percent per billion dollars of revenue since 1998—the company reduced hazardous waste 20 percent in 2007 alone.[35] Also in the aerospace and defense industry, Lockheed Martin pledged to reduce its greenhouse gas emissions 30 percent per dollar of revenue by 2010, using 2001 as the baseline. Lockheed Martin Space Systems took a further step to purchase about 10 percent of its energy from wind and solar sources.[36] Similarly, Honeywell is working to reduce its greenhouse gas emissions 30 percent and to increase energy efficiency 20 percent by 2012, using 2004 as the baseline year.[37] All these efforts improve environmental impact, as well as reduce bottom-line costs and increase profitability.

However, companies must pay attention to whether such pronouncements are made in absolute terms or in terms of revenue dollars. When expressed in terms of revenue dollars, total emissions can still increase even when stated reduction targets are met, where revenue growth is sufficiently high. Of course, any kind of waste reduction represents a step in the right direction, but standards for setting targets and reporting progress toward them are not yet in place across companies and industries.

Companies around the world are making environmental stewardship a top priority and using it to transform every aspect of their businesses. The green movement is driving changes in product and service offerings, business partnerships and alliances, infrastructure and office space, equipment and plants, information technology and computing capabilities, and organizational capabilities and governance. Governments are also working to facilitate the transformation to a more sustainable planet by providing incentives to adopt green practices and technology, providing funding to develop more efficient technology, and legislating new policies that enterprises must follow. Trends are now firmly in place, with drivers of those trends strongly aligned so that long-term prominence of the green movement can continue until environmental stewardship is a natural a part of everyday business activity. Perhaps Colin Harrison, who leads a number of environmental strategy activities from IBM's corporate headquarters, is right when he remarks that "changing the light bulbs will not be enough" and that humankind in the late twenty-first century "will probably pity us for our addiction to fossil fuels."[38]

Endnote References

Chapter 1

1. Accolo, Inc., "About EcoPartnership." See www.accolo.com/ecopartnership/about/.

2. The Marlin Company, "14th Annual 'Attitudes in the American Workplace' Poll of 2008," conducted by Zogby International for The Marlin Company. See www.themarlincompany.com/MediaRoom/PollResults.aspx.

3. A. Gore, *An Inconvenient Truth: The Planetary Emergency of Global Warming and What We Can Do About It* (New York: Rodale, Inc., 2006).

4. C. J. Campbell, *Oil Crisis,* (Essex, U.K.: Multi-Science Publishing Co. Ltd., 2005).

5. M. Lynas, *Six Degrees: Our Future on a Hotter Planet* (New York: Random House, 2008).

6. J. H. Kunstler, *The Long Emergency: Surviving the End of Oil, Climate Change, and Other Converging Catastrophes of the Twenty-First Century* (New York: Grove Press, 2006).

7. O. Brown, "Migration and Climate Change" (Geneva, Switzerland: International Organization for Migration, 2008). See www.iisd.org/pdf/2008/migration_climate.pdf.

8. D. C. Esty and A. S. Winston, *Green to Gold: How Smart Companies Use Environmental Strategy to Innovate, Create Value, and Build Competitive Advantage* (Hoboken, New Jersey: John Wiley & Sons, Inc., 2009).

9. Answers.com, "Global Warming." See www.answers.com/topic/global-warming.

10. R. Spencer, *Climate Confusion: How Global Warming Hysteria Leads to Bad Science, Pandering Politicians, and Misguided Policies That Hurt the Poor* (New York: Encounter Books, 2008).

11. K. E. Trenberth, P. D. Jones, P. Ambenje, R. Bojariu, D. Easterling, A. Klein Tank, D. Parker, et al., "Observations: Surface and Atmospheric Climate Change," in Climate Change 2007: The Physical Science Basis. Contribution of Working Group I to the Fourth Assessment Report of the Intergovernmental Panel on Climate Change (New York: Cambridge University Press, 2007). See http:// ipcc-wg1.ucar.edu/wg1/wg1-report.html.

12. N. L. Bindoff, J. Willebrand, V. Artale, A. Cazenave, J. Gregory, S. Gulev, K. Hanawa, et al., "Observations: Oceanic Climate Change and Sea Level," in Climate Change 2007: The Physical Science Basis. Contribution of Working Group I to the Fourth Assessment Report of the Intergovernmental Panel on Climate Change (New York: Cambridge University Press, 2007). See http:// ipcc-wg1.ucar.edu/wg1/wg1-report.html.

13. P. Lemke, J. Ren, R. B. Alley, I. Allison, J. Carrasco, G. Flato, Y. Fujii, et al., "Observations: Changes in Snow, Ice and Frozen Ground," in Climate Change 2007: The Physical Science Basis. Contribution of Working Group I to the Fourth Assessment Report of the Intergovernmental Panel on Climate Change (New York: Cambridge University Press, 2007).
See http://ipcc-wg1.ucar.edu/wg1/wg1-report.html.

14. Global Warming Trends, "Global Warming—Climate."
See www.globalwarmingtrends.com/.

15. *Ibid.*

16. S. Solomon, G. K. Plattner, R. Knutti, and P. Friedlingstein, "Irreversible Climate Change Due to Carbon Dioxide Emissions," *Proceedings of the National Academy of Science of the United States of America (PNAS)* 106, no. 6 (10 February 2009): 1704–1709. See www.pnas.org/content/early/2009/01/28/0812721106.full.pdf.

17. McKinsey & Company, "Pathways to a Low-Carbon Economy: Version 2 of the Global Greenhouse Gas Abatement Cost Curve" (2009). See http://mckinsey.com/clientservice/ccsi/pathways_low_carbon_economy.asp.

18. U.S. Environmental Protection Agency, "Inventory of U.S. Greenhouse Gas Emissions and Sinks: 1990–2006," *U.S. Greenhouse Gas Inventory Reports* (15 April 2008). See http://epa.gov/climatechange/emissions/downloads/08_CR.pdf.

19. B. Kenney, "Green Spot: United Technologies: Think Global, Act Global," *Industry Week* (14 November 2007). See www.industryweek.com/articles/green_spot_united_technologies_think_global _act_global_15296.aspx.

20. J. Brodkin, "Dell Says It's 'Carbon Neutral,'" *NetworkWorld* (7 August 2008). See www.networkworld.com/news/2008/080708-dell-carbon-neutral.html.

21. J. Ball, "Green Goal of 'Carbon Neutrality' Has Limits," *The Wall Street Journal* (30 December 2008). See http://online.wsj.com/article/SB123059880241541259.html.

22. United Nations Population Division, "The World at Six Billion," (12 October 1999): Part 1, p. 5. See www.un.org/esa/population/publications/sixbillion/sixbilpart1.pdf.

23. United Nations Environment Programme, "Millions at Risk of Hunger and Water Stress in Asia Unless Global Greenhouse Emissions Cut" (10 April 2007). See www.unep.org/Documents.Multilingual/Default.asp?ArticleID=5551&DocumentID=504&l=en.

24. R. E. Schmidt, "Climate warming gases rising faster than expected," USAToday.com (16 February 2009). See www.usatoday.com/tech/science/2009-02-14-climate-report_N.htm.

25. Live Science, "Earth's Limited Supply of Metals Raises Concerns" (19 January 2006). See www.livescience.com/strangenews/060119_scarce_metals.html.

26. S. L. Nunes, "Big Green Innovations" presentation, Surface Mount Technology Association (2008). See www.smta.org/files/Nunes_SMTAI_presentation.pdf.

27. P. Déry, and B. Anderson, "Peak Phosphorous," *Energy Bulletin* (13 August 2007). See www.energybulletin.net/node/33164.

28. K. P. Green, "Are Polar Bears Really an Endangered Species?" *The American: A Magazine of Ideas* (13 May 2008). See www.american.com/archive/2008/may-05-08/are-polar-bears-really-an-endangered-species.

29. B. Knickerbocker, "Charismatic Bears on Thin Ice: As the Arctic Heats Up Sooner Than Scientists Anticipated, Animals Like the Polar Bear Are Losing Ground," *The Christian Science Monitor* (13 September 2007). See www.csmonitor.com/2007/0913/p03s03-wogi.html.

30. A. Westervelt, "Seeing Green: And Why It Matters to Your Business and Clients," *California Real Estate Magazine: The Green Issue* 8: no. 7 (September 2008): 7. See www.car.org/newsstand/crem/past-issues/september2008/seeinggreen/.

31. Interview with David O'Reilly, chairman and CEO of Chevron Corp., *CNN Larry King Live* (30 June 2008), See http://transcripts.cnn.com/TRANSCRIPTS/0806/30/lkl.01.html.

32. J. W. Schoen, "Oil Prices Include a Growing 'Risk Premium': Fears of Attack, Supply Disruptions Add to Crude Costs," msnbc.com (12 May 2004). See www.msnbc.msn.com/id/4962032/.

33. T. Wu and A. McCallum, "Do Oil Futures Prices Help Predict Future Oil Prices?" Federal Reserve Bank of San Francisco, FRBSF Economic Letter no. 2005-38 (30 December 2005). See www.frbsf.org/publications/economics/letter/2005/el2005-38.html.

34. FreshPlaza.com, "The British Government and Carbon Trust Will Devise the New Label System—UK: Carbon Reduction Label for All Products" (26 June 2007). See www.freshplaza.com/news_detail.asp?id=3424.

35. GreenBiz.com, "New Cars in California Must Display Global Warming Score" (7 July 2008). See www.greenbiz.com/news/2008/07/07/cars-california-global-warming-score.

36. Green Seal, "About Green Seal." See http://greenseal.org/about/index.cfm.

37. NYDAILYNEWS.COM, "G-8 Endorses Halving Global Emissions by 2050" (8 July 2008). See www.nydailynews.com/news/us_world/2008/07/08/2008-07-08_g8_endorses_halving_global_emissions_by_.html.

38. Office of Public Sector Information, "Climate Change Act 2008, Chapter 27" (United Kingdom: The Stationary Office Limited, 2008). See www.opsi.gov.uk/acts/acts2008/pdf/ukpga_20080027_en.pdf.

39. Army Energy Program, "The U.S. Army Strategy for Installations" (8 July 2005). See http://army-energy.hqda.pentagon.mil/docs/strategy.pdf.

40. D. Eng, "Finding Green Financing: Green Mortgages Reward Green-Minded Clients for Audits, Upgrades, and Enhancements," *California Real Estate Magazine: The Green Issue* 8: no. 7 (September 2008): 22. See www.car.org/newsstand/crem/past-issues/september2008/findinggreenfinancing/.

41. R. Freedman, "Climate-Change Crossfire," *Realtor Magazine* (August 2007): 15. See www.realtor.org/archives/frontlinesledeaug07.

42. Forest Stewardship Council, "The Chain of Custody Certification Process," Fact Sheet. See www.fscus.org/images/documents/COC%20Process%20Sheet.pdf.

43. U.S. Green Building Council, "Frequently Asked Questions about the LEED Green Building Certification System." See www.usgbc.org/ShowFile.aspx?DocumentID=3330.

44. Water-L News, "Indian State Cuts Water Supply to Coca-Cola Plant," *The International Institute for Sustainable Development* 8 (16 January–20 February 2004). See www.iisd.ca/water-l/Water-L_News_8.pdf.

45. *Food & Water Watch*, "All Bottled Up: Nestlé's Pursuit of Community Water" (January 2009). See www.foodandwaterwatch.org/water/pubs/reports/all-bottled-up/download?id=pdf.

46. J. Lumborg, J. Kelley, and P. Beygirci, "Overview of the WEEE, RoHS, and Elek-troG Environmental Legislation," *U.S. Commercial Service Germany* (29 July 2005). See www.buyusa.gov/europeanunion/64.pdf.

47. GreenBiz.com, "California Considers Product Stewardship Bill" (3 March 2009). See www.greenbiz.com/news/2009/03/03/california-considers-product-stewardship-bill.

48. Dell, Inc., "Dell to Launch Free Recycling of Dell-Branded Products for Consumers Globally," company press release (28 June 2006). See www.dell.com/content/topics/global.aspx/corp/pressoffice/en/2006/2006_06_28_rr_001.

49. Electronics TakeBack Coalition, "Which Manufacturers Take Back Their Products?" See www.electronicstakeback.com/corporate/who_takes_back.htm.

50. Sony Electronics, Inc., "Trade-In Program" and "Recycling Program." See www.sonystyle.com/webapp/wcs/stores/servlet/CategoryDisplay?catalogId=10551&storeId=10151&langId=-1&categoryId=8198552921644513777.

51. Electronics TakeBack Coalition, "Which Manufacturers Take Back Their Products?" See www.electronicstakeback.com/corporate/who_takes_back.htm.

52. G. Pohle and J. Hittner, "Attaining Sustainable Growth through Corporate Social Responsibility," *IBM Institute for Business Value* (Endicott, New York: IBM Global Business Services, 2008). See www-935.ibm.com/services/us/gbs/bus/pdf/gbe03019-usen-02.pdf.

53. A. Collier, "You Can't Go Green Without Adding a Little Blue," GreenBiz.com (15 December 2008). See www.greenbiz.com/feature/2008/12/15/cant-go-green-without-a-little-blue.

54. G. Pohle and J. Hittner, "Attaining Sustainable Growth through Corporate Social Responsibility," *IBM Institute for Business Value* (Endicott, New York: IBM Global Business Services, 2008). See www-935.ibm.com/services/us/gbs/bus/pdf/gbe03019-usen-02.pdf.

55. Environmental Leader, "Tesco Powers Distribution Center on Straw" (22 July 2008). See www.environmentalleader.com/2008/07/22/tesco-powers-distribution-center-on-straw/.

56. Environmental Leader, "Tesco U.S.A. to Install $13 Million Solar Roof" (19 January 2007). See www.environmentalleader.com/2007/01/19/tesco-usa-to-install-13-million-solar-roof/.

57. Wal-Mart, "Wal-Mart Mexico Inaugurates Largest Sun-Operated Photovoltaic Installation in Latin America," company press release (19 January 2009). See http://walmartstores.com/FactsNews/NewsRoom/8913.aspx.

58. EcoSecurities and ClimateBiz, "Carbon Offsetting Trends Survey 2008" (2008). See www.carbonflow.com/files/ECO_Carbonoffsettingtrendssurvey2008_US.pdf.

59. A. J. Hoffman, "Getting Ahead of the Curve: Corporate Strategies That Address Climate Change," Prepared for the Pew Center on Global Climate Change (October 2006). See www.pewclimate.org/docUploads/PEW_CorpStrategies.pdf.

60. Deloitte U.S. Manufacturing Industry Practice, "Creating the 'Wholly Sustainable Enterprise'—A Practical Guide to Driving Shareholder Value Through Enterprise Sustainability" (January 2007). See www.deloitte.com/dtt/cda/doc/content/Creating%20the%20wholly%20sustainable%20enterprise%281%29.pdf.

61. Harvard Business Review Paperback Series, *Harvard Business Review on Green Business Strategy* (Boston, Massachusetts: Harvard Business School Press, 2007).

Chapter 2

1. Internal Revenue Service, "Internal Revenue Manual (IRM)," Part 1, Chapter 14, Section 12, Paragraph 1.14.12.6.1.D (27 June 2008). See www.irs.gov/irm/part1/ch10s10.html.

2. J. Senxian, "The Greening of Business Culture: Comparing the Best-in-Class," *Environmental Leader* (11 September 2008). See www.environmentalleader.com/2008/09/11/the-greening-of-business-culture-comparing-the-best-in-class/.

3. BHP Billiton, "BHP Billiton Climate Change Policy" (June 2007). See www.bhpbilliton.com/bbContentRepository/bhpbclimatechangepolicy.pdf.

4. BHP Billiton, "BHP Billiton Launches Revised Climate Change Policy." company news release (18 June 2007). See www.bhpbilliton.com/bb/investorsMedia/news/2007/bhpBillitonLaunchesRevisedClimateChangePolicy.jsp.

5. Intel Capital, "Cogentrix Energy, PCG Clean Energy and Technology Fund, Solon AG Also Invest in SpectraWatt to Deliver Solar Cells," investor news release (16 June 2008). See www.intc.com/releasedetail.cfm?ReleaseID=316866.

6. Applied Materials, "Applied Materials to Accelerate Its Solar Roadmap with Acquisition of Baccini," company news release (19 November 2007). See www.appliedmaterials.com/news/pr2007.html.

7. Applied Materials, "Applied Materials Revolutionizes Solar Module Manufacturing with Breakthrough SunFab Thin Film Line," company news release (4 September 2007). See www.appliedmaterials.com/news/pr2007.html.

8. Applied Materials, "Applied Materials Launches Strategy to Reduce the Cost Per Watt of Solar Power," company news release (5 September 2006). See www.appliedmaterials.com/news/pr2006.html.

9. B. Caulfield, "Intel, IBM Get Solar Exposure," Forbes.com (16 June 2008). See www.forbes.com/technology/2008/06/16/solar-intel-ibm-tech-cx_bc_0616tech-solar.html.

10. General Electric—Ecomagination, "Welcome to Our Vision of a Healthier World." See http://ge.ecomagination.com/site/vision.html.

11. *USA Today*, "Branson Commits $3B to Fight Global Warming" (21 September 2006). See www.usatoday.com/money/2006-09-21-branson-warming_x.htm.

12. Virgin Green Fund, "Khosla Ventures and Virgin Fuels Invest in Gevo, Inc. (19 July 2007). See www.virgin-fuels.net/images//gevo%20press%20release%20vf%20final%20_3_.pdf.

13. Virgin Green Fund, "Odersun Secures US$90 Million Financing Round" (1 February 2008). See www.virgingreenfund.com/images/odersun%20release%20final.doc.

14. Virgin Green Fund, "Masdar Clean Tech Fund and Virgin Green Fund Complete Buy-Out of Texas Petroleum and Metal Recycling Business" (7 July 2008). See www.virgingreenfund.com/images//mctf%20vgf%20announcement%20%28final%29.doc.

15. Virgin Green Fund, "Sir Richard Branson's Virgin Fuels and Gemini Lead Investment Round in Metrolight," August 16, 2007; see http://www.virgin-fuels.net/images/metrolight%2012%208%2007.pdf.

16. Virgin Green Fund, "Virgin Green Fund and Benchmark Capital Lead $14.5 Million Investment Round in GreenRoad Technologies" (31 January 2008). See www.virgingreenfund.com/images/virgin_green%20road%20series%20final.doc.

17. Office Depot, "Office Depot Unveils Company's First: New Retail Location Incorporates Sustainable Building Design and Innovative Green Visual Merchandising," company press release (10 July 2008). See http://investor.officedepot.com/phoenix.zhtml?c=94746&p=irol-newsCorporateArticle&ID=1173598&highlight=green.

18. Office Depot, "Office Depot Survey Shows Half of Business Professionals Seek 'Greener Offices,'" company press release (30 June 2008). See http://investor.officedepot.com/phoenix.zhtml?c=94746&p=irol-newsCorporateArticle&ID=1170510&highlight=green.

19. GreenBiz.com, "USPS Aims to Cut Energy Use by a Third" (3 October 2008). See www.greenbiz.com/news/2008/10/03/usps-aims-cut-energy-use-a-third.

20. PepsiCo, Inc., "PepsiCo Marks Progress Toward Sustainability Goals: Advancing on Water, Electricity and Fuel Conservation Initiatives," company news release (2 October 2008). See http://phx.corporate-ir.net/phoenix.zhtml?c=78265&p=irol-newsArticle&ID=1204941&highlight=.

21. The Coca-Cola Company, "The Coca-Cola System Announces New Global Targets for Water Conservation and Climate Protection in Partnership with WWF," company news release (30 October 2008). See www.thecoca-colacompany.com/presscenter/nr_20081030_wwf.html.

22. The Coca-Cola Company, "Act. Inspire. Make a Difference. A Dialogue of Progress and Responsibility," *2007/2008 Sustainability Review* (September 2008): 35. See www.thecoca-colacompany.com/citizenship/pdf/2007-2008_sustainability_review.pdf.

23. GreenBiz.com, "PricewaterhouseCoopers to Cut CO2 by a Fifth" (26 September 2008). See www.greenbiz.com/news/2008/09/26/pricewaterhousecoopers-cut-co2-a-fifth.

24. GreenBiz.com, "JPMorgan Chase Aims for 20 Percent Carbon Reduction" (24 April 2008). See www.greenbiz.com/news/2008/04/24/jpmorgan-chase-aims-20-percent-carbon-reduction.

25. PR Leap, "On-line Entertainment Guide Goes Carbon Negative" (20 October 2007). See www.prleap.com/pr/99137/.

26. GreenBiz.com, "Clinton Global Initiative Brings Big Corporate, NGO Commitments" (26 September 2008). See www.greenbiz.com/news/2008/09/26/clinton-global-initiative-big-corporate-commitments.

27. U.S. Environmental Protection Agency, "Private Sector Tops Green Power List" (29 January 2007). See http://yosemite.epa.gov/opa/admpress.nsf/4b729a23b12fa90c8525701c005e6d70/70628d9a3fdd05ac85257272005a8efe.

28. IBM Corporation, "IBM Honored by EPA for Climate Protection," company press release (11 May 2006). See www-03.ibm.com/press/us/en/pressrelease/19660.wss.

29. E. Rabin, "Green Performance Creates Value and Competitive Advantage," GreenBiz.com (17 July 2003). See www.greenbiz.com/blog/2003/07/17/green-performance-creates-value-and-competitive-advantage.

30. IBM Corporation, "IBM Ranks #1 on Climate Change Strategies in Ceres Report," company press release (11 December 2008). See www-03.ibm.com/press/us/en/pressrelease/26269.wss.

31. Corporate Knights, Inc., and Innovest Strategic Advisors, "Global 100 Most Sustainable Corporations Announced in Davos," company press release (28 January 2009). See www.global100.org/PR_Global_2009.pdf.

32. Ceres, "Southern, Massey Energy and Chevron Among Nine 'Climate Watch' Companies Targeted by Investors," company press release (18 February 2009). See www.ceres.org/Page.aspx?pid=1033.

33. GreenBiz.com, "Wineries Embrace Green Business Practices but Hesitate Telling Customers" (29 September 2008). See www.greenbiz.com/news/2008/09/29/wineries-embrace-green-business-practices-hesitate-telling-customers.

34. GreenBiz.com, "Consumers Still Buying Green Through Economic Changes" (9 February 2009). See www.greenbiz.com/news/2009/02/09/consumers-buying-green.

35. C. Jackson and D. Houlihan, "Greening Today's Products: Sustainable Design Meets Engineering Innovation," Aberdeen Group (August 2008). See www.aberdeen.com/summary/report/benchmark/5147-RA-green-sustainable-innovation.asp.

36. Indiatimes Infotech, "Sony's Green TV" (21 June 2008). See http://infotech.indiatimes.com/articleshow/3136428.cms.

37. The Hindu BusinessLine, "Sanyo to Unveil 'GreenTV' Next Year," (14 February 2007). See www.thehindubusinessline.com/2007/02/14/stories/2007021403490500.htm.

38. IBM Corporation, "IBM and APC Partner to Create Energy Efficient Green Data Center for Bryant University," company press release (13 July 2007). See www-03.ibm.com/press/us/en/pressrelease/21858.wss.

39. IBM Corporation, "IBM Helps Religare Go Green in a US$3.1 Million Agreement," company press release (2 February 2009). See www-03.ibm.com/press/us/en/pressrelease/26584.wss.

40. GreenerDesign.com, "Cradle to Cradle Certification Now Available for Product Ingredients" (28 January 2009). See www.greenerdesign.com/news/2009/01/28/cradle-cradle-ingredients.

41. Arrowhead Brand, "The Eco-Shape Bottle." See www.arrowheadwater.com/DoingOurPart/EcoShapeBottle.aspx.

42. Poland Brand, "The Eco-Shape Bottle." See www.polandspring.com/DoingOurPart/EcoShapeBottle.aspx.

43. Treehugger, "A World of Reasons to Ditch Bottled Water" (9 July 2007). See www.treehugger.com/files/2007/07/reasons_to_ditch_bottled_water.php.

44. GreenBiz.com, "Wal-Mart, Kmart Stock Up on Organic Jeans" (18 February 2009). See www.greenbiz.com/news/2009/02/18/walmart-kmart-organic-jeans.

45. IBM Corporation, "IBM Data Center Technology Helps Solar-Powered Web Hosting Firm AISO.Net Build on Its 'Green' Commitment to Customers," company press release (18 June 2007). See www-03.ibm.com/press/us/en/pressrelease/21740.wss.

46. Discussion with Peter Williams, IBM CTO for Big Green Innovations, 14 April 2009.

47. GE Money's My Earth Rewards, "My Earth Rewards." See www.myearthrewards.com/creditcard.html.

48. The Nature Conservancy, "The Nature Conservancy Visa Credit Card." See www.nature.org/joinanddonate/corporatepartnerships/tnccard/.

49. E. Pilloton, "Chicago Green Roof Program," Inhabitat.com (1 August 2006). See www.inhabitat.com/2006/08/01/chicago-green-roof-program/.

50. A. Kriscenski, "Green Roofs for Healthy Cities Awards 2008," Inhabitat.com (12 May 2008). See www.inhabitat.com/2008/05/12/green-roofs-for-healthy-cities-awards-2008/.

51. Green Roofs for Healthy Cities, "Green Roofs Goes to Washington—Category: Intensive Institutional." See www.greenroofs.org/washington/index.php?page=schwab.

52. Green Century Funds, "Our Finds: Overview—Since 1991, the Green Century Funds Have Offered Environmentally Responsible Mutual Funds." See www.greencentury.com/funds/.

53. Hewlett-Packard, "HP Makes It Easy to Make Smart Environmental Choices with Unrivaled Portfolio of Printing Solutions," company news release (22 May 2008). See www.hp.com/hpinfo/newsroom/press/2008/080522xa.html.

54. Xerox Company, "Xerox Creates Calculator That Measures Environmental Efficiency; First in the Industry to Answer 'How Green Is Your Office?'," company

news release (25 March 2008). See www.xerox.com/go/xrx/template/
inv_rel_newsroom.jsp?app=Newsroom&ed_name=NR_2008March25_
Xerox_Sustainability_Calculator_Green_Office&format=article&view=
newsrelease&metrics=NWS_Link1&Xcntry=USA&Xlang=en_US.

55. M. Studley, "Energy Audit: Making Your Small Business Greener," Capital.com.
    See www.capital.com/business-planning/energy-audit.aspx.

56. Microsoft Corporation, "Environmental Sustainability Dashboard for Microsoft
    Dynamics AX." See www.microsoft.com/environment/business_solutions/
    articles/dynamics_ax.aspx.

57. Accenture, "Accenture Introduces Green Technology Suite to Help Organizations
    Use IT to Assess and Improve Green Agenda," company news release (23 July
    2008). See http://newsroom.accenture.com/article_display.cfm?article_id=4724.

58. Bank of America, "San Jose Unified School District, Chevron, and Bank of
    America Establish Largest K–12 Solar Power and Energy Efficiency Program in
    the United States," joint press release (25 July 2007). See
    http://newsroom.bankofamerica.com/index.php?s=press_releases&item=7843.

59. Green Highways Partnership, "ACAA and Chevron Support GHP." See
    www.greenhighways.org/new.cfm?Page=1&NewsID=35625.

60. Ricoh Group, "Green Partnership." See www.ricoh.com/environment/
    green/index.html.

61. U.S. Environmental Protection Agency, "Green Power Partnership." See
    http://epa.gov/greenpower/index.htm.

62. Global Water Challenge, "Our Mission." See www.globalwaterchallenge.org/
    about-us/mission.php.

63. International Paper, "Ecotainer Partnership Receives Sustainability Award" (21
    May 2007). See
    www.internationalpaper.com/packaging/Packaging%20Stand%20Alone%
    20Pages/Foodservice/Press_Release/ecotainerTM_Partners1.html.

64. J. Ball, "Green Goal of 'Carbon Neutrality' Has Limits," *The Wall Street Journal*
    (30 December 2008). See http://online.wsj.com/article/
    SB123059880241541259.html.

65. Sustainable Supply Chain Summit, "Green Purchasing," 2nd Green Purchasing
    Summit 2008, San Francisco, Calif., July 2008. See www.eyeforprocurement.
    com/green/report.pdf.

66. Accenture, "Only One in 10 Companies Actively Manage Their Supply Chain Carbon Footprints, Accenture Study Finds," company news release (25 February 2009). See http://newsroom.accenture.com/article_display.cfm?article_id=4801.

67. M. Kistler, "Save More. Live Better," Awareness into Action. See www.awareness-intoaction.com/whitepapers/Wal-Mart-Supply-Chain-Packaging-Scorecard-sustainability.html.

68. B. Alter, "Tesco Goes Green," TreeHugger.com (15 May 2006). See www.treehugger.com/files/2006/05/tesco_goes_gree.php.

69. J-P. Rodriguez, B. Slack, C. Comtois, "Green Logistics (The Paradoxes of)," from *The Handbook of Logistics and Supply-Chain Management, Handbooks in Transport #2* (London: Pergamon/Elsevier, 2001). See http://people.hofstra.edu/Jean-paul_Rodrigue/downloads/Green%20Logistics.pdf.

Chapter 3

1. GreenBiz.com, "Ben & Jerry's Trial Cleaner Freezers" (2 October 2008). See www.greenbiz.com/news/2008/10/02/ben-jerrys-trials-cleaner-freezers.

2. J. Gogek, "Construction for the Sustainable Energy Program at UC San Diego Begins," *UC San Diego Environment and Sustainability Initiative* (21 July 2008). See http://esi.ucsd.edu/esiportal/index.php?option=com_content&task=view&id=183&Itemid=101.

3. ReCellular, "Motorola Races to Recycle during Boston's 14th Annual Earthfest, Memorial Day Weekend" (16 May 2007). See www.recellular.com/about/news46.asp.

4. Nokia, "Recycle Your Nokia Phone." See www.nokiausa.com/A4761433.

5. Sony Ericsson Mobile Communications AB, "Our Commitment, Why Recycle? How to Recycle." See www.sonyericsson.com/recycling/en_us/.

6. The Home Depot Investor Relations, "The Home Depot Launches National CFL Bulb–Recycling Initiative," company news release (24 June 2008). See http://ir.homedepot.com/releasedetail.cfm?releaseid=317987.

7. Greenpeace, "Greenpeace Light Bulb FAQ." See www.greenpeace.org.uk/climate/light-bulb-faq.

8. Best Buy, "Best Buy Tests Free Electronics Recycling Program in 117 Stores," company news release (2 June 2008). See http://bestbuymedia.tekgroup.com/article_display.cfm?article_id=4565.

9. C. Hanebeck, M. Lunani, "RFID-Enabled Returnable Container Management," On Publishing S. A.'s global-identification.com, GID no. 39, (July 2008). See www.global-identification.com/index.php?id=1147.

10. International Paper, "Certification." See http://internationalpaper.com/Our%20Company/Environment/SUSTAINABILITY/Certification.html.

11. PR Leap, "On-Line Entertainment Guide Goes Carbon Negative," (20 October 2007). See www.prleap.com/pr/99137/.

12. L. Buhl, "'Green Collar' Jobs Are Poised for Growth," Yahoo! HotJobs. See http://hotjobs.yahoo.com/career-articles-_green_collar_jobs_are_poised_for_growth-229.

13. Green For All, "Frequently Asked Questions (FAQ) about the Green Jobs Act of 2007." See www.greenforall.org/files/faq-greenjobsact07.pdf.

14. Goodwill Industries International, Inc., "Green Jobs Act," Policy Fact Sheet (June 2008). See www.goodwill.org/c/document_library/get_file?folderId=1142299&name=DLFE-11505.pdf.

15. MyBarackObama.com, "New Energy for America." See http://my.barackobama.com/page/content/newenergy.

16. L. Buhl, "'Green Collar' Jobs Are Poised for Growth," Yahoo! HotJobs. See http://hotjobs.yahoo.com/career-articles-_green_collar_jobs_are_poised_for_growth-229.

17. Scania, "Scania and Sveaskog Join in Environmental Effort," company press release (18 September 2008). See www.scania.com/news/Press_releases/2008/Q3/N08023EN.asp.

18. T. Young, "IT Industry Failing to Meet Low-Carbon Challenge: Report," *Greener-Computing News* (10 November 2008). See www.greenercomputing.com/news/2008/11/10/it-failing-low-carbon-challenge.

19. S. McGillicuddy, "Green Computing Slow to Take Hold in U.S. Businesses," *CIO News: Headlines from SearchCIO.com* (23 May 2007). See http://searchcio.techtarget.com/news/article/0,289142,sid182_gci1256091,00.html.

20. GreenBiz.com, "Enterprise and Wal-Mart Boost Their Alternative Fuel–Vehicle Fleets" (4 February 2009). See www.greenbiz.com/news/2009/02/04/enterprise-and-wal-mart-boost-their-alternative-fuel-vehicle-fleets.

21. U.S. Environmental Protection Agency, "Lighting Unlimited: Investing in Energy Star," Energy Star (2006). See www.energystar.gov/ia/products/lighting/fixtures/Unlimited.pdf.

22. D. Wegge, "'Going Green' Seen As Important for Business: Large Majority of Area CEOs in Survey Believe It's Right Thing to Do Regardless of Cost," *The Business News—Nicolet National Bank* (23 June 2008). See www.nicoletbank.com/upload/mediaroom/filepath_1214839826231.8872_NB16-0508_AR_Going%20Green.pdf.

23. Sustainable Live Media, "Competitive Advantage Driving Green Retail Efforts, Survey Says," (22 August 2008). See www.sustainablelifemedia.com/content/story/strategy/competitive_advantage_driving_green_retail_efforts.

24. S. L. Hart, "Beyond Greening: Strategies for a Sustainable World," *Harvard Business Review* (January–February 1997): 66–76.

25. G. Hirshberg, "The CEO of Stonyfield Farm Made Green by Going Green," *Southwest Airlines Spirit Magazine* 16:8 (August 2007): 38–40. See www.harvest-graphics.net/ceottsept07.pdf.

26. L. Swinton, "Kurt Lewin's Force-Field Analysis: Decision Making Made Easy," *Management for the Rest of Us* (8 February 2005). See www.mftrou.com/Lewins-force-field-analysis.html.

Chapter 5

1. E. Pinero, "Leading by Example," *Report to the President on Federal Environmental and Energy Management* (October 2007). See http://ofee.gov/leadingbyexample/LeadingbyExample2004-2006.pdf.

2. U.S. Environmental Protection Agency, "Working Smart for Environmental Protection: Improving State Agency Processes with Lean and Six Sigma," (September 2006). See www.epa.gov/NCEI/lean/primer.pdf.

3. U.S. Department of Transportation Federal Highway Administration, "Federal Lands Highway: Finding an Efficient Method to Track Environmental Commitments," *Successes in Stewardship Newsletter* (May 2007). See http://environment.fhwa.dot.gov/strmlng/newsletters/may07nl.pdf.

4. PepsiCo, Inc., "Our Sustainability Journey: Overview 2007" (2008). See www.pepsico.com/Downloads/2008_Summary_final.pdf.

5. Burt's Bees, "Environment and Sustainability." See www.burtsbees.com/webapp/wcs/stores/servlet/ContentView?storeId=10001&langId=-1&catalogId=10051&contentPageId=62.

6. Ricoh Group, "Ricoh Group Sustainability Report (Environment) 2007" (August 2007). See www.ricoh.com/environment/report/pdf2007/all.pdf.

7. IBM Corporation, "IBM Ranks #1 on Climate Change Strategies in Ceres Report," company press release (11 December 2008). See www-03.ibm.com/press/us/en/pressrelease/26269.wss.

8. M. Kenber, "Reducers Reap Rewards: Low-Carbon Leaders Profiting from Emissions Reductions," supplement to *Environmental Finance* (December 2004–January 2005). See www.ctclimatechange.com/documents/Lowcarbonleaders.pdf.

9. IBM Corporation, "IBM Helps People Stay Connected with New Software and Mobile Devices," company press release (8 August 2008). See www-03.ibm.com/press/us/en/pressrelease/24854.wss.

10. IBM Corporation, "IBM Poughkeepsie Facility Named 'Assembly Plant of the Year 2008,'" company press release (23 October 2008). See www-03.ibm.com/press/us/en/pressrelease/25748.wss.

11. R. Kumar, "IT for Water Management," *Water India—V: International Conference and Exhibition,* New Delhi, India (4 November 2008). See http://waterindia-v2008.com/Pdf/raji_kumar.pdf.

12. R. L. MacInnes, *The Lean Enterprise Memory Jogger: Create Value and Eliminate Waste throughout Your Company* (Salem, New Hampshire: GOAL/QPC, 2002).

13. D. Ginn and E. Varner, *The Design for Six Sigma Memory Jogger: Tools and Methods for Robust Processes and Products* (Salem, New Hampshire: GOAL/QPC, 2004).

14. IBM Corporation, "IBM and SAP—SAP Benefits Realization," Gartner Group 2002 study findings. See www-05.ibm.com/ie/sap/index.shtml?section=sap3.

15. ClimateBiz.com, "Carbon Market Worth $118B in 2008" (12 January 2009). See www.climatebiz.com/news/2009/01/12/carbon-market-worth-118b-2008.

16. J. Stillman, "What Is Carbon Credit?" *BNET Briefing* (February 2008). See www.bnet.com/2403-13241_23-187036.html.

17. Carbon Trust, "Types of Emissions." See www.carbontrust.co.uk/carbon/PrivateSector/emissions.htm.

18. The Greenhouse Gas Protocol Initiative, "Frequently Asked Questions." See www.ghgprotocol.org/calculation-tools/faq.

19. International Organization for Standardization, "ISO 14001:2004." See www.iso.org/iso/search.htm?qt=ISO+14001%3A2004&searchSubmit= Search&sort=rel&type=simple&published=on.

20. Emerald, "Emerald's Green and Quality Credentials Are Internationally Recognized," company press release (December 2008). See http://info.emeraldinsight. com/about/news/story.htm?PHPSESSID=u9kmutnrqa893c9k31nh079l70&id =958.

21. Emerson Process Management, "Smart Wireless: Self-Organizing Network." See www.emersonprocess.com/.

22. Department for Environment, Food, and Rural Affairs, "Consultation on Implementation Proposals for the Carbon-Reduction Commitment" (June 2007). See www.defra.gov.uk/environment/climatechange/uk/business/crc/pdf/ crc-implement-consultation.pdf.

23. Department for Environment, Food, and Rural Affairs, "Guidelines to DEFRA's GHG Conversion Factors: Annexes Updated April 2008," (June 2008). See www.defra.gov.uk/environment/business/envrp/pdf/ghg-cf-guidelines- annexes2008.pdf.

24. Department for Environment, Food, and Rural Affairs, "Energy and Carbon Conversions: 2008 Update," Fact Sheet CTL018 (1 December 2008). See www.carbontrust.co.uk/publications/publicationdetail?productid=CTL018.

25. FIJI Water, "FIJI Water Becomes First Bottled-Water Company to Release Carbon Footprint of Its Products: Unveils FIJIGreen.com to Report Progress on Its Negative Carbon-Footprint Commitment," company press release (9 April 2008). See www.fijiwater.com/PR_carbon.aspx.

26. Press Release Newswire, "Ski Company Goes Carbon Negative to Combat Global Warming" (16 October 2007). See www.prweb.com/releases/ skiing/holidays/prweb560656.htm.

Chapter 6

1. The Climate Group, "Carbon Down, Profits Up: Third Edition" (February 2007). See www.theclimategroup.org/assets/resources/cdpu_newedition.pdf.

Chapter 7

1. The Climate Group, "SMART 2020: Enabling the Low-Carbon Economy in the Information Age" (2008). See www.theclimategroup.org/assets/resources/publications/Smart2020Report.pdf.

2. S. Palmissano, "A Smarter Planet: The Next Leadership Agenda," speech to the Council on Foreign Relations (New York: 6 November 2008). See www.ibm.com/ibm/ideasfromibm/us/smartplanet/20081106/sjp_speech.shtml.

3. National Academy of Sciences, "International Geophysical Year." See www.nas.edu/history/igy/.

4. K. Ridley, "Global Mobile Phone Use to Pass 3 Billion," Reuters U.K. See http://uk.reuters.com/article/technologyNews/idUKL2712199720070627.

5. P. Harrop and R. Das, "Active RFID and Sensor Networks 2008–2018," IDTechEx.com. See www.idtechex.com/research/reports/active_rfid_and_sensor_networks_2008_2018_000166.asp.

6. Global Sources, "Car GPS Product Adoption Growing; Market Uptrend Seen" (3 April 2008). See www.globalsources.com/gsol/I/Car-GPS-product/a/9000000096102.htm.

7. Tekrati, "Networking/IP to Drive Video Surveillance Market Growth, Says iSuppli" (20 March 2007). See http://semiconductors.tekrati.com/research/8608/.

8. G. Tibbetts, "Millions Face Compulsory Water Metering," *The Telegraph* (18 August 2007). See www.telegraph.co.uk/news/uknews/1560575/Millions-face-compulsory-water-metering.html.

9. W. J. Broad, "A Web of Sensors, Taking Earth's Pulse," *New York Times* (10 May 2005). See www.nytimes.com/2005/05/10/science/earth/10wire.html?_r=1.

10. A. Mainwaring, J. Polastre, R. Szewczyk, D. Culler, and J. Anderson, "Wireless Sensor Networks for Habitat Monitoring," *Proceedings of the First ACM International Workshop on Wireless Sensor Networks and Applications* (Atlanta, Georgia: 28 September 2002): 88–97. See www.polastre.com/papers/wsna02.pdf.

11. J. Krausmann, "Sensors Watch Barrier Reef Coral," *BBC News* (17 January 2006). See http://news.bbc.co.uk/2/hi/technology/4618086.stm.

12. K. Martinez, P. Padhy, A. Riddoch, H. L. R. Ong, and J. K. Hart, "Glacial Environment Monitoring Using Sensor Networks," *Workshop on Real-World Wireless Sensor Networks* (Stockholm, Sweden: 20–21 June 2005). See www.sics.se/realwsn05/papers/martinez05glacial.pdf.

13. The Nature Conservancy, "The Great Rivers Center for Conservation and Learning." See www.nature.org/wherewework/greatrivers/science/art21888.html.

14. NASA, "NASA, Cisco Partnering for Climate Change Monitoring Platform," press release (3 March 2009). See www.nasa.gov/home/hqnews/2009/mar/HQ_09046_NASA_Cisco.html.

15. D. H. Meadows, D. L. Meadows, J. Randers, and W. W. Behrens, III, *The Limits to Growth* (Washington D.C.: Potomac Associates, 1972).

16. D. H. Meadows, J. Randers, D. L. Meadows, *Limits to Growth: The 30-Year Update* (White River Jct., Vermont: Chelsea Green Publishing, 2004).

17. M. Wackernagel, N. B. Schulz, D. Deumling. A. C. Linares, M. Jenkins, V. Kapos, C. Monfreda, et al., "Tracking the Ecological Overshoot of the Human Economy," *Proceedings of the National Academy of Sciences* 99, no.14 (Washington D.C: 2002): 9266–9271.

18. United Nations Environment Programme, "Global Environment Outlook 4 (GEO4)" (2007). See www.unep.org/geo/geo4/report/GEO-4_Report_Full_en.pdf.

19. United Nations Population Fund, "World Population Growth Projection." See www.unfpa.org/6billion/pages/worldpopgrowth.htm.

20. U.S. Census Bureau, "World Population Information." See www.census.gov/ipc/www/idb/worldpopinfo.html.

21. Energy Information Administration, "World Oil Supply," *International Petroleum Monthly* (November 2008).See www.eia.doe.gov/emeu/ipsr/t22.xls.

22. The Global Education Project, "Food and Soil." See www.theglobaleducationproject.org/earth/food-and-soil.php.

23. *Business Week,* "Food vs. Fuel" (5 February 2007). See www.businessweek.com/magazine/content/07_06/b4020093.htm.

24. H. Askari and N. Krichene, "Inflationary Trends in World Commodity Markets: 2003–2007," *GW Center for the Study of Globalization.* See http://gstudynet.org/spotlight/workingpapers/InflationaryTrendsinWorldR1_Askari.pdf.

25. IBM Corporation, "Smarter Food Systems Required to Improve Safety and Availability of World's Food Supplies," company press release (8 December 2008). See www-03.ibm.com/press/us/en/pressrelease/26241.wss.

26. R. Cleetus, "We Need a Well-Designed Cap-and-Trade Program to Fight Global Warming," Union of Concerned Scientists. See www.ucsusa.org/ global_warming/solutions/big_picture_solutions/cap-and-trade.html.

27. Pacific Northwest National Laboratory, "Department of Energy Putting Power in the Hands of Consumers through Technology." See www.pnl.gov/ topstory.asp?id=285.

28. IBM Corporation, "AEP Selects IBM as Systems Integrator for gridSMART(SM) Initiative," company press release (25 November 2008). See www-03.ibm.com/press/us/en/pressrelease/26178.wss.

29. IBM Corporation, "IBM and Singapore's Land Transport Authority Pilot Innovative Traffic Prediction Tool," company press release (1 August 2007). See www-03.ibm.com/press/us/en/pressrelease/21971.wss.

30. A. Witze, "Earth Observation: Not Enough Eyes on the Prize," *Nature* 450, no. 6 (5 December 2007): 782–785. See www.nature.com/news/2007/ 071205/full/450782a.html.

31. Goddard Space Flight Center, "Ask an Astrophysicist" (2 February 1998). See http://imagine.gsfc.nasa.gov/docs/ask_astro/answers/980202e.html.

32. D. Jones, "Speed Equals Efficiency: Delivering NPOESS Data on the Ground for Better Weather and Climate Forecasts and Environmental Monitoring," *Envirocast* 3:1 (April 2008). See www.ipo.noaa.gov/IPOarchive/ED/Articles/ Envirocast_NPOESS_200804_Ground_System.pdf.

33. Orbital Sciences Corporation, "Orbiting Carbon Observatory." See www.orbital.com/SatellitesSpace/ScienceTechnology/OCO/.

34. NASA, "NASA Announces Mishap Board Members for OCO Investigation" (3 March 2009). See www.nasa.gov/home/hqnews/2009/mar/HQ_09-047_OCO_MIB.html.

35. Japanese Aerospace Exploration Agency, "Greenhouse Gases Observing SATellite (GOSAT)" (7 April 2008). See www.jaxa.jp/press/2008/04/ 20080407_gosat_e.html.

36. Japan Aerospace Exploration Agency, "Greenhouse Gases Observing Satellite 'IBUKI' (GOSAT) 'First Light' Acquired by Onboard Sensors," press release (9 February 2009). See www.jaxa.jp/press/2009/02/20090209_ibuki_e.html.

37. K. Ridley, "Global Mobile Phone Use to Pass 3 Billion," Reuters U.K. See http://uk.reuters.com/article/technologyNews/idUKL2712199720070627.

38. Path Intelligence, "Pedestrian Path Measurement Technology." See www.PathIntelligence.com.

39. Cellint.Com, "Cellint's Solution for Road Traffic Monitoring." See www.Cellint.com.

40. INRIX, Inc., "Dynamic Bayesian Predictions." See www.inrix.com/techbayesian.asp.

41. *Science Daily,* "Catching Earthquake Details with Ordinary Laptop Computers" (30 October 2008). See www.sciencedaily.com/releases/2008/10/081027140823.htm.

42. N. Klein, "China's All-Seeing Eye," *RollingStone* (29 May 2008). See www.rollingstone.com/politics/story/20797485/chinas_allseeing_eye/.

43. Stockholmforsoket, "Facts and Results from the Stockholm Trial" (Stockholm: August 2006). See www.stockholmsforsoket.se/upload/Hushall_eng.pdf.

44. H. S. Mahmassani, "Regime Change: Uncongesting Traffic Flow through Dynamic Pricing and Real-Time Information," *NEXTRANS Seminar Series* (Purdue University, 22 April 2008). See www.purdue.edu/discoverypark/nextrans/NEXTRANS%20Seminar_04-22-08.pdf.

45. A. Visser, A. J. van der Wees, and L. O. Hertzberger, "Discrete Event Modelling Methodology for Intelligent Transport Systems," Paper 2016 of *Proceedings of the World Congress on Intelligent Transport Systems* (Torino, Italy: November 2000). See www.science.uva.nl/~arnoud/publications/ITS_Torino.pdf.

46. I. Winz and G. Brierley, "The Use of System Dynamics Simulation in Integrated Water Resource Management," *25th International Systems Dynamics Conference* (Boston, Massachusetts: 29 July–2 August 2007). See www.systemdynamics.org/conferences/2007/proceed/papers/WINZ302.pdf.

47. J. T. Villarin, F. A. Cruz, E. C. Castillo, K. U. Cheng Chua, W. Y. Yu, and G. T. Narisma, "High Resolution Numerical Simulation of Philippine Weather and Climate Using the Agila Beowulf Cluster," *Loyola Review* (Manila, Philippines: Ateneo de Manila University, December 2001). See http://cng.ateneo.edu/cng/wyu/works/papers/LSR-MM5.pdf.

48. M. Kandlikar and B. Morel, "Accelerating the Mitigation of Greenhouse Gas Emissions: The Influence of Uncertainties in Economic Growth and Technological Change," *The Integrated Assessment Journal* 7:1 (2007): 81–101. See http://journals.sfu.ca/int_assess/index.php/iaj/article/view/259/231.

49. A. Rose, J. Benavides, D. Lim, and O. Frias, "Global Warming Policy, Energy, and the Chinese Economy," *Resource and Energy Economics* 18, no. 1 (March 1996): 31–63.

50. A. S. Ko and N. B. Chang, "Optimal Planning of Cofiring Alternative Fuels with Coal in a Power Plant by Gray Nonlinear Mixed Integer Programming Model," *Journal of Environmental Management* 88, no. 1 (July 2008): 11–27. See http://greenhouseeffect.researchtoday.net/archive/4/5/135.htm.

51. U. Diwekar, "An Efficient Algorithmic Framework for Environmental Modeling," *Summit on Environmental Modeling Software, 3rd Biennial Meeting of the International Environmental Modeling and Software Society* (9–13 July 2006). See www.iemss.org/iemss2006/papers/s4/255_Diwekar_2.pdf.

52. Y. Frayman, B. F. Rolfe, and G. I. Webb, *Solving Regression Problems Using Competitive Ensemble Models* (Berlin, Germany: Springer-Verlag, 2002). See www.csse.monash.edu.au/~webb/Files/FraymanRolfeWebb02.pdf.

53. Lawrence Livermore National Laboratory, "Applied Mathematics at the U.S. Department of Energy: Past, Present. and a View to the Future" (May 2008). See http://brownreport.siam.org/Document%20Library/Brown_Report_May_08.pdf.

54. IBM Corporation, "IBM to Implement 70 Million Euro Smart Grid System for Malta," company press release (4 February 2009). See www-03.ibm.com/press/us/en/pressrelease/26596.wss.

55. Discussion with Peter Williams, IBM CTO for Big Green Innovations (9 January 2009).

56. United States Department of Energy, "Mathematical Research Challenges in Optimization of Complex Systems," *Report on a Department of Energy Workshop* (7–8 December 2006). See www.courant.nyu.edu/ComplexSystems/literature/ComplexSystemsReport.pdf.

57. VTT (Technical Research Centre of Finland), "Small Customer Dynamic Pricing Pilots in Denmark and Norway (EFFLOCOM-project) vs. DR of Electric Heating in Finland" (19 April 2005). See www.demandresponseresources.com/Portals/0/FinDRWS%20Kärkkäinen%20SeppoEFFLOCOM-SK.ppt.

58. Electric Power Research Institute, "Advancing the Efficiency of Electricity Utilization: 'Prices to Devices[SM],'" *EPRI Summer Seminar Background Paper* (2006). See http://mydocs.epri.com/docs/CorporateDocuments/Newsroom/SummerSeminar2006/Advancing%20Efficiency_20060720.pdf.

59. M. N. Azaiez, M. Hariga, and I. Al-Harkan, "A Chance-Constrained Multiperiod Model for a Special Multireservoir System," *Computers and Operations Research* 32, no. 5 (2005): 1337–1351.

60. K. Ponnambalam, A. Vannelli, and T .E. Unny, "An Application of Karmarkar's Interior-Point Linear Programming Algorithm for Multireservoir Operations Optimization," *Stochastic Environmental Research and Risk Assessment* 3, no.1 (1989): 17–29.

61. K. Westphal, R. Vogel, P. Kirshen, and S. Chapra, "Decision Support Systems for Adaptive Water Supply Management," *Journal of Water Resources Planning and Management* 129, no.3 (2003): 165–177.

62. T. J. Rasmussen, A. C. Ziegler, P. P. Rasmussen, and T. C. Stiles, "Continuous Water-Quality Monitoring—A Valuable Tool for TMDL Programs," *Proceedings of National TMDL Science and Policy 2003 Specialty Conference* (Chicago, Illinois: 16–19 November 2003): 17.

63. K. P. Georgakakos, N. E. Graham, T. M. Carpenter, A. P. Georgakakos, and H. Yao, "Integrating Climate-Hydrology Forecasts and Multiobjective Reservoir Management for Northern California," *Eos, Transactions, American Geophysical Union* 86, no. 12 (2005): 122.

64. Maryland Department of Natural Resources, "Continuous Water Quality Monitoring in the Maryland Coastal Bays," *2004 Annual Report*. See www.dnr.state.md.us/coastalbays/2004report.pdf.

65. United States Fish and Wildlife Service, "Klamath River Water Quality Monitoring," Arcata Fish and Wildlife Office. See www.fws.gov/arcata/fisheries/activities/waterQuality/klamathWQ.html.

66. N. Cressie, *Statistics for Spatial Data* (New York: Wiley, 1993).

67. R. Smith, G. Schwarz, and R. Alexander, "Regional Interpretation of Water-Quality Monitoring Data," *Water Resources Research* 33, no. 12 (1997): 2781–2798.

68. A. Anandkumar, L. Tong, A. Swami, and A. Ephremides, "Minimum Cost Data Aggregation with Localized Processing for Statistical Inference," *Proceedings of IEEE INFOCOM* (2008): 780–788.

69. P. Brandt and D. Lauria, "Derivation of Water Rationing Rules Using Goal Programming," *Proceedings of the 29th Annual Water Resources Planning and Management Conference* (Tempe, Arizona: 6–9 June 1999):182.

70. H. Bjornlund and J. McKay, "Aspects of Water Markets for Developing Countries: Experiences from Australia, Chile, and the United States," *Environment and Development Economics* 7, no. 4 (2002): 769–795.

71. F. Harvey, "A Costly Thirst," FT.com (3 April 2008). See www.ft.com/cms/s/0/3c12a800-0197-11dd-a323-000077b07658.html?nclick_check=1.

72. W. Min, L. Wynter, and Y. Amemiya, "Road Traffic Prediction with Spatiotemporal Correlations," *IBM Research Report, RC24275* (5 June 2007). See http://transp-or2.epfl.ch/tristan/FullPapers/010wynter.pdf.

73. J. R. Saenz, G. Tapia, X. Ostolaza, A. Tapia, R. Criado, and J. L. Berasategul, "Simulation of a Wind Farm Performance under Wind Speed Changes," *16th International Conference and Exhibition on Electricity Distribution (CIRED)* (2001): 5.

74. G. C. Vineel, A. Sarkar, A. Saha, and A. Anbarasu, "A Simulation Model for Assessing the Uncertainties of Wind Farm Production," *Proceedings of the 18th IASTED International Conference: Modeling and Simulation* (Montreal, Canada, 2007): 90–95.

75. J. Dudhia and J. F. Bresch, "A Global Version of the PSU-NCAR Mesoscale Model," *Monthly Weather Review* 130, no.12 (2002): 2989–3007.

76. E. Delarue, P. Luickx, and W. D'haeseleer, "The Effect of Implemented Wind Power on Overall Electricity Generation Costs, Carbon Dioxide Emissions and Reliability," *TIME Working Paper, Toegepaste Mechanica en Energieconversie* (Katholieke Universiteit, Leuven: Department of Mechanical Engineering: June 2008). See www.mech.kuleuven.be/energy/resources/docs/papers/pdf/WP%20EN2007-005.pdf.

77. E. Delarue, P. Luickx, and W. D'haeseleer, "The Effect of Generation Mix on Wind Power Introduction," *TIME Working Paper, Toegepaste Mechanica en Energieconversie* (Katholieke Universiteit, Leuven: Department of Mechanical Engineering: June 2008). See www.mech.kuleuven.be/energy/resources/docs/papers/pdf/WP%20EN2008-005.pdf.

78. F. Kazuhiko, K. Shunji, K. Hiroyasu, and S. Yoshio, "Monitoring System Based on BOTDR Optical Fiber–Sensing Technology for Road Slope and River Embankment," *Proceedings of Sensor Symposium, Sensors, Micromachine, and Applied Systems* (Japan, 2006): 529–532.

79. F. Bastianini, A. Rizzo, N. Galati, U. Deza, and A. Nanni, "Discontinuous Brillouin Strain Monitoring of Small Concrete Bridges: Comparison between Near-to-Surface and 'Smart' FRP Fiber Installation Techniques," *Smart Structures and Materials 2005: Nondestructive Evaluation for Health Monitoring and Diagnostics, Proc. SPIE* 5765 (2005): 612–623. See http://utc.mst.edu/documents/P-7.pdf.

80. R. Kumar, "IT for Water Management," *Water India—V: International Conference and Exhibition* (New Delhi, India: 4 November 2008). See http:// waterindia-v2008.com/Pdf/raji_kumar.pdf.

81. R. Harrabin, "Climate Prediction: No Model for Success," BBC News (6 May 2008). See http://news.bbc.co.uk/2/hi/science/nature/7381250.stm.

82. R. Bonneau, M. T. Facciotti, D. J. Reiss, A. Schmid, M. Pan, A. Kaur, V. Thorsson, et al., "A Predictive Model for Transcriptional Control of Physiology in a Free Living Cell," *Cell* 131, no. 7 (2007): 1354–1365.

Chapter 8

1. D. Ford, J. Kaufman, and I. Eiron, "An Extensible Spatial and Temporal Epidemiological Modeling System," *International Journal of Health Geographics* 5, no. 4 (2006). See http://www.ij-healthgeographics.com/content/pdf/1476-072X-5-4.pdf.

2. Geophysical Fluid Dynamics Laboratory, "The Flexible Modeling System." See www.gfdl.noaa.gov/~fms/.

3. C. Hill, C. DeLuca, V. Balaji, M. Suarez, and A. da Silva, "Architecture of the Earth System Modeling Framework," *Computing in Science and Engineering* 6, no.1 (2004): 18–28.

4. S. J. Zhou, "Coupling Climate Models with the Earth System Modeling Framework and the Common Component Architecture," *Concurrency and Computation: Practice and Experience* 18 (2006): 203–213.

5. C. Xu, E. Widen, and S. Halldin, "Modeling Hydrological Consequences of Climate Change—Progress and Challenges," *Advances in Atmospheric Sciences* 22, no. 6 (2005): 789–797.

6. Moody's Investors Service. See www.moodys.com/cust/default.asp.

7. The Carbon Rating Agency, "Bloomberg Now Features Carbon Reduction Project Ratings," company press release (January 2009). See www.ideacarbon.com/Bloomberg_IDEAcarbon_press_release.pdf.

8. IBM Corporation, "IBM and OECD to Focus on Global Collaboration for Innovation," company press release (25 June 2007). See www-03.ibm.com/press/us/en/pressrelease/21782.wss.

9. IBM Corporation, "Exploratory Stream Processing Systems." See http://domino.research.ibm.com/comm/research_projects.nsf/pages/esps.index.html.

10. Dust Networks, "Embedded Wireless Sensor Networking." See www. dustnetworks.com/index.shtml.

11. IBM Corporation, "Smart Surveillance System." See http://domino.research.ibm. com/comm/research_projects.nsf/pages/s3.index.html.

12. Pacific Northwest National Laboratory, "Pacific Northwest GridWisee Testbed Demonstration Projects. Part I. Olympic Peninsula Project," PNNL-17167 (2007). See www.gridwise.pnl.gov/docs/op_project_final_report_pnnl17167.pdf.

13. The Nature Conservancy, "The Great Rivers Center for Conservation and Learning." See www.nature.org/wherewework/greatrivers/science/art21888.html.

14. IBM Corporation, "Water for Tomorrow" (16 October 2007). See www.ibm.com/ibm/ideasfromibm/us/environment/100807/images/ IFI_10082007.pdf.

15. The Nature Conservancy, "Water Monitoring Equipment Provides Window into Restoration Project," The Great Rivers Partnership (February 2006). See www.nature.org/wherewework/greatrivers/namerica/art17426.html.

16. The Beacon Institute, "River and Estuary Observatory Network (REON)." See www.thebeaconinstitute.org/institute/innovation.php.

17. Ministry of Research, Sciences and Technology, "Environmental Sensing for Real Time Resource Management" (July 2007). See www.morst.govt.nz/ current-work/transformational-rst/sensing/.

18. Consortium of Universities for the Advancement of Hydrologic Science, Inc., "Hydrologic Information System" (12 July 2008). See http://his.cuahsi.org/ documents/HISOverview.pdf.

19. U.S. Environmental Protection Agency, "Bear River Watershed, Utah, Idaho, Wyoming—Water Quality Trading Program and Model" (December 2006). See www.epa.gov/watershed/winnews/2006/0612.html#5.

20. U.S. Environmental Protection Agency, "State and Individual Trading Programs." See www.epa.gov/owow/watershed/trading/tradingmap.html.

21. National Oceanic and Atmospheric Administration, National Data Buoy Center, "Deep-Ocean Assessment and Reporting of Tsunamis (DART) Description." See www.ndbc.noaa.gov/dart/dart.shtml.

22. Singapore Land Transport Authority, "Electronic Road Pricing." See www.lta.gov.sg/motoring_matters/index_motoring_erp.htm.

23. IBM Corporation, "Driving Change in Stockholm," How It Works (3 April 2007). See www.ibm.com/podcasts/howitworks/040207/images/HIW_04022007.pdf.

24. Masdar—Abu Dhabi Future Energy Company, "Welcome to Masdar." See www.masdaruae.com/home/index.aspx.

25. General Electric, "Masdar and GE Announce World's First ecomagination Centre at Masdar City," company press release (20 January 2009). See www.genewscenter.com/Content/Detail.asp?ReleaseID=5514&NewsAreaID=2&MenuSearchCategoryID=.

Chapter 9

1. Interview with David Cote, chairman and CEO of Honeywell International, Inc., "Honeywell's CEO on the Economy," *CNBC Power Lunch,* aired 28 January 2009. See www.cnbc.com/id/15840232?video=1015760906&play=1.

2. N. Mims, M. Bell, and S. Doig, "Assessing the Electric Productivity Gap and the U.S. Efficiency Opportunity," Rocky Mountain Institute (January 2009). See http://ert.rmi.org/files/documents/CGU.RMI.pdf.

3. IBM Corporation, "The Planet Will Be Instrumented, Interconnected, Intelligent." See www.ibm.com/ibm/ideasfromibm/us/smartplanet/20081106/index.shtml.

4. IBM Corporation, "IBM Unveils New Carbon Management Analysis Tool to Optimize Supply Chain Efficiencies," company press release (22 May 2008). See www-03.ibm.com/press/us/en/pressrelease/24296.wss.

5. TerraPass, "TerraPass Carbon Balanced Business Program." See www.terrapass.com/business/.

6. Carbon Footprint, "Business Carbon Footprint Calculator." See http://www.carbonfootprint.com/index.html.

7. EcoForests.org, "Carbon Footprint Calculator." See http://carbon.ecoforests.org/.

8. The Climate Trust, "Business and Organization Carbon Calculator." See www.climatetrust.org/content/calculators/Business_&_Org_Calculator.pdf.

9. The Carbon Neutral Company, "Business Carbon Calculator." See www.carbonneutral.com/business-carbon-calculator/index.asp.

10. Carbon UK, "Your Company Carbon Footprint Calculator." See www.carbonuk.co.uk/carbonemission.asp.

11. Center for Sustainable Innovation, "Corporate Water Gauge," Version 3.0. See http://www.sustainableinnovation.org/Corporate-Water-Gauge.pdf.

12. IBM Corporation, "Foxconn Teams with IBM to Fight Asia Pacific Region's Carbon Emissions," company press release (4 March 2009). See www-03.ibm.com/press/us/en/pressrelease/26836.wss.

13. C. Bottrill, "Internet-Based Carbon Tools for Behaviour Change," Environmental Change Institute at the Oxford University Center for the Environment (November 2007). See www.scribd.com/doc/7964527/Internetbased-carbon-tools-for-behaviour-change.

14. Stockholm Environment Institute and Tufts Climate Initiative, "Voluntary Carbon Offset Information Portal: Airtravel Emissions Calculator." See www.tufts.edu/tie/carbonoffsets/aircalculator.htm.

15. C. Reich-Weiser, G. Bullock, J. Hartnett, E. J. Jin, P. Mittal, S. Parthasarathy, "Creating a Greenhouse Gas Calculator for Consumer Goods: A Methodological Case Study of the VW Golf," Berkeley University of California (11 December 2006). See http://www.me.berkeley.edu/~corinne/CE268EFinalReport.pdf.

16. Supply Chain Consulting—Carbon View, "Carbon Management Maturity Model (CM^3)." See www.carbon-view.com/cmmm.htm.

17. IBM Corporation, "Lead Now or Be Left Behind—the Choice Is Yours." See www-935.ibm.com/services/au/gbs/pdf/ibm_carbonview_brochure.pdf.

18. J. Murray, "IBM Outlines Carbon Management Ambitions," businessGreen.com (17 March 2008). See www.businessgreen.com/business-green/news/2212191/ibm-outlines-carbon-management.

19. Cygnus Supply & Demand Chain Executive, "Green Enterprise Maturity Model Debuts," *Decision Support News* (4 August 2008). See www.sdcexec.com/web/online/Decision-Support-News/Green-Enterprise-Maturity-Model-Debuts/37$10592.

20. B. Schneiderman, "Winners and Losers in Sustainability: Accelerating Green Enterprise Maturity for Competitive Advantage," presentation from The Results Group at the 2nd Sustainable Supply Chain in Summit, San Francisco (16 October 2008). See www.resultsgroup.com/pdf/Eye_For_Transport_Presentation.pdf.

21. M. Wheeland, "Intel, Microsoft, Sap and Others Unveil Lean, Green IT Toolbox," GreenBiz.com (12 February 2009). See http://www.greenbiz.com/news/2009/02/12/lean-green-it-toolbox.

22. Accenture, "Accenture Introduces Green Technology Suite to Help Organizations Use IT to Assess and Improve Green Agenda," company press release (23 July 2008). See http://newsroom.accenture.com/article_display.cfm?article_id=4724.

23. European Photovoltaic Industry Association, and Greenpeace, "Solar Generation V—2008: Solar Electricity for over One Billion People and Two Million Jobs by 2020" (September 2008). See www.epia.org/fileadmin/EPIA_docs/documents/EPIA_SG_V_ENGLISH_FULL_Sept2008.pdf.

24. *UD Daily,* "UD-Led Team Sets Solar Cell Record, Joins DuPont on $100 Million Project," University of Delaware (23 July 2007). See www.udel.edu/PR/UDaily/2008/jul/solar072307.html.

25. RenewableEnergyWorld.com, "PV You Can Drive On: Promising Technology in Solar Roads" (6 March 2008). See www.renewableenergyworld.com/rea/news/story?id=51755.

26. A. Blakers and K. Weber, "The Energy Intensity of Photovoltaic Systems," Australian National University (October 2000). See www.ecotopia.com/apollo2/pvepbtoz.htm.

27. E. A. Alsema, M. J. de Wild-Scholten, and V. M. Fthenakis, "Environmental Impacts of PV Electricity Generation—a Critical Comparison of Energy Supply Options," Energieonderzoek Centrum Nederland (ECN), presented at the 21st European Photovoltaic Solar Energy Conference in Dresden, Germany (4–8 September 2006; published November 9, 2006). See www.ecn.nl/docs/library/report/2006/rx06016.pdf.

28. BP p.l.c., "Going for grid parity," *Frontiers Magazine* 12 (April 2005). See www.bp.com/genericarticle.do?categoryId=9013609&contentId=7005395.

29. BP p.l.c., "Gaining on the Grid," *Frontiers Magazine* 19 (August 2007). See www.bp.com/sectiongenericarticle.do?categoryId=9019305&contentId=7035199.

30. U.S. Climate Change Technology Program, "Transmission and Distribution Technologies," Technology Options for the Near and Long Term (November 2003): 34–35. See http://climatetechnology.gov/library/2003/tech-options/tech-options-1-3-2.pdf.

31. V. M. Fthenakis and P. D. Moskowitz, "The Value and Feasibility of Proactive Recycling," National Photovoltaics Environmental Research Center, Brookhaven National Laboratory. See www.bnl.gov/pv/abs/abs_142.asp.

32. R. Neal, "Storm over Mass. Windmill Plan: Plan for Nantucket Sound Wind Farm Raises Debate," *CBS News* (23 June 2003). See www.cbsnews.com/stories/2003/06/26/sunday/main560595.shtml.

33. N. Pierpont, *Wind Turbine Syndrome* (Santa Fe, New Mexico: K-Selected Books, 2009). See www.windturbinesyndrome.com/.

34. F. Pearce, "Sea Birds Might Pay for Green Electricity," *New Scientist* (7 May 2005). See www.newscientist.com/article/dn7350-sea-birds-might-pay-for-green-electricity.html.

35. The British Wind Energy Association, "Birds and Wind Energy: Wind Farm and Ornithological Interests Can Co-exist" (3 March 2004). See http://web.archive.org/web/20060113010247/http://www.bwea.org/media/news/birds.html.

36. Public Interest Energy Research (PIER) Program, "Development of a Cost-Effective System to Monitor Wind Turbines for Bird and Bat Collisions: Phase I, Sensor System Feasibility Study," California Energy Commission (March 2007). See www.energy.ca.gov/2007publications/CEC-500-2007-004/CEC-500-2007-004.PDF.

37. The British Wind Energy Association, "Wind Energy: Top Myths About Wind Energy." See www.bwea.com/energy/myths.html.

38. U.K. Parliament Publications & Records, "Energy Payback Times" (28 June 2004). See www.publications.parliament.uk/pa/ld200304/ldselect/ldsctech/126/12620.htm.

39. U.S. Geological Survey, "Hydroelectric Power Water Use." See http://ga.water.usgs.gov/edu/wuhy.html.

40. U.S. Department of the Interior, "Reclamation: Managing Water in the West—Hydroelectric Power," Bureau of Reclamation, Power Resources Office (July 2005). See www.usbr.gov/power/edu/pamphlet.pdf.

41. U.S. Geological Survey, "Hydroelectric Power Water Use." See http://ga.water.usgs.gov/edu/wuhy.html.

42. M. Scherber, "How Tides Could Power the Future," *Live Science* (16 July 2008). See www.livescience.com/environment/080716-pf-tidal-current.html.

43. *Taipei Times*, "Generating Power from Ocean Currents Is Promising: CEPD" (3 July 2007). See www.taipeitimes.com/News/taiwan/archives/2007/07/03/2003367869.

44. M. G. Richard, "Wave Power: Spotlight on Ocean Power Delivery Ltd.," TreeHugger (10 October 2006). See www.treehugger.com/files/2006/10/wave_power_ocean.php.

45. GreenBiz.com, "Disneyland Resort Greens Transportation in Its Small World" (11 February 2009). See www.greenbiz.com/news/2009/02/11/disneyland-resort-greens-transportation-its-small-world.

46. J. Leckie, G. Masters, H. Whitehouse, and L. Young, *More Other Homes and Garbage: Designs for Self-Sufficient Living* (San Francisco, California: Sierra Club Books, 1981).

47. J. Winters, "The Sunshine Solution," *Mechanical Engineering: The Magazine of ASME* 130, no. 12 (December 2008): 24–29. See http://memagazine.asme.org/articles/2008/december/Sunshine_Solution.cfm.

48. Calpine, "Welcome to The Geysers." See www.geysers.com.

49. International Energy Agency, "Key World Energy Statistics: Total Primary Energy Supply—2008." See www.iea.org/textbase/nppdf/free/2008/key_stats_2008.pdf.

50. IBM Corporation, "A Measured Approach to Going Green: IBM 'Green Sigma (TM)' Consulting Offering to Help Clients Reduce Energy and Water Usage," company press release (18 August 2008). See www-304.ibm.com/jct03001c/press/us/en/pressrelease/24945.wss.

51. Microsoft Corporation, "Environmental Sustainability Dashboard for Microsoft Dynamics AX." See www.microsoft.com/environment/business_solutions/articles/dynamics_ax.aspx.

52. Accenture, "Accenture Introduces Green Technology Suite to Help Organizations Use IT to Assess and Improve Green Agenda," company press release (23 July 2008). See http://newsroom.accenture.com/article_display.cfm?article_id=4724.

53. IBM Corporation and Enterprise Storage Group, "IBM Information Infrastructure to Meet New Emerging Green Initiatives and Needs in IT" (June 2008). See www-03.ibm.com/systems/resources/Green_IIIS_07222008.pdf.

54. *Ibid.*

55. GreenBiz.com, "Ben & Jerry's Trials Cleaner Freezers" (2 October 2008). See www.greenbiz.com/news/2008/10/02/ben-jerrys-trials-cleaner-freezers.

56. Southwest Airlines *Spirit* Magazine, "For a Green Time Call" advertisement, Avis Rent a Car System, LLC (September 2008).

57. P. Muncaster, "PowerDown Tool Could Save Thousands in Energy Bills," BusinessGreen.com (6 February 2009). See www.businessgreen.com/vnunet/news/2235955/software-save-thousands-energy.

58. IBM Corporation, "Made in IBM Labs: IBM Creates Software for Holding Face-to-Face Meetings in Virtual Worlds," company press release (4 March 2009). See www-03.ibm.com/press/us/en/pressrelease/26837.wss.

59. C. Lockwood, "Building the Green Way," *Harvard Business Review* (June 2006): 129–137.

60. C. J. Kibert, *Sustainable Construction: Green Building Design and Delivery, 2nd Ed.* (Hoboken, New Jersey: John Wiley & Sons, Inc., 2008).

61. C. Werthmann, *Green Roof—A Case Study* (New York: Princeton Architectural Press, 2007).

62. J. Clark, "What Is Gray Water, and How Can It Solve the Global Water Crisis?" HowStuffWorks. See http://home.howstuffworks.com/gray-water.htm.

63. Epuramat, "Box4Water—Turning Wastewater into Drinking Water," company news release (12 February 2009). See www.epuramat.com/en/news/newsItem.asp?id=56.

64. IST Energy Corporation, "IST Energy Announces Waste-to-Energy System That Turns Trash into Clean Energy," company press release. (19 January 2009). See http://www.istenergy.com/index.php?option=com_content&view=article&id=174:gem-annoucement&catid=54:press-releases&Itemid=83.

65. K. C. Bhasin, "Plasma Arch Gasification for Waste Management," Electronics for You (February 2009). See www.electronicsforu.com/EFYLinux/efyhome/cover/February2009/Plasma-Arc-2.pdf.

66. GreenBiz.com, "Terracycle Sets Up Waste Collection Bins in Home Depot, Petco" (25 February 2009). See www.greenbiz.com/news/2009/02/25/terracycle-sets-up-waste-collection-bins-home-depot-petco.

67. U.S. Tile Company company press release (10 November 2008). See http://ustile.com/pressReleases/CradleToCradle.html.

Chapter 10

1. R. Bowden, "Long-Term CO_2 Reduction Targets May Lead to 'Dangerously Misguided' Government Policies," *The Tech Herald* (1 September 2008). See www.thetechherald.com/article.php/200836/1912/Long-term-CO2-reduction-targets-may-lead-to-dangerously-misguided-government-policies.

2. J. Clark, "Have We Reached Peak Oil?" HowStuffWorks. See http://science.howstuffworks.com/peak-oil.htm.

3. S. J. Berman and P. J. S. Korsten, "Corporate Strategy for the New Millennium," IBM Institute for Business Value (2003). See www-935.ibm.com/services/in/igs/pdf/corporate_strategy_for_the_new_milleninium.pdf.

4. S. L. Nunes, "Big Green Innovations" presentation, Surface Mount Technology Association (2008). See www.smta.org/files/Nunes_SMTAI_presentation.pdf.

5. P. Déry and B. Anderson, "Peak Phosphorous," *Energy Bulletin* (13 August 2007). See www.energybulletin.net/node/33164.

6. D. Smolen, "The Rise of the Chief Green Officer," Sturdy Roots Blog (11 July 2008). See http://sturdyroots.wordpress.com/2008/07/11/the-rise-of-the-chief-green-officer/.

7. Georgia-Pacific, "Georgia-Pacific Names Chief Sustainability Officer," company press release (5 November 2007). See www.gp.com/newsroom/newsReleases/news.asp?NewsID=6148.

8. C. H. Deutsch, "Companies Giving Green an Office," *The New York Times* (3 July 2007). See www.nytimes.com/2007/07/03/business/03sustain.html.

9. Discussion with Peter Williams, IBM CTO for Big Green Innovations, 14 April 2009.

10. GreenBiz.com, "Sustainability Reporting Grows Dramatically Among Multinationals" (29 October 2008). See www.greenbiz.com/news/2008/10/29/sustainability-reporting-grows-dramatically-among-multinationals.

11. GreenBiz.com, "Underwriters Laboratories Launches Green Verification Service" (26 January 2009). See www.greenbiz.com/news/2009/01/26/underwriters-labs-launches-green-service.

12. B. Westley, "Hybrid Vehicles Threaten Commuters' Trip in the Fast Lane," SignOnSanDiego.com (7 July 2005). See www.signonsandiego.com/news/nation/20050707-2335-hybrids-carpoollanes.html.

13. *Texarcana Gazette,* "California Adopts Tough Greenhouse Gas Restrictions" (12 December 2008). See www.texarkanagazette.com/news/WireHeadlines/2008/12/12/california-adopts-tough-greenhouse-gas-r-48.php.

14. Chicago Climate Exchange, "Exchange Overview." See www.chicagoclimatex.com/.

15. Environmental Defense Fund, "Companies Across U.S. Poised for Growth under Cap on Carbon," company press release (27 February 2009). See www.edf.org/pressrelease.cfm?contentID=9307.

16. MyBarackObama, "New Energy for America." See http://my.barackobama.com/page/content/newenergy.

17. J. Fichera and J. Kueter, "Considering Brazil's Energy Independence," George C. Marshall Institute Policy Outlook (September 2006). See www.marshall.org/pdf/materials/455.pdf.

18. M. Reel, "Brazil's Road to Energy Independence: Alternative-Fuel Strategy, Rooted in Ethanol from Sugar Cane, Seen as Model," *Washington Post* (20 August 2006): A1. See www.washingtonpost.com/wp-dyn/content/article/2006/08/19/AR2006081900842.html.

19. J. Moody, "A Green Lesson from Iceland," *The Christian Science Monitor* (2 November 2008). See http://features.csmonitor.com/environment/2008/11/02/a-green-lesson-from-iceland/.

20. GreenBiz.com, "Google, U.S. Chamber Offer Energy Plans" (6 October 2008). See www.greenbiz.com/news/2008/10/06/google-us-chamber-offer-energy-plans.

21. *Ibid.*

22. S. Rishi, B. Stanley, and K. Gyimesi, "Automotive 2020: Clarity beyond the Chaos," IBM Global Business Services—IBM Institute for Business Value (2008). See www-935.ibm.com/services/us/gbs/bus/pdf/gbe03079-usen-auto2020.pdf.

23. *San Francisco Chronicle,* "Rolling Blackouts Hit Southern California" (25 August 2005). See www.sfgate.com/cgi-bin/article.cgi?f=/chronicle/archive/2005/08/25/BABlackouts25.DTL.

24. IBM Corporation, "'Smarter' Food Systems Required to Improve Safety and Availability of World's Food Supplies, Says IBM," company press release (8 December 2008). See www-03.ibm.com/press/us/en/pressrelease/26241.wss.

25. J. Bonasia, "IBM Plans to Put Its Fingerprint All over Smart Sensor Industry," *Investor's Business Daily* (8 December 2008): xx. See www.investors.com/editorial/IBDArticles.asp?artsec=17&issue=20081208.

26. *Ibid.*

27. General Electric Company, "GE Debuts World's First Truly Incandescent-Shaped Energy Smart CFL Bulb," company press release (11 December 2008). See www.genewscenter.com/Content/Detail.asp?ReleaseID=4933&NewsAreaID=2.

28. A Closer Look, Inc., "Guests Want Hotels to Be More Environmentally Conscious: Survey Reveals Guests Will Reuse Towels, Use Recycle Bins and Even Bulk Amenities, If Offered These Choices" (12 November 2007). See www.a-closer-look.com/ACLInTheNews.aspx.

29. Hospitality Trends, "Survey—Guests Say Hotels Not 'Green' Enough" (14 November 2007). see www.htrends.com/article30124.html.

30. CERES Green Hotel Initiative, "Best Practice Survey" (May 2001). See www.bluegreenmeetings.org/HostsAndPlanners/PDFs/GHIsurvey.pdf.

31. D. L. Goodison, "'Green Hotel' Program Gets Nod from Corporations," *Boston Business Journal* (8 June 2001). See www.accessmylibrary.com/coms2/summary_0286-10718952_ITM.

32. Motorola, "Motorola Unveils World's First Mobile Phone Made Using Recycled Water Bottle Plastics and New 3G Touch Tablet with Customizable Home Screen," company press release (6 January 2009). See http://mediacenter.motorola.com/content/Detail.aspx?ReleaseID=10464&NewsAreaID=2.

33. Motorola, "Citizens Advisers Releases Top Ten Corporate Citizens List," company press release (7 October 2004). See www.motorola.com/mediacenter/news/detail.jsp?globalObjectId=4752_4048_23&page=archive.

34. S. Rishi, B. Stanley, and K. Gyimesi, "Automotive 2020: Clarity beyond the Chaos," IBM Global Business Services—IBM Institute for Business Value (2008). See www-935.ibm.com/services/us/gbs/bus/pdf/gbe03079-usen-auto2020.pdf.

35. Raytheon Company, "Environment." See www.raytheon.com/stewardship/environment/.

36. Lockheed Martin, "Energy Program Improves Efficiency, Reduces Emissions." See www.lockheedmartin.com/aboutus/energy_environment/energy-program.html.

37. Honeywell International, Inc., "Honeywell's Environmental Values: A Comprehensive Commitment." See www51.honeywell.com/hser/our-values-our-commitments.html.

38. C. Harrison and M. Fleming, "Life on an Instrumented Planet," presentation at Stanford University (5 May 2008). See http://weigend.com/files/teaching/stanford/2008/guest%20speaker%20powerpoints/ColinHarrisonMartinFleming.Stanford2008.05.05.ppt.

Index

D

E

U

V

W–Z